D1714911

MINSTREL

To Jerry —

Always make
your life your
art —

& have a joyous
Christmas
Jim K Christie

MINSTREL

My Adventure in Newspapering

Jim Klobuchar

University of Minnesota Press
Minneapolis
London

The author and publisher wish to extend their thanks to the *Star Tribune* of the Twin Cities, Rod Wilson, and Rose Klobuchar for permission to publish the photographs that appear in this book.

Published by the University of Minnesota Press
111 Third Avenue South, Suite 290
Minneapolis, MN 55401-2520

Printed in the United States of America on acid-free paper

Library of Congress Cataloging-in-Publication Data

Klobuchar, Jim.
    Minstrel : my adventure in newspapering / Jim Klobuchar.
        p.   cm.
    Includes index.
    ISBN 0-8166-2991-9 (pbk. : alk. paper)
    1. Klobuchar, Jim.   2. Journalists—United States—Biography.
    I. Title.
    PN4874.K573A3   1997
    070'.92—dc21
    [B]   97-11088
                                                                        CIP

The University of Minnesota is an equal-opportunity educator and employer.

For the men and women of the newsroom who shared my joys and sometimes contributed to my bewilderment in forty-three years of daily journalism. They have my love, thanks, and forgiveness.

Contents

Preface

On my last day at the *Star Tribune* in Minneapolis, I closed my office door and for fifteen or twenty minutes drifted through a self-inflicted performance review. It was part dreamy, part painful. This was the finish of forty-three years in daily journalism that included thirty years as a columnist. In longhand I wrote some questions, made an examination. An advice giver in one of the magazines had suggested this as a civilized way to achieve a condition now described as "closure," which may be one of the ugliest words in the English language.

"OK," I said, "how is it, closing down after forty-three years?"

I wrote a question.

"Was it worth it?" Meaning forty-three years, dead-of-night plane flights, writing against the clock, absorbing the jocks' screaming curses in the losers' dressing room, keeling over from the cops' tear gas offensive against the hippies in a Miami street outside the Republican convention; railing into the wind against the gambling blight a hundred times, knowing most of it was time wasted for both the author and the reader; trying to keep the mother of a dead marine on the phone although she was crying and alone in the house while I struggled with my revulsion for doing this.

Clinical psychologists insist that you should write out the answers to these private inquisitions. I didn't. It would have meant one more file in my computer terminal on my last day. That meant another printout and pages more of paper. It had the look of a dossier. So I tumbled the answers around in my head.

Was it worth it?

God, yes. I got out of the swivel chair and stared through the office window, trying to resist the unspoken stage instructions that seemed to go with the scene. Hey, no melodrama, I told myself. Strike no atti-

tudes of reverie. Why not? Well, isn't that thick, the aging newspaperman amiably scudding around in a fog of sentimentality?

Yes, it's thick.

Do I want it or need it?

Sure.

I looked toward the gray and russet buildings of the University of
Minnesota a mile away, trying to picture the faces of George Hage
and Mitchell Charnley of the journalism school of forty-five years before. George was a man with a long, crevassed face that invited trust.
He didn't mess with trivialities when the subject was journalism. If
you were serious about wanting to go into newspapering, George
would walk you through every paragraph, every syllable, all the
busted syntax. He was my adviser, a sort of Scandinavian Mr. Chips.
Two years after I graduated, I telephoned George from the Great
Northern Depot in Minneapolis on a Saturday morning, passing
through. I'd been in the army and was on my way back to my first job
in newspapering in Bismarck, North Dakota. George invited me to
lunch at Coffman Union on campus. He took three hours with a dimly
remembered young man whose phone call must have wrecked his
plans for a day off. We talked army, newspapering, politics, and the
creeping shabbiness of the Minneapolis streetcars. When we stood to
leave, George shook my hand and looked at me gravely, making one
of those measured evaluations of the college professor. He said, "I
think you could use a wider audience."

He couldn't have realized how much his words mattered to me.
Teachers often don't. Mitch Charnley might not have. He had one of
those flawless little mustaches and a voice of glass-cutting precision
that spoke of hundreds of hours teaching the sons and daughters of
Minnesota dirt farmers how to write radio news and how to read it.
Mitch pronounced it "nyews" in the diction-conscious microphone
style of the day. But he was very much the conscience of good (meaning clear) journalism. In class, he had read a piece I wrote about a visit
to the old Lincoln Rec pool hall on Hennepin Avenue. A jock celebrity
was there. An old man in grungy clothes came up to him and asked
for an autograph for his grandson. I don't think the jock believed that.
The autograph was for the old man, a nobody who had met his hero
and would revere that moment and that scribbled signature. Mitch
said he thought the piece had warmth because, in a very ordinary
scene, it gave a glimpse into human vulnerability. He then went on to

another paper, but I didn't hear his next critique. His words bobbed around in my mind. A small encounter I'd described had touched an emotion. The professor's approval was spare, but he didn't toss around his approval like sunflower seeds. It was a beginning for me. It set a direction. To tell the truth, it had me in flames leaving the classroom. It told me there might be something good ahead, a lifetime roaming through the clangor of convention halls and arenas, of unlocking doors and locating skeletons.

And that is pretty much what happened.

But on this December morning in 1995 I had a hard time seeing the faces of Mitch and George from the window because the grounded blimp of the Metrodome got in the way. So I laughed away the reverie. Here was a building uproariously scorned and damned for years. The denunciation was voiced without mercy by ballplayers, by baseball fans who adored the sun, by football fans who adored blizzards, and by the usual snarling cliques in the press box.

And I was one of the guys who campaigned for it, this homely blob that always looks as though it needs laundering. The city, I'd said, needed a stadium more than the suburbs did. At the time, you could walk the empty streets of downtown Minneapolis at night on the way to a movie and theoretically get arrested for vagrancy. And if you were going to put the arena in the city, I wrote, you might as well put a roof on it because winter arrives sometime around the beginning of school in September. They built the Metrodome. I can't claim to have stampeded the legislature into it. The legislature didn't want the stadium but finally wore down after years of guerrilla warfare by a handful of downtown Minneapolis corporate pleaders. The sun lovers screamed and the tailgaters mourned, and baseballs got lost in the ceiling. But the Twins ultimately won two World Series they wouldn't have won on God's good grass. The Vikings made millions and the lights glowed again on Nicollet Avenue.

I closed the blinds. Was it worth it? The newspapering. Yes, of course. I loved it. I couldn't remember a day walking into a city room when I didn't feel a beat of suspense. That was almost always the best hour. Something new today, something around the corner. Where did the electricity I felt come from? The people around me in the city room were by and large good and competent people. Some of them were superb writers or reporters or editors, and I admired them. But I was never a social animal in the newsroom, and its environment was not my energy. That came from the voice of a farmer in Kandiyohi, howling about what the newspaper was doing to truth and justice and didn't anybody down there know a damned thing about farming and what was happening to farmers.

We talked for a half hour. He grumped about being driven to the edge of poverty and ended up bellyaching about liberals and the banks. But it was a fair fight and we both got scuffed up. I can't remember whether I wrote a column about it, but either way I learned something new about crops and also about the eight-week vacation he was about to take on his meager earnings.

The readers of the newspaper were my ignition. They were also my recreation and my sparring partners. They were my sources and, now and then, my confessors. Everybody who writes a column likes the feel and sound of being a prophet, casting laser streaks of insight into the political brawls of the day. Some days, a lot of days, I did that with relish. On a few days, I did it with enough evidence or enough hot blood to move some minds or reverse a wrong. But newspaper columnists, no matter how entertaining or perceptive, don't change many votes or start many revolutions. It was the obscure people I met in a gas station or on the phone or by mail who opened the doors to a more fruitful kind of writing, at least as I reflect now. In sharing a story that told of a child's indomitability in facing cancer, I didn't consciously try to offer comfort or hope to a newspaper reader who might have needed them, although if that happened we were both graced. Very often the people I wrote about simply humbled me. The sight of two people genuinely in love did that, maybe because I'd grappled so ineptly and so thoughtlessly with love in my own life.

I attended a wedding in which an attractive young woman was pushed down the aisle in a wheelchair. She'd lost her legs to the propeller blades of a drunken motorboat driver. She was engaged at the time of the accident and lived through weeks of fright and disorientation, facing her new disability and a rising terror that her fiancé would abandon her. He didn't. That never entered his mind. On the evening of the wedding, as they said their vows, he sat on a stool beside her instead of standing, so that they would begin their life together as equals. Love at that level of commitment is a majestic sight. I told that story to the newspaper's readers. I don't think I did it to extract tears from an emotional episode, but to invite the reader to share a recognition: here was an undefeatable love, so strong it was capable of lifting two people beyond pain and insecurity and even beyond their fairy tales.

It was always the time when I felt the most legitimate and worthwhile in newspapering, in the revealing of a life, worthy or desperate, grubby or successful, that could reach into the homes of thousands who were unaware of that life until the newspaper arrived on their doorsteps.

My private inquisition went on. I asked another question: Was it worth the needless hurt I sometimes caused when I could have built the case against a sloppy bureaucrat or a self-enriching corporate CEO without piling it on?

There I tried to give myself some room to maneuver. Isn't this how you argue, I said, sorting the facts, finding the most persuasive ones, and skirting or ignoring the evidence that makes your opponent a little more believable? Lawyers do it. Economists do it. Preachers do it, and car dealers.

Right. But doing it to persuade three hundred thousand newspaper readers doesn't give it any more respectability.

How many times did I overstretch deliberately, make the wound deeper than I had to?

Not that many, I told my invisible confessor.

Then wouldn't it have been the decent thing, the next day, to pick up a telephone and apologize to the victim for excess and unfairness?

It would.

Did you?

No.

Why not?

Because on those days I was as self-indulgent as the CEO or the bureaucrat.

But do you think that on other days, when you were trying to defend a scraggly old bag woman against the wardens of law and order, you wrote with enough generosity to satisfy your conscience and Mitch Charnley's? In other words, were your forty-three years worth it to the readers, when you balance it out?

Lord, I hope so.

The interrogation was now getting nearer to Scrooge and the ghosts, close and flinty. I thought: If as a columnist I'd been misleading or a manipulator or just putting on a show in a prolonged way, the readers would have discovered it long before now. I didn't mind the ranting from readers in Edina and Wayzata and West Bloomington when I wrote politics, or the fuming red eyes from gun lovers when I wrote gun control.

I would have minded the dismissive contempt that average readers will show when they don't trust a guy in the newspaper.

A last question.

Was all of that energy and running and electricity worth two broken marriages and alcoholism?

There I stopped the grilling. That wasn't a question. It was a red herring. Why blame all of that grief and destruction on the job? If being sober meant anything, it meant seeing truth better than I once did. Newspapering for me had meant speed and gratification and some sort of tumult that made the blood run every day. But newspapering had nothing much to do with broken marriages and alcoholism.

I managed those without needing an alibi. But newspapering in the later years became more comfortable because recovery from drinking forced me into attitudes that made me more whole. They peeled back some of the alibis and self-deceptions I'd invented to explain my rudeness and rashness.

I don't mean I stopped being rude or rash. I mean I recognized it when I saw it or heard it.

Acknowledgments

Excerpts from several of my columns that appeared in the Minneapolis newspaper are included in this book. For permission to use the material I wish to thank the *Star Tribune* of the Twin Cities. I also want to express my appreciation to David Lebedoff, Arthur Rolnick, and Chuck Slocom for our lively discussions on "where to, Minnesota?" To Otto Silha, David Nimmer, and Lou Gelfand I want to say thanks for our noodlings and memory-jogging sessions about the *Star* and *Tribune* past. I'm also much appreciative of the skills and cooperativeness of the employees of the Minneapolis Public Library's history section for giving me access to its files, and of Barbara Schmitt's priceless tutelage in the mysterious arts of operating a personal computer. Finally, I want to thank the readers of the *Minneapolis Star*, the *Minneapolis Tribune*, and the *Star Tribune* of the Twin Cities for their interest and loyalty, and their uncommon durability in following my column all those years.

1/ Start by Electing a President

At midmorning of November 9, 1960, the day after the American presidential election, the world fidgeted in suspense. More than twelve hours after the last vote was cast, the Americans still had no certified new president. Editors and producers prowled the teletype machines in hundreds of newsrooms, trying to coax the name of the winner from the printers' reluctant keys: Richard Nixon or John F. Kennedy? The counting of votes in the three undecided states, Illinois, California, and Minnesota, droned on past dawn.

In the world's capitals, the tension radiated to the chambers of premiers, the palaces of kings, and the sanctums of dictators. All had monumental stakes in the course of American politics and the new American president.

The word came from an improbable place. In a wire service office in Minneapolis, not far from the alfalfa fields of mid-America, a man set his fingers skittering across the keyboard of his typewriter and gave the world the name of the next American president.

Although I wrote the story, I doubt that I'm going to be immortalized as the man who elected John Kennedy president. But was this one of those once-in-a-generation stories to stir up the continents and bring the fairy tale back to respectability? It probably was. John Kennedy, charming young millionaire, Irish Catholic, war hero, wins the American presidency. A prince vanquishes the frog and rides into the White House on a yacht and the echoes of a PT boat.

And the news whirled around the planet from a clicking old teletype machine whose operator was getting the copy one paragraph at a time, ferried to him by the office bureau chief, who tore it out of my

1

typewriter on the fly and hurdled chairs to keep the story running on the international wire.

In retrospect, more than thirty-seven years later, I remember it as a day thrumming with newsroom theatrics that barely escaped vaudeville. It was pressure stuff and I'd have to be a gold medal liar to tell you that I didn't crave that hour and later put it in a private trophy case. But wire service newsrooms aren't demonstrative, and nobody in the office cheered when I signed off the story. High fives were still twenty years away. The most vivid satisfaction I remember was a handshake from the winded bureau chief, George Moses. I said, "Hey, we got it right." He sighed and said, "Nice work doing the story. I almost died twice and barely missed a hernia." After which I walked to the corner café on Portland Avenue and had two coffees and a glazed doughnut in celebration. When I got back to the office a half hour later, the first story I wrote after electing Kennedy was about two dogs who got stuck in a mud pit near Faribault and needed the county grader to bail them out.

Years later I sorted through that brief entangling of John Kennedy's life with mine. For one thing, if I had suspected that Kennedy's ordination to the Oval Office would be coming out of my typewriter on November 9, I don't think I would have picked the morning of election day to spend three hours banging my skull and knees on the rocks above the St. Croix River. I owed the bureau chief's sanity more generous treatment than that.

Before heading for the cliffs with a climbing friend, I cast one wan suburban vote for John Kennedy. His candidacy didn't enthrall all of my friends and neighbors in the rustic precincts of Plymouth, west of Minneapolis. My own view of JFK was more charitable. But Kennedy's chances on election day were shaky. There was the hobgoblin of his Catholicism. There was the carryover of the country's lingering fondness for the departing Dwight Eisenhower.

My vote owed more to my origins than to any hot zeal for JFK. I acquired most of my early political attitudes and animosities from the ore pits of northern Minnesota, where a certain amount of righteous ferocity is expected in candidates. I thought Kennedy's chief endowment as a candidate was his opponent, Nixon, the only politician I've ever seen with the power to make millions of voters queasy simply by looking into a camera. I thought Kennedy had some sensible ideas as well as his obvious energy and glamour. But the guy was an ordeal for the Midwestern ear. Kennedy sounded like a Boston lawyer peddling clams. Each time I heard him rip into the Castros in Cuber, I shivered. How was this striped-pants millionaire with his hanging *r*'s playing among my clansmen on the Range, where speech is delivered with big tonsils and vowels land with a thud?

En route to the St. Croix, I stopped fretting about that particular sideshow of the election. If you grew up on Minnesota's Iron Range in the middle of the twentieth century, you knew that Dick Nixon's prospects in northeastern Minnesota in 1960 were as bright as the temperance movement's chances in West Duluth.

Nobody has ever tabulated the exact number of prophets who claimed to have forecast a Kennedy victory. I wasn't one of them. I know this: on the day of the election, my one sure connection with political reality in Minnesota was knowing how the Iron Range would behave. The Range's distaste for Republicans was deep. It was exuberant. It was one of those laws of nature, like gravity and the windchill index, and only political dreamers and idiots could afford to doubt that.

What I didn't know and couldn't have imagined was that within twenty-four hours, this phenomenon of Minnesota politics was going to push me into the middle of the election as the sweaty and anonymous herald of a Kennedy victory that was cemented by the voters of Minnesota.

On the way to meet my climbing partner the morning of election day, I drove into Minneapolis and stopped for a few minutes at the Minneapolis bureau of the Associated Press, where I worked, across Portland from the *Minneapolis Star* and *Tribune*.

The usual clatter escorted me through the doorway. It was the noisy pulsation of the working newsroom of the midcentury: the rhythmic clippety-clop of the teletype machines, jangling telephones, somebody typing dictation from the South St. Paul stockyards—all about the quoted prices of feeder pigs today—and somebody else pawing at his headset, yelling into the phone to find out if anybody died in the fire on a farm near the Red River.

These people were my confederates, at work on the AP desk. George Moses looked up from the bureau chief's desk through a mushroom fog rising from one of his smoking pipes. As I approached, George smiled, not with total conviction. George was sociable but twitchy. All wire service bureau chiefs are nervous on election days. At least they

were then, years before the television networks routinely began announcing the names of the election winners with .3 percent of the total
vote counted. But in 1960 there were no exit polls. There were no
giant computers to ingest a sprinkling of votes, run them through electronic laundries of data in microseconds, and nail the eventual result
with a mathematical sureness that numbs mortal minds.

There was no such wizardry in 1960, thank God, although there
was no shortage of mortal minds. The chief mortal mind in the Minneapolis AP belonged to Moses, a muscular man with a bald head and
a round pink face, usually cordial. He had a yen for operatic music
and a relaxed style of command. None of this disappeared on election
day. But the rosiness in George's face did tend to bleach. Election days
in the big wire service bureaus were blockbuster events. The election
results on American radio and television and in the newspapers in that
age originated with the wire services, not with the networks. The tabu-
lations came from multitudes of county auditor offices, funneled into
the wire services. And so the twin mantras of the wire service gods,
speed and accuracy, were squared and multiplied in their urgencies
on election night. The AP's competition came from the other major
American news service at the time, the smaller but feisty United Press
International. Yet that was just the surface pressure for the George
Moses types of the AP.

The hard, mostly unspoken pressure came from thousands of newspaper, radio, and television editors around the country. They were
more than clients. They were also proprietors. The AP corporately
calls itself a cooperative, owned by the member newspapers and stations it serves. So when the AP screws up, when it tells a story late,
badly, or erroneously, it is doing something more than embarrassing
its member stations and papers. It makes a mess inside the corporate
family. And if the offense is bad enough—botched election results, for
example—the ensuing bricks fall on bald heads like the one belonging
to George Moses. He stood when I got to the desk and made a joke
about my training for election night by hanging by my fingernails over
a precipice, not the posture to impress a jittery bureau chief. My job
on election night was to write the election stories as they developed
in Minnesota, North Dakota, and South Dakota. Much of this material was intramural, for newspapers and stations in Minnesota. If any
of it had national impact—the election of a governor or a member of
Congress—my job was to handle the story for the national wire. The

work was important but didn't merit any drum rolls. Most of it was routine bean counting, translated into the lingo of the election writing of the time: "Scattered and fragmentary returns today gave Josh Murgatroyd the early lead . . ."

And later: "Josh Murgatroyd, an obscure county judge from Hayloft, Minn., tonight appeared headed for a surprise congressional victory . . ."

And on.

Moses was a good fit for most of the people in his office, including me. We had something like fifteen full-time writers and editors, a photographer, and a dozen teletype operators, darkroom workers, and copy aides to work two shifts. It was an office in which there were few intimate friends, but it was bound by a strong if unspoken camaraderie of people working under sustained shared stress. In those years, except for the elections and the random big stories of crime or natural disasters, the steamy cauldrons of wire service competition were the University of Minnesota football games. I wrote the game stories; George sat next to me, editing and dictating to the office downtown. The holy grails of wire service football coverage were speed and action language. The need for literate, zingy writing was clear. Football was action, and the stories we wrote had to be competitive. What really mattered, though, was speed of delivery. The newspaper sports desks on late Saturday afternoons around the country were jungles in the midcentury. Early deadlines collided with cascades of wire service and local copy and mountains of photos. The clutter was compounded by screeds of statistics—the lineups, scoring summaries. Owly creatures on the desk sifted through this anarchy of information and images. All of it came together at the hour of panic, 5:00 P.M. But if your wire service story reached the newspaper's sports copy desk first in the face of all that mess, and if it had the nouns and verbs plus the score in presentable order, you were going to win your battle with the competing wire service and later feel the glow of seeing that dateline and logo in print:

"Minneapolis, Minn. (AP)—"

Or, God forbid, if the black hats won you were going to see the unthinkable:

"Minneapolis, Minn. (UPI)—"

In the old Memorial Stadium press box, George the bureau chief was the soul of hands-off managerial restraint. When the crux of the game approached, or when the game clock was bleeding away and I got ready to write, he did no prodding or meddling. He did squirm. I could feel the anxiety seeping through the skin of George's hairless head and guess his thoughts:

"How's the guy going to write this?"

I usually wrote it in time to spare George arterial blockage. The mania for swift movement of copy to the impatient fingers on America's sports desks sometimes spilled into comedy. On a few days I actually wrote optional leads, or provisional opening paragraphs, before the game ended. One said Gophers win. Another, Gophers lose. A third, Gophers tie. All three were put on hold in the downtown office to await a phone call from Moses in the Memorial Stadium press box, alerting the desk to which of the three versions was the live one. With this identification in hand, the desk could rush the bulletin onto the wire. The scheme was intended to buy us the minute or so it would take to write the game-ending lead if we waited for the gun. The idea always had more theater in it than common sense. If you dictated the optional leads into the office, with instructions to the copy handlers to drop dead if the wrong one got on the wire, there was still a fighting chance that the wrong one would get on the wire and into somebody's newspaper.

It happened in wire service reporting more than once. As far as I can remember, it never happened out of the Minneapolis AP office during Moses' tenure or mine. Moses tolerated those optional leads for two or three years. He did it in the manner of a bomb detonator standing in the crater of a two-thousand-pounder and hearing sudden clicking sounds. We abandoned the strategy with mutual relief well before Moses needed therapy.

So we hit it off well in the eight years I worked for the AP and respected each other in our fashion. "Don't fall off the mountain today," Moses said helpfully as I left for Taylors Falls. "We're not set up to handle election copy from a man in traction." I reminded him that there were no mountains at Taylors Falls, only perpendicular black cliffs. He made a face of martyrdom, blew a puff of pale smoke, and went back to his mail and election jitters.

I have to say this of George: he mattered to me then, and he always has. He has mattered as a colleague, a friend, and a man who influenced the course of my professional life. The mark of his relationships in the workplace was decency. He was a manager of easy competence who knew the human condition well enough to sift through the hothouse turmoil of the wire service office. Doing that, he could look past the surface stresses that wore on the men and women who churned out the news. He found himself fascinated by their personalities. He admired the craft and ingenuity he saw in many of them and resigned himself to the plodders, with thanks, because they were probably the real glue of the operation. He never probed into private lives, although he was a counselor if he was asked. I met him a few days before my college graduation in June of 1950, when George acted as a screening agent for John O. Hjelle, editor of the Bismarck, North Dakota, *Tribune,* which had offered me a job: starting pay forty dollars a week if I survived the first two weeks.

First-job offers deserve respect. The *Tribune*'s had mine with no argument. So what if it was a newspaper on the prairie, megayears from the *Washington Post*? It was a sturdy prairie newspaper with a Pulitzer Prize in its history, and I honestly didn't look on it as a launching pad. As far as I could predict, I was going to be a Bismarcker for the rest of my life, a condition I admit wouldn't have electrified all young journalists of the time.

I reached Bismarck by train in mid-June and bought a copy of the *Tribune* to read at dinner in a drugstore café. It was a standard-size newspaper with an eight-column front-page banner headline that immediately pinned me to the back of the booth.

"A Thousand Elks in Bismarck Today."

Nothing in the ore pits had prepared me for this. Bismarck was going to be a place of mind-stretching time warps. I thought, My first day in town and they unleash a stampede of wildlife. How deep in the prairie does this place go?

But no antlered hordes materialized as I walked to the hotel. A street banner announced that the Order of Elks was holding its state convention in Bismarck—and the newspaper wasn't going to be accused of overlooking it.

John O. Hjelle confided on my first day at the newspaper that it was highly likely I was going to become one of the world's great wire editors. Wire editing was not my conception of the road to journalistic immortality, but it was the job I was hired to do. They also called the wire editor the telegraph editor, a charmingly antique title that forged a nice bridge between the mid–twentieth century and the newspapering days of spittoons and kids in stocking caps yelling "wuxtra" on the street corners. On small dailies, the telegraph editor was a one-man international desk. He (or she) edited all of the national and international news that entered the newsroom on the wire service printers. The telegraph editor designed the front page, scheduled the wire stories and photos that appeared on page one, edited the copy, and wrote the headlines on all the stories outside the city news.

If the newspaper had two editions daily, which the Bismarck newspaper did, the wire editor performed this exercise twice a day. It meant writing headlines on more than a hundred stories daily, deciding the style of headlines and making sure they fit the space allotted for them. It meant editing all of those stories and fighting every day with the fat guy in the composing room who actually handled the hot metal type in the page frame and couldn't stand cheeky boy editors fresh out of college.

It was a buzz saw. For the rookie newspaperman it was also a loony Armageddon every day. It was filled with breaking stories from Washington, with paper jams in the printer machines on deadline, with John O. Hjelle striding into the newsroom wondering why the speech by his Republican chum running for governor wasn't scheduled above the front page fold, with other crises that had to stand in line.

I probably don't have to confess that I was lit up by the job from the start. I couldn't get to the newsroom fast enough. I was the first one in at 6:00 A.M., greeted by the yammering of the AP printer beside my desk. The appeal of it was the tingly hands-on connection it gave me with the events and faces of the world. Now, this minute. One day it was a rescue in the South Pacific. Or Caribbean political fanatics turning the U.S. House of Representatives into a shooting gallery. The world with all of its misery and violence and greed and gallantry showed up each morning on the wire service printer, and someplace in my brain a voice was humming constantly, asking, "How are you going to show this to the readers today?"

The other magnetic part of it was the demand for speed. It charged me up and shaped the role of time and deadlines in the rest of my years in the newspaper business. Deadlines were never villains in my life. They were more the adrenaline. I can't say they pitched me into superhuman leaps of rhetorical brilliance. What they did was to put discipline near the head of my commandments when the time came to write.

The job was so captivating that I reached a conclusion fairly early. Hjelle was probably right in his assessment of my historic potential as a wire editor. Hjelle was a breezy and agreeable busybody. He was slim and athletic with a fine stream of sandy Scandinavian hair, and he was usually up to his earlobes in Republican politics. He was also smitten by the newsroom bulletin board as a teaching tool. His news sleuths responded to this technique with smirky amusement. Spying a spelling blunder in the newspaper one day, the editor pinned an all-points memo on the board. "Remember," it read, "there's no 'e' in judgment."

For the next five days in the news columns of the *Bismarck Tribune*, every rendering of the word came up "judgmnt."

On my third week on the job, John inquired about my draft status. I wasn't surprised. About the time I arrived in Bismarck, the North Korean army crossed the Thirty-Eighth Parallel. I was twenty-two, registered for the draft, single, healthy, and thoroughly eligible for the American army.

Single. Yes, eagerly. One of the hypes of the summer of 1950 for me was the liberation of it. The fences disappeared. The nighthawk tentatively emerged.

At *what* age?

All right, twenty-two. Not exactly adolescence. You want to remember the mid-1950s were a time of order and sensible behavior and noses to the grindstone in high school and college. You didn't get a car if you made the graduation program in high school, and you didn't get twelve weeks in Europe to learn environmental awareness in your freshman year at college. The summer before I graduated from the University of Minnesota, I worked fifteen hundred feet underground in an iron mine, read the *Duluth Herald* for my nighttime recreation, and listened to my worried mother hounding me to go to confession.

But now it was five o'clock in the afternoon in Bismarck, North Dakota, and the horizons stretched to the buttes across the wide Missouri River and so did my time. I didn't have to read Schopenhauer for extra credit tonight or wash the red ore stains off my work clothes. The country roads and outdoor theaters were wide open. Fresh coin from my expanded forty-five-dollar-a-week salary clinked in my pockets. There was nothing to tie down the boulevardier from Big Minny.

There was one small impediment, at that. I was immobile, without wheels. There was one thing more. As a swashbuckling bachelor, I posed very little threat to the local swells. For that I could probably blame the outcome of my first date in Bismarck. The young woman was pleasant and undemanding, an attractive farm girl from Medina, North Dakota. To give myself a fair chance to reveal my sophistication, I borrowed Carl Arp's automobile. Arp was the *Tribune*'s city editor, a man of murky intelligence who was not easy to befriend. But he was a sympathetic man and gave me the keys, carefully. He said first dates should always be a time of moderation, words I had cause to remember six hours later.

For dinner, my date and I drove to one of the roadhouses between Bismarck and Mandan on the west side of the Missouri. I felt a surge of adventure in the tradition of the great frontiersmen Lewis and Clark. But a few hours later I finished closer to Custer. We had dinner and then headed back to Bismarck via a county road renowned for its clusters of secluded cottonwoods.

We parked. I made complimentary mewlings that seemed well received. Our mutual friendliness advanced. The usual gymnastics began. Unfortunately, Arp's automobile didn't match the expectations of the moment. Without warning it went into reverse. I'd parked the car on the edge of a gravel pit, one window lined up with a nearly full moon. I'd forgotten the hand brake. At about the time our exertions were reaching critical mass, the car rolled twenty-five feet backward to the bottom of the gravel pit.

This event totally defused all incitements to amour inside the car. The final embarrassment was that I had to climb out of the pit in the mud and walk two miles to a gas station to get a tow, using the North Star as a navigational aid.

The episode largely ended my after-hours schemes for the summer. But remembering those postcollege bunglings today puts the America I knew in the early 1950s in a frame edged with both gratitude and some guilt. Setting Korea aside, life didn't present much crisis or pain for the young white male just out of college. Most of us were children of the Depression. The memory of the fear and ignominy it inflicted on the elders was soaked into our brains. By the 1950s World War II and America's ascent to world leadership had loosed the country's enormous energies and lifted it to richness and power. For us, it meant jobs, college, and emancipation from the fears of our parents. The legacy of the Depression for its children was the enshrinement of Work. Almost any work. This was ten years before Vietnam. The passionate embracing of social causes by America's young came later, along with the volatility and rebellion those causes generated. The orthodoxies for us in the early 1950s were less dramatic and less visionary—finding work, going to school, getting married, trying to save money, and building a family. We didn't hold seminars on the effect of rural values in our lives, but when I think about it now, there was a heavy overlay of small-town attitudes and traditionalism in how we acted and what we believed. Another value that was hard to evade was the carryover into our own lives of the immigrants' obsession to make it in America.

Partly because of this, the fashion in the past few years among nostalgists has been to idealize those years as the last slice of clean-jean American wholesomeness. Families lived in houses they owned. There was a husband who had a job that could support the family. There was a wife who kept the house and the family together, bought the groceries, paid the bills, and probably worked harder and longer than the husband but was not considered part of the workforce and didn't think much about emancipation until later. The families went together to movies in which everybody wore clothes. Nobody swore on the screen or fornicated with the boss's wife. The family paid its bills on time and rode in a car that didn't incur a twenty-five-hundred-dollar repair bill when the bumper brushed against a vagrant juniper branch. The family usually went to church and didn't hate the government, which it probably saw more as a guardian than as a warden. People didn't go crazy when the employment rate went up, in the hysterical style of stockholders today. More employment and upsurges in business are bad news on Wall Street today. They're supposed to mean that inflation is ready to engulf us. This in turn is supposed to trigger the threat of higher interest rates. This means that when good business news comes, the stock market goes out of its gourd in despondency. And almost *everybody* owns stock today and therefore curses the good economic news because Wall Street is cursing the good news, which allegedly depresses the stock.

In the 1950s, people actually cheered when the business news was good.

The 1950s were the decade in which I graduated from college, got a job, went into the army, got married, and, with my wife, built a house in the suburbs with a 4¾ percent GI home loan. The lives of millions of white males followed roughly the same course. If you had some drive, schooling, a presentable brain, and good health, you could set yourself up for life at a serviceable level of comfort and stability. Millions did, especially the ones who got entrenched with a strong and durable employer early enough to insulate themselves against the nightmares of downsizing and mercurial job changes and the fast-lane syndrome that overtook the boomers in the 1980s and 1990s.

Yet I know now this was not every American's America.

We did talk civil rights and human rights in the early 1950s. We listened to Hubert Humphrey and the other Fair Dealers, and we said, "They're right." I'm not sure whether we talked much about women's rights and Indians' rights and gay rights or thought much about Hispanics and the mentally retarded and others with disabilities. We listened sympathetically when the talk got to the underclass. Sometimes we gave money and friendship. But not many of us walked out into the street to proclaim unfairness in America's society or hounded the politicians to change it. We listened to the offensive language of the casual bigots without challenging it.

That came later, and we can now call this process evolutionary.

It's a comfort, the long view of history. We were better about recognizing the chasms between the haves and the have nots than the generations before us, and that's another consolation. But I do remember now what it was that we left unsaid and undone when I remember the well-documented serenity and good order of life in the 1950s in America.

It wasn't the same country for millions of others. The evidence of that was the muted but rising rumbling we were hearing about injustice. If we couldn't hear the voices, we needed only to look at the faces of hopelessness we saw on the street.

That recognition came later. The war in Korea dominated the news if not the country's psyche in the summer of 1950. Don Whitehead's AP dispatches from the battlefield crossed my desk often—scenes of death and bewilderment and bravery drawn by one of the century's great war correspondents. The war began badly for the Americans and South Koreans, both of them unprepared and undermotivated. The dispatches told of men cursing and dying. I edited the stories and wrote the headlines in the wheat basin of America; Korea did not register on me personally with any power until late summer. And then it landed. The men who were fighting and dying were my age, my peers.

The draft began filling the training camps of America. My notice came from Duluth in the fall. By then the Americans had landed in Inchon, had recaptured Seoul and advanced deep into North Korea, under Douglas MacArthur's orders to carry the offensive to the banks of the Yalu River on the border of Communist China. That set off a new war. Chinese forces by the thousands poured across the Yalu, driving the U.N. armies into retreat.

Right about there, I was welcomed into the U.S. Army at Fort Riley, Kansas. The army experience was a watershed in my life. It could have killed me or embittered me. It did neither. It made me an adult.

With the country suddenly facing communist threats in Korea and in the cold war in Europe, the draft boards sent their deadpan summons—beginning with the chummy "your friends and neighbors"—to hundreds of thousands of young men to fill the regiments and to appease the war gods' appetite. The great majority of the draftees went without protest. Ten years later, forced military service in Vietnam incited rage and rebellion in the cities and on the campuses of America. At home, Vietnam was an ocean-to-ocean confrontation that mocked the social inertia of a comfortable America. It erupted in flames in the street and launched a generational war. It produced an atmosphere of hatred and alienation not witnessed in America since the Civil War. But it also shook the country into realizing the neglect and abuse it had systematically inflicted on its voiceless.

I wasn't twenty-two at the time of Vietnam. I don't know how I would have acted at the thought of getting blown up in a war filled with so much political deceit and scrambled aims. Being yanked out of work to wear a uniform in 1950 wasn't the same kind of trauma. If you were in your early twenties then, you remembered the shared purpose that embraced the country during World War II. You remembered the stars in the windows of proud—if fearful—parents. You remembered the sight of devastated mothers and fathers attending church service a week after learning of their son's death on a tiny Pacific atoll whose name they couldn't pronounce. They didn't blame the government or God or even the Japanese. They were immigrants or the children of immigrants. The country had given them shelter and work and hope. There was an understanding that went with this.

Belonging to the country and accepting its gifts meant accepting the other half of the contract. Sometimes belonging meant grief, or death in a jungle five thousand miles away. Sometimes the blood trail was as mindless as the political slogans that created it. But World War II was an emotional national commitment. When the politicians and generals said "We have to fight," the young went to fight. They might have felt fear, but no true resentment. The national commitment was hardly the same for Korea, but for the young the idea of an obligation to serve hadn't changed much. Today, that sounds like a terribly romanticized portrait of the citizen's relationship with the America of the earlier 1950s. But it was pretty much the attitude not only of the immigrants but also of rural and small-town America—in fact, of most of America. So when I boarded the train in Duluth for Fort Riley with a contingent of draftees from Minnesota, I had nothing in particular to wail about, didn't think a lot about getting blown up, and looked at military service as part of a young man's passage.

To be candid about it, I found something in it that gave me a lift. Going into the army at the time of Korea put me in a moral fraternity with the veterans from my hometown who fought in the Big War. I even remembered the mock horror stories from training camp, stocked with the gargoyles from the drill field. And here was the first gargoyle, on my first full day in the army, standing in the company street in front of rows of barracks and five hundred recruits. He wore the stripes of a master sergeant, and he was well launched into a speech terrorizing us with the muck that lay ahead if we forgot that we were now in the army of the United States. Nothing in life was going to be the same, he said. He carried a swagger stick. It was a genuine swagger stick, right out of the time of Kipling and Kitchener. He bounced it in the palm of his left hand. He rammed it under his armpit. He paced up and down the street. He bellowed and mugged. He was loving it, and he had us scared witless.

"You screw up, and may God have mercy on your soul, because your ass is mine."

He may have been right. But the sergeant and his swagger stick disappeared the next day. I don't know in what burlesque casting bureau they found this guy, or where they hid him between indoctrinations. But he was succeeded the next day by a working sergeant who had a more pragmatic message: "You're probably all going to Korea. If you listen to us, you've got a chance of coming home standing up instead of in a box."

In the ancient field of motivational rhetoric, more inspirational speeches have been given. He had the look and sound of the real army, although he wasn't quite right about all of us going to Korea. After basic training, one of the personnel officers at Fort Riley saw my newspaper background in the files and assigned me to a new company forming at Riley. It was bound for Germany to conduct psychological warfare in support of combat troops if war broke out with the Soviets.

The Fifth Loudspeaker and Leaflet Company.

This is truth. That was its actual military designation. A few months later when we were installed in a reformed German army barracks outside of Stuttgart, we had a hard time defining the exalted role of the Fifth Loudspeaker and Leaflet to the wind-reddened men of the First Infantry Division, the Big Red One. The company's mission statement made it a little more palatable. We were there to induce enemy troops to surrender and to convince natives in the battlefront towns that we were their friends bent on liberation. This seemed to put a lot of faith in the power of loudspeaker microphones and propaganda leaflets fluttering in the Russian sky above ten thousand Voroshilov tanks. But the system had scored some successes in World War II, and a sister company of ours was already operating in Korea. The L&L was taken seriously by the army's psychological warfare eggheads as an instrument of persuasion against the Russians. Toward that end, we were stocked with linguist-émigrés from Eastern Europe, young engravers and silk screeners from the states, and four or five scriptwriters, including me. We learned what we could about the mentality of Soviet soldiers and how to appeal to Soviet citizens under siege at home, although sometimes it got flaky.

This was only six years after the end of World War II. The streets of Frankfurt and Munich crawled with clandestine characters, spies, double agents, pornographers, prostitutes, pimps, and miscellaneous hustlers. When you walked around at night you fully expected to see Orson Welles popping out of a sewer from the reels of *The Third Man*. At the elevated rank of corporal, wearing civilian clothes and given the cover name and identity of Frank Novak, a researcher from Princeton, I represented the U.S. Army in Europe in dialogue with two dozen other shadowy conferees (all of them with bogus names and titles) at a gathering of the Allies' psychological warfare experts in Frankfurt. We were there to interrogate Soviet expatriates. The idea was to get a psychological composite of Soviet warriors and citizens. It got more fascinating when one of the Soviet defectors at the conference approached me on my way to dinner in a Frankfurt restaurant. He talked in Russian. I shook my head. In wobbling German I said I didn't understand Russian and asked if he spoke English. He did. He said he recognized me instantly as a member of a dissident group in

Leningrad, under investigation by the KGB, or whatever they called it in those years. I said he had it wrong, but we could talk about it at the next day's conference. I never saw him again. He might have disappeared into a sewer, looking for Welles.

For me, it was Europe instead of the foxholes of Korea. I've thought of it a hundred times. My short work history, six months with a small newspaper in North Dakota, insulated me from the battlefield. I've always felt uneasy about that, especially when I'd encounter somebody from our basic training company years later and we talked about who went to Korea, and what happened. And after that, I got myself into a corner and had to reflect: "What did you want? Absolution? Glory? What? If you had wanted that, you could have volunteered for Korea."

Not many draftees did. When I finished with the acrobatics of logic and with the adolescent images I had of the soldier in time of war, I was left with this: the army and the war were a numbers game. Some got shot up. Some went the other way. Somebody at an assignment desk, faceless and nameless to the one whose life he was controlling, punched the numbers. Today, no human hand would decide life or death. The computers, without obligation to God, country, or adolescent images, would make the decision.

Whoever or whatever made the decision in my case shaped my life in a way I couldn't have foreseen. The army was a compass of chance, steering me into places and relationships that molded my attitudes for a lifetime. It could have been Korea, but it became Europe. It could have been death or disability, but it became an open door to the world. It thrust me into cultures that had mingled richly and violently for centuries, that had created America. It led me into friendships with German, Swiss, Austrian, English, and Italian people that lasted for life. It introduced me to their music, their food, their homes, and their neuroses. I was impressionable and sometimes naive. But this was the formative time of my life, and my walks to the mountains of Switzerland put me into a land of snow peaks and thousand-foot waterfalls I'd only imagined from the pages of the child's geography book. They whipped up fantasies about high-altitude climbing and stuck in my glands with an insistence that ultimately made adventure in the high country one of the passageways of my life.

And there was the effect of the army experience itself. It inflicted its casual and zany humilities. But in the gruff way armies do, it imbued the idea of belonging to something large and important. The army fiercely cherished its tradition of ostrich-headed bureaucracy then, and I assume it still does. But long after I've forgotten that, I'll remember the relaxed intelligence and friendship of David E. Lillienthal Jr., my best friend in the army and an uncommonly good writer who became a novelist and adventurer a little more restrained than I. We traveled Switzerland together and amused each other with shaggy-dog stories about our separate travels. Dave's were often in Italy and mine included London, where one morning I saw Winston Churchill in action in Parliament, deriding his baiters from the ranks of Labor. It was a show. The excuse was a mediocre dispute over the price of the metal wolfram. It took me a couple of hours to figure out that wolfram had something to do with tungsten. I forgot what the fight was about the next morning. But the picture of Winston Churchill, rumbling and posturing, mixing pugnacity with mischief, will stay with me forever. For that alone, I'll be a friend of the army to the end.

Europe and the cold war didn't dull my fondness for prairie journalism. A few weeks after my discharge from the army, I took the train back to Bismarck to discover that I'd been reincarnated as a legislative reporter. John Hjelle was anxious that I should not be overcome by calm and tedium after my liaisons with spies and other slippery characters in Europe. To guard against this threat, he assigned me to cover the North Dakota House of Representatives, an institution that had never been intimidated by calm and order. To preserve its reputation for squirrelly behavior, the House early in the 1953 session proposed a bill to ban dancing in the dark in North Dakota. A week later it introduced another landmark in frontier statesmanship, a bill to prohibit buying by the round in all licensed bars and taverns in North Dakota. Nobody was able to explain whether the bill was meant to serve the interests of the abstinence groups or the cheapskates. I was filing furiously one week trying to find a glimmer of social value in this legislative wackoland when I got a call from Moses offering me a job with the AP in Minneapolis. He said he'd asked Hjelle's permission to tamper with a client's employee—me—and Hjelle said go ahead. North Dakota is crazy only when the legislature is in session, Hjelle said, and he couldn't guarantee legislative reporters much hysteria during the wheat-growing season.

In Minneapolis, Moses said, I could expect to cover political strife, tornadoes, blizzards, floods, murders, traffic accidents, and hairy fish stories like everybody else, plus the Gophers, golf tournaments, and ice-chunk kicking. I asked when did I start. He said how about today. Three days later I was at Stillwater Prison covering an inmate riot. A few hours earlier I'd taken the dictation of Jack Mackay, the Minnesota AP's St. Paul and capitol correspondent. Jack's story was about intramural brawling among the state Senate's policy makers. He dictated ad lib from notes. Some of the syntax was rough, but I marveled at his ability to craft a comprehensible and readable story off the wall. On the day of the riot, I picked up a phone in the prison, intending to give the rewrite man in the Minneapolis office material for a new lead on the prison riot.

"Waddya have?" Gale Tollin asked.

I was about to give him the notes when I remembered Mackay writing that five-hundred-word story off the top of his skull. I sucked in some air and said, "See how far we can go with this." I gave him the dateline and then plowed into the action. Several kinds of anguish promptly squeezed in on me. How many prisoners were rioting? Who knew? It was dozens. It could have been hundreds. Don't estimate. Leave it to the warden. I started dictating. "Inmates at the Minnesota State Prison in Stillwater rioted today, filling the corridors with smoke from burning mattresses to enforce demands against prison authorities." Something on that order. It got stickier a few paragraphs later. Trying to keep the story running, I grubbed through my notes for quotes from prison guards and their superiors. None of the notes were legible. I started the quoted paragraph again. Pause. Tollin was kind. "We've got time," he said. I'm not sure we did. I attacked the notes again. Three pages of them fell into a puddle of water created when a water glass spilled off the desk I was working on. I ducked to picked them up and the line disconnected.

I dialed again and Tollin was back on the line. "We've sent your first six grafs," he said. "You're going great."

I felt like Napoleon.

"But we could use more."

I paraphrased the notes I remembered. With the rest of them submerged, I switched to description—the acrid smell of the burning mattresses, the obscenities coming from the smoking cells, the threats and the hatred.

The dictation came hard, dragged haltingly out of my brain, emerging more or less full grown. When I finished I thanked Tollin and asked if he would mind, well . . .

"Cleaning it up?"

Yeah.

"Sure." Tollin was a pudgy, talkative guy. In the tight spots, he was also cordial and accommodating. He didn't tell me about all of the double negatives and homeless clauses he'd already flushed out. Yet it was a beginning for me of a peculiar form of wire service journalism, beating the clock and conserving the resources of understaffed offices with extemporaneous dictation. I saved no time that first day, nor the next time I dictated. But eventually I found myself in sync with the idea. I liked the discipline it demanded and the satisfaction it gave. I found that I could organize paragraphs and sections of a piece if I was not intimidated by soundless pauses and if I didn't squirm at the thought of the guy on the other end of the phone squirming. It didn't have to be frantic. It was a dumb idea if it deteriorated into that. Once you were confident with it, you could take the time to deliver insight if it was that kind of piece, or to tell a funny story with punch lines.

But the mechanics of delivering a story, and sometimes even the writing of it, dimmed in emotional wallop alongside the encounters with some of the unforgettable faces of history. Here was Haile Selassie, Ethiopia's tiny Lion of Judah, looking unbearably solemn in his beard and uniform, holding a reception in St. Paul in what was supposed to be a ceremony of state. But the sight of this man, his every movement brushed by the tragedy of his people and his archaic reign, sent the young reporter's mind racing back to the old newsreels of the 1930s, when the Lion of Judah stood before the League of Nations and hopelessly asked it to stop Mussolini's invasion of his country. And now in St. Paul, twenty years later, he was going through the motions of conducting a press conference, which produced absolutely nothing newsy or notable other than a face out of the ages of human struggle and human folly.

And not long later here was an elderly woman, tall and superficially awkward in how she walked, her voice breaking into split pitches and cackles that might have seemed comical if this were not Eleanor Roosevelt. She walked into a Minneapolis department store out of a long-playing, rough-and-tumble fairy tale. She came out of an American political revolution, out of a personal torment Americans were just beginning to understand, and out of a White House soap opera. She was promoting her last book, escorted by an obscure Minnesota politician, Joe Robbie, who later became the owner of the Miami Dolphins. There were only two or three of us to talk about her book there among the shelves at Dayton's. Local television in those years didn't have people to staff an event like this. And besides, Eleanor Roosevelt was an institution who no longer seemed relevant; she was a little musty, a little shrill in her plugs for Adlai Stevenson, and definitely past tense.

But I couldn't take my eyes from her, from the movements of her hands and her homely-elegant face and the spontaneity in her eyes. I admit it wasn't entirely her personality I found hard to resist. She breathed the America of the Depression years and the great sweep of its World War II victory. Her husband was gone, but what remained was enough—Eleanor with her conscience, Eleanor with her lanky awkwardness and her stubborn awareness of the neglected. We had five minutes of private conversation. I asked the obligatory questions and did some fencing with her answers. But I don't think I fooled her. I didn't see her as a book peddler or a politician. When I saw her I saw FDR and Henry Morganthau and Harry Hopkins and the Hyde Park upper crust, bread lines and lawn parties with parasols and Eleanor, a lonely, vanishing icon of a time that became part of the country's soul.

Because the newspaper reader has a stake in it, I'd like to offer an aside here on the attitudes most sensible reporters will try to carry into a meeting with celebrities, newsmakers, and the notorious. Often they are the legitimate heroes and heroines of society. Writers' attitudes toward those personalities can bear on the stories they write. No reporter wants to go into a session with one of those megastars feeling awed. If he does, transfer him to advertising. There is practically no danger of anybody in the business getting starstruck in today's era of commercial cynicism among the talking and writing heads and the growing trend toward ambush journalism. And most of today's heroes and high-profile characters have had enough of their warts exposed to insulate the public against any threat of blind adulation. Nobody is saddled with many illusions anymore, least of all the people with the microphones and tape recorders. But I felt then as a young man in the trade, and I still feel, that you can respect a person's achievements or character, without compromising your responsibility to probe and to nag.

A peculiar but real fellowship seasoned the AP office where I worked, and it sticks with me forty years later. It didn't necessarily generate close friendship. Some of us, in fact, weren't friends at all. We were a small, mostly anonymous clump of reporters and editors sharing the charter of taking care of the clients' needs, in a business that brought with it peculiar but lasting gratification. A breaking story would develop out in the country. A man with a shotgun runs amok. Children fall in a farmyard. The first news comes at 1:30 P.M., at about deadline time for dozens of small dailies in the area where we distribute the news. The Twin Cities metropolitan morning newspapers will play this story prodigiously on their front pages tomorrow. No small afternoon daily wants to get shut out on that big midday story and have to look sleepy and inept to its subscribers when the big morning papers gallop into their towns.

So there was—and is—a collective busting of butts in the wire service office to get something into those small newspapers before they shut down for the day. The process took more than quick feet and sweat. A certain sort of trust had to be stirred into the mix, a confidence in the judgment and skills of the person working next to you— whether it was the benevolent, bald-headed day city editor, Arn Pearson, or the curmudgeon from the journalism of the Roaring Twenties, George Bradley, heavy-handed and irreverent but reliable.

Or Joe Kane.

Joe and I had been classmates at the university and found our way to the Minneapolis AP by separate routes. He wrote with a minimum of flash, but clearly and with an impact. He was frugal with color in his personality stories, but what he did use was almost always tasteful and enriching. Years later he moved to Washington, D.C., and became one of the AP's most respected senior editors before he died. We were friends and often worked the same shift. I walked into the office from lunch one day and found Joe alone at the desk, taking notes on his typewriter by phone. He turned away from the phone when I sat down and said hurriedly, "It's a bank robbery in a little town in western Minnesota." He went back to banging his typewriter with notes from our stringer. I glanced at what he'd taken. It was a Toonerville-sized town, but the haul was big and the robber was evidently racing through the back roads ducking the gendarmes. This was forty years ago. There wasn't that much major league crime in rural Minnesota, and a bank hardly ever got held up. Joe was in a sweat hammering out his notes, and I didn't feel very valuable standing around and watching. I rolled my typewriter next to his, pulled out his first sheet of notes, and started writing. I'd done three or four paragraphs and then stopped Joe and asked him to read it. "This OK?" Joe read and nodded. I handed the copy to the filing editor, Bob Brugere, and worked through the next batch of Joe's notes. We had most of the story on the wire about the time Joe hung up, dripping. Kane was a basically reserved guy with streaks of droll behavior.

"If the money is wrong"—the figure we had used—he said, "I'm going to say you were trigger-happy and should have waited until the sheriff verified it instead of blindly following my notes."

I called his attention to the fact that the sheriff at the moment was charging through western Minnesota at eighty miles an hour in hot pursuit of a bank robber and was in no position to count cash. The figure, though, stood up. So did the story. No applause was heard. None was needed. The reward was in putting the story together, knowing each other, and being willing to risk our credibility on each other's judgment.

But on the day after the election in 1960, the risk ran substantially deeper.

The Kennedy-versus-Nixon returns were dribbling in slowly by early morning on November 9. A couple of the confirmed insomniacs on the staff stayed on to handle the vote count over the graveyard hours. The rest of us went home for a few hours of sleep. My wife, Rose, an unrepentant Democrat who had proudly worn a pin celebrating the hole in Adlai Stevenson's campaign shoe in the 1950s, asked how it was going with Kennedy and Nixon in Minnesota.

"It'll probably end in a tie," I said. "They could have a recount lasting until Christmas."

I was back in the office at 7:00 A.M. Kennedy had been favored in Minnesota, but it was already a momentous election for the state. The incumbent Democratic-Farmer-Labor governor, Orville Freeman, was being defeated by Elmer Andersen, a popular state senator and liberal Republican who benefited from Freeman's involving the National Guard in a violent labor dispute in the Albert Lea packing industry. The effect of that race on the presidential battle in Minnesota could only be guessed at. But shortly before 9:00 A.M., Adolph Johnson, the office's designated maven on Minnesota politics, brought some news to Moses. He said Kennedy and Nixon were running practically even with Minnesota's votes counted except for a significant batch running into the tens of thousands from northeastern Minnesota.

The count always dragged out in northeastern Minnesota in those years. There were several reasons—the remoteness, the habits of the county auditors, the pace in tallying, and maybe a little bit of the perversity of the Iron Range.

Adolph Johnson was the portrait of restraint as a wire service man. Sometimes his caution was painful to see; it was like watching a man check the sky for hail and lightning before crossing the street. As a reporter and analyst at the capitol, he weighed and he calculated and he looked on the other hand. But he was as reliable as four feet of ice on the lake. This ultimate man of discretion now advised Moses, "If the voting patterns of the last ten years mean anything in northeastern Minnesota, Kennedy is going to win three-fourths of those votes. If he does, and that's practically a cinch, he wins in Minnesota."

Which meant that Kennedy was the new president of the United States, because he was only six votes short of a majority in the electoral college and Minnesota counted eleven. Moses called me into the discussion. "Adolph says Kennedy will wrap it up in Minnesota when all the votes come in from the Range and Duluth," he said. "You have any thoughts about it?"

I said Adolph knew the numbers better than anybody in Minnesota and that nothing I'd been hearing from Rangers all fall was going to turn them into flaming Nixonites the day of the election. Moses said he appreciated this seat-of-the-pants evaluation, but the real reason he was asking me had to do with professional courtesy. If the Minneapolis AP was going write Kennedy into the presidency, I was going to be the author.

I sat down to a typewriter scanning Adolph's numbers. But the judge on the call—all right, the Solomon—had to be Moses. It was his call as the price or the curse of his command. He thanked us, rolled his eyes, and walked to a telephone to tell the AP's general desk in New York that we were going to elect Kennedy from Minneapolis. He explained why.

The general desk mahatma listened and said he was persuaded. He wished us well and then, Moses recalled later, offered what he thought was a useful suggestion: "Be right."

In the 1960s we typed on onionskin paper with three carbon copies beneath. Sometimes the stuff jammed in the typewriter. I grabbed a sheet of rough copy paper instead and started writing. The general desk in New York hung a number for us on the national trunk wire.

This put up a green light on the teletype circuit for MP, or Minneapolis. It said, in effect, "Come on with your blockbuster, Minneapolis."

I didn't spend much time in the clutches of creation. The news was that John F. Kennedy had won Minnesota's electoral votes and clinched the U.S. presidency, becoming the first Roman Catholic elected to the White House.

That's about what I said in the first paragraph. Moses yanked it out of the typewriter, scanned it for typographical errors and syntax, and ran it to the teletype machine with a BULLETIN label. He was back a few seconds later, trying not to hover, but hovering nonetheless. I felt all the juices of the chase, but the story had to say why Nixon could not now overcome Kennedy's lead. It had to describe the tautness of their duel in Minnesota. And, although this lead from Minnesota climaxing the election would soon be superseded by a new general election story from New York, ours had to hit the big accent points of the Kennedy victory—its narrowness in the popular vote, how it reflected on the major issues in the campaign, and what it might bring to the White House.

I can't remember any special tension. But I do remember feeling the goad to keep it rolling. I flew through it one and two paragraphs at a time. Moses ferried them to the printer. Halfway through it, without a copy in front of me, I needed information and yelled to the teletype operator, maybe Bob Mexner, "How does that last paragraph end?"

He tried his level best to oblige.

"With a period," he shouted.

We won the battle with the tough and combative UPI by about an hour. The world's newspapers and broadcast stations gave the news to their millions by way of a teletype machine in Minneapolis, Minnesota.

And when they finally got around to tabulating the Iron Range vote, it was about three to one for Kennedy. Adolph Johnson, the cautious oracle, went home and celebrated the day with a glass of milk.

2/ Echoes of Cool Red Tunnels

The call of the wolf won wide popularity among nature lovers as the symbolic sound of northern Minnesota winter in later years. But in the mining town where I grew up, the sound that brought the snow and north wind of approaching winter suddenly close to the skin was the squeal of a dying pig.

Once every late November in my hometown of Ely on the Iron Range, the families gathered at Grandma Rose's to slaughter a pig and make sausage for the winter. It was also Grandpa Joe's, of course, but Rose was the empress of the family and especially of the grandchildren. She gave presents and kisses in profusion. In the family, she combined the highest callings of counselor and chair of the board. You couldn't confuse it with a corporate board. We wouldn't be making blood sausage in her backyard on a November morning if it were that. But there was a roughly constituted round table of family affairs on the Iron Range then. Its moral leadership usually fell to a woman like Rose, whose memory of America reached back to the throngs at Ellis Island, where she could not understand the voices but could understand the surge of excitement she felt and the bewilderment she saw in the faces of the others as they pressed toward the gates of their new land and its deep void of the unknown. That had been nearly a half century before. The country they left, Slovenia in what became Yugoslavia, was a dead end for Rose, for her husband, and for thousands like them. It was dominated by Austria, which, exercising the overlord's prerogative, decided which of the native children could go to school. Sometimes it was as primitive and as cruel as a lineup in the street. Every fifth or tenth child would be selected. The rest had no appeal.

Rose's kids rarely groused about cold rooms in the middle of winter in Minnesota or about rock-headed teachers at school. If she heard it, she listened for a while and then slapped the table. In her broken English, she recalled the scenes of what the immigrants called "the old country." The sound of her hand banging the oak tabletop needed no translation. "Enough," it said.

To her children, she spoke Slovenian most of the time. It was easier all around because they grew up hearing and speaking their parents' tongue, learning the names of the unpronounceable towns where their parents grew up, the Ribnicas and the Crnomelces. The grandchildren didn't bother grappling with the rest of those Slavic syllables. When they bitched, they did it in English, and when they were told off by the family matriarch, it was prompt and in English and didn't allow for rebuttal.

If you were a linguistic expert, you could have unscrambled dialogue like that in the Finnish and Italian homes as well. Add Croatian, Bulgarian, and Greek. I don't know how many made blood sausage on a November morning in the 1930s and 1940s. As children, we assumed it was some kind of ethnic food, unaware that this was common fare among the Scandinavians in town as well as some of the other nationalities. But I don't know how many others gathered the clans on a November Saturday and turned the grinding of sausage into a family festival where wine flowed when the pig was well and truly dead. And Rose brought out a stumpy grinding machine two feet high, and with it a washtub full of boiled pig intestines she used for sausage casings. The sight foreshadowed an axiom I learned years later: if you want to enjoy feasting on hot dogs at a picnic, never tour a sausage factory.

Re-creating the day years later on a drive back to Ely for my grandmother's funeral, I was struck by the tribal quality of that scene of sausage making and reunion on the brink of winter. There couldn't have been much aesthetic content in all of that mess. What I did remember warmly was the sociable sense of ritual that went with a day like that on the Range. Sausage making for the immigrants was a bridge to the old country. The memory of Europe brought them few glints of rekindled joy—the old country with its thin pantries and the boots of the emperor's army and the dead ends. But it was, after all, their homeland and the cradle of their family, and it taught them their songs. So they sang the songs and spoke the language, but the Iron Range was the new frontier of their lives. If they had ever envisioned

America as a place where lotus gardens flowered outside their windows and velvet carpets carried them into the streets, they didn't find the gardens and the carpets. Most of them got shantytowns on the edge of the mining pits. The men went into the mines. The women hung the family clothes on the line when the temperature was fifteen degrees below zero. The plumbing, when it came in, was erratic. It wasn't the Austrian government that ruled their lives now, or the czar in Russia, or the kings and queens. Now the mining companies disbursed the money and made most of the rules.

But in the mining town of Minnesota there was one abiding difference from the times and places that had squashed them down before they came to America. Fear had gone out of their lives. So had futility. True, the dirt of the mining town might have been a little deeper than the dirt of the old country. They were embarrassed by their ignorance of the language and having to sequester themselves in their self-protective colonies, where people spoke a language they could understand and nobody laughed at their crudities. But there were schools in this town. Their children would grow up speaking English. If they did their lessons, they could escape the shantytowns and the dark red pits where the immigrant men worked.

On the way to my last visit to my grandmother, driving old Highway 61 from the Twin Cities to the Iron Range, I prayed for forgiveness and said a prayer of thanks. I came back to my hometown as a newspaper columnist in the midst of a life seasoned with action and familiar with the faces of celebrity. But until that day in December of 1969, I hadn't realized what the mining town on the edge of the wilderness had implanted in my life. I don't think I really comprehended until then the tang and the richness and the wonderful looniness that all of those mixed tongues and cultures had conspired to produce. The names and the insults we threw at each other would probably put us in court in a seventy-five-page defamation suit today. They were thick with derision and mockery, mean and naked. They did eventually take on a softer coat of good-natured ribbing, but that took a while. The nationalities came together, the light-skinned Finns and the darker, maybe faintly menacing South Slavs and Italians and the rest. Color me a darker, maybe faintly menacing South Slav. The other settlers called the Slovenians and Croatians "garlic gabbers." You can believe that this was one of the politer terms of odium. And when the rest of us heard an unexplained boom from somewhere above the ore tunnels, somebody in Zenith Location (dominated by the Slavs) would smirk with the answer: "The Finnish navy is back in action"—meaning that they were dynamiting fish out on the lake. It didn't matter whether *all* of the Slovenians smelled of garlic or whether there really was a Finnish dynamite flotilla out there on the water. The backbiting gossip and name calling were games, mostly harmless. But they did establish little pieces of turf for the nationalities in town.

The Vermilion Range and its enclaves were isolated from the larger and more prominent Mesabi. Ely was not the Mesabi's Hibbing or Eveleth. Its red riches did not lie in the caverns called open pits, where men could see the sun—or feel the hard clamp of subzero cold—while they and their machines dug those giant concentric circles of the oval mining strip. On the Vermilion Range, where Ely and Tower and Soudan grew, the ore that would become the steel of the automobiles and artillery of America was buried more than a thousand feet beneath the surface. To pry it out of its subterranean lodes, men had to descend into the red tunnels with lamps on their helmets, carrying lunch pails in which their wives or daughters had packed pork chop sandwiches or pasties or Polish sausages, a thermos of coffee, and a chocolate bar or a wedge of homemade pie. In a large elevator suspended beneath a two-inch steel cable, they were lowered into the claustrophobia of a mine shaft sunk a quarter of a mile deep below the mine's head frame. No one ever called it the elevator. It was, simply, "the cage." In the summer between college terms when I worked underground to help pay tuition, I never heard a miner refer to "the cage" with any trace of martyrdom or sarcasm. It was a blunt, unlovely word for a blunt and unlovely vehicle. Nothing much else seemed to fit. Elevators ran in hotels. This was the underground mine. Call it the cage.

Oddly, the cage and the damp tunnels became a gruff forum for the beginnings of mutual tolerance in a laboring town of so many mixed tongues and ethnic feuds transported from the old world. Sensitivity it wasn't. The Range mining towns in those years were outposts of hardcore macho. But if you were an immigrant or a first-generation Finn and your mining partner was a Croatian, the suspicions and the crude jokes tended to dissolve. The bridges were built slowly. They asked about one another's families. They shared the work and the bonus pay that came with harder work. They shared the intramural horseplay and sometimes the fear. Even into the 1940s and 1950s, after much of the mining had been mechanized and federal law had mandated safety practices and the mining companies cooperated, death underground was always a risk. Once or twice a year during the catechism classes of my childhood, I'd look down the aisle of our church and see a black-draped catafalque placed near the altar to bear the coffin of a member of the church killed in a cave-in fourteen hundred feet beneath the surface. It was chilling. It frightened me because my father went underground each day or each night five days a week, round the calendar. Once he was trapped in a cave-in and buried to his waist. He had been mining since the age of fifteen, when his mother and father died of cancer within a few months of each other, leaving ten children. My father was the oldest. There weren't many foster homes on the Iron Range in the early 1920s. Even if there had been, the creed in the mining town was to keep the family together. There were no trips to the office for aid to the families of dependent children. Nearly twenty years after his death, I still have no idea what my father wrote on the line for "age" in his application to the mining company. There may not have been such a line. If there was, the supervising mining captain ignored it. Here was a kid from the eighth grade trying to support his brothers and sisters, his parents gone.

The captain gave him a helmet and a carbide lamp. In the eighth grade he'd received good grades in arithmetic, and in another time he might have been an honor roll student and a college grad. He'd hoped some day to go to sea. It was the one fantasy of his life. He'd read books and listened to sailors, and in his walks to the schoolhouse through the snowdrifts he imagined a career in the United States Navy, visiting the exotic ports of call and breathing the ocean air.

There were no exotic places for a fifteen-year-old swinging a pick a thousand feet below ground. His youngest sister was sheltered in an orphanage in Duluth for a few years, but was restored to the family when the older sisters and the other two brothers were old enough to work. The family survived. The kid who would never see the ocean became a shift boss underground after a few years and married a young woman named Mary, the child of Slovenian immigrants, as he was. Four of his sisters and a brother eventually moved to Milwaukee and married. The two other sisters married and stayed in Ely. So did the two younger brothers. There was no dramatic rise to riches for any of these people, but all lived worthwhile lives. Sympathetic poets might have seen in the underground mine an oblivion of the spirit. No such poetry appeared in our family's archives. The iron mine became the family's salvation, the mine and the teenage boy who would never see the world.

It happened much that way for scores of families in my hometown. It was not enough reason for them to love the underground mine or the mining companies that gave them work. There wasn't much humanitarianism in the relationship of company, miner, and mine. But one of the reasons I gave thanks on the drive to my grandmother's funeral was seeing the whole sweaty but glorious metaphor of the American idea summarized by the lifetime of this woman who came out of the Slovenian highlands and landed on Ellis Island, scared but thrilled. I remembered her comforting bosom when I was a child. I remembered her sitting beside that funny black meat grinder, churning out dozens of fat and squishy sausages, filling the casings with rice and pork chunks and pig's blood and running a pointed peg through the sausage ends to create a ringlet that would be frozen and kept for the long northern winter.

At that moment she was not a portrait to be confused with Whistler's mother. But she provided, and she made the family unbreakable.

On the Range, and over a wider geography than that, she was an Everywoman of her time, the immigrant matriarch of her family. She and the Finnish and Croatian and Jewish and Polish and Bulgarian and Scandinavian and English and Irish women and the women of a dozen other nationalities were priceless to the country's future. Their people were disgorged from the steamers by the thousands, expecting no peppermint canes and lemon trees in the new country and without illusions about what lay ahead: leaky roofs and muddy streets in the mining towns, a mole's life in the pits for the men.

They were carried on the corporate books of the time as Cheap Labor. They might not have been aware of that, but it wouldn't have bothered them much if they had been. America was their redemption. It might laugh at their clumsy English and be scared by their foreign faces. But it would pay if they worked. It was huge and unstoppable, America. I didn't know what Grandma Rose's dreams were in the highlands before she left the old country. But in my newspaper column a few days after her funeral, I explored what those dreams might have been and what her reality became. Doing it, I found a different kind of mine on the Iron Range, one not likely to run dry. This one yielded its riches in the thick broth of the mining town's personalities. They carried to Minnesota's north their cacophonous tongues and yearnings, their furies and hilarities. I began bringing the Range into the newspaper. The stories seemed to fascinate our readers, city dwellers and farm people who had always been inquisitive about what lay out there on that strange frontier of ore canyons and people who talked with their hands.

Grandma Rose. I never did decide what she imagined she would find or what she would become. Her husband worked underground for thirty years. His pension amounted to a few bucks a week when he retired. He didn't feel exploited or underpaid. His kids went to school. He had food on the table and pin cherry wine in the basement. In some years it was zinfandel wine, the years when he and a few hundred others contracted with the Casagrandes in Virginia for a load of Michigan grapes. It was legal, more or less, depending on how much wine you made. The cops didn't usually inquire, because the cops had some sizable barrels in their own basements.

Grandma Rose gave me my first Christmas present and a grandmother's last embrace. She saw the country in terms of the bread and the integrity it gave her family, in the beans and the dandelion salad they ate in the early years and something better as they grew older and the unions got stronger and the wages went up. The day after she died I wrote:

> I don't think it occurred to her that the road ran two ways, that the genius and greatness of America flows more profoundly from the conflicts and struggles of its people than from its treasure; and that by this measurement, one of its small but imperishable gifts came from the lady who spoke broken English and sang the songs of her native village. Most of the immigrants are dead now or dying, the Scandinavians and Germans, Italians, Finns, Slavs, Welsh, the others. On the Iron Range, the mines with their 12-hour days of the 1920s first tyrannized them, but later welded a rough democracy among their sons and daughters.
>
> Here for three or four decades was the essence of the American destiny—the meshing of the immigrant's hunger for identity with the nation's restless reach for fulfillment. The mining headframes have been dismantled now and the tunnels have been left to the echoes of the grinding tuggers and bantering miners. The old men on the hills have outlasted the pits that might have entombed them. My grandmother lived to see her youngest son become an internationally renowned scientist in the microchip field, and a global lecturer. She lived to enjoy the modest luxury of a TV in her living room. In the fashion of the mining town society, she was the unquestioned conscience of her family. In this,

she stood only a half step below the church, and there were times when that was a close call. Of the several tests of passage to manhood on the Range, I can't remember one more expressive than when the lady wordlessly included my glass in the pouring of wine for a New Year's toast at the family table. The devotion to family up there is fierce and sometimes melodramatic. As it was in the sodhouse on the prairie, it was the refuge against ordeal, the one invincible reality for the immigrant. So there was no gold-paved street for the girl from the Balkan highlands. I don't know what she envisioned, but I do know what she meant to us. And her requiem is in the faces of the once-hungry who trusted her and do not want today.

On the Range, the tenderness and guidance came from the mother. The father set the rules. When necessary, he gave the whacks. This was not exactly gender equality, nor did that form of family discipline pay much attention to the Beatitudes. In fact, it would horrify family counselors today, and conceivably get the old man tossed in jail. It's simply the way it was, the last stand of the patriarchal fiefdom brought over from old Europe. Neither my brother nor I got many whacks from our father, or many embraces. Mike never felt comfortable revealing affection. He was the father in the style of his own father, who acquired the style in the hills of Slovenia, where the idea went back a few millennia. The stoical, distant father was hardly peculiar to the Iron Range. Not many social attitudes have clung so obstinately in humanity's stumbling attempts over the centuries to arrange its roles and privileges. It took the revolutions of the 1960s and the new-age psychology plus the courts and a million television sitcoms to produce some symptoms of democracy in the house. What might have been different on the Iron Range was the harshness of the work, which heightened the husband and father's role as the Provider.

Although I spent twenty years in his house, I didn't know my father well. I was proud of him and, by my lights, I loved him. I know that cut both ways, but my father didn't speak of love. He wasn't an especially stern man. At work he was a leader as the foreman of a mining crew, but that role rarely transmitted itself to the living room at a time when we might have been sifting through what today we'd call family issues. At the table our conversation was frugal. It wasn't until I came home from college and the army that his questions and responses seemed genuinely animated. Our best times were later in my adulthood and near the end of his life, after the mine had shut down and he was working part time in a lumberyard to stay busy. He and mother visited at my home for a week or two at a time. I'd take him to a ball game and our talk afterward was lively and lasted late into the night. And the next evening I'd come home from work and find some new architecture going up on the house, a deck or railing or whatever he had time for. We'd reached the level of good friends at ease with each other.

But something was missing, and I'll always regret that. We never achieved a relaxed relationship like the one between Dick and our dad. My brother, four years younger, was a hunter. The two of them spent days together in the fall prowling the woods for deer, enjoyed the times immensely, and valued them. But my recollection of our earlier days was that while life in the family was relatively normal, there weren't many tidal waves of laughter in our house. My mother deferred to Mike on most questions except for finance, which she ran efficiently and without much consultation. He brought home the check. When he did, he often went "uptown" for some beers and brandies with his cronies at Garni's Bar, one of forty or fifty taverns in a village of five thousand. This was mining country. It was still a frontier in the 1940s. If Mike limited himself to two or three drinks, he'd come home at nine o'clock and become—to my brother's and my amazement (we were lying in bed listening to the performance in the kitchen)—a standup comedian. A few drinks gave him permission to escape from his straitjacket as the reticent Provider. He had a good mind and, when he was loose, a gift for storytelling. His audience was my mother, who pretended to scoff at his exaggerations, drawn from the deer stands and the fishing holes in the Shagawa ice. But she delighted in those interludes because for her, too, they were a holiday from the laconic formality of their workaday dialogue.

Was there a place for genuine love in this house?

Yes, there was. Love may have been defined differently in a home like ours in a mining town in the 1930s and 1940s, in marriages like that of my mother and father. In today's relationships and families, love is intimacy and awareness of each other's feelings; it is respecting differences, sharing and forgiving.

Most of those qualities were present in our house and the houses of our neighbors, but not as candidly and self-consciously as we know them today. It was not written then that love means showing affection in spontaneous ways, although every now and then I'd see outbursts at a family gathering and I remember enjoying the sight. In our house, the love that my mother and father expressed for each other and for their children began with the sanctity of the marriage. Most people in my town and in most of the towns of America in those years believed that the marriage vow meant what it said: for better or for worse. Until death do us part. One man, one woman, one marriage, one family. That was their commitment. It meant acceptance of the other—which did not have to be the same as docility—as long as that acceptance did not condone lifelong brutality. It meant loyalty and it meant dividing the burden. It meant my mother praying at midnight when my father was late getting home from work; she was afraid there'd been a cave-in. The only time I ever saw my father cry was when I was ten, and my mother went to the hospital for an examination that both were afraid would reveal cancer, but didn't. My brother said the one time he saw Mike in tears was while he was writing an accident report at home the day after a timber collapse killed one of his crew members in the tunnel where they worked.

Marriage counselors of today might look at that stoical nuclear family of the mining town with a certain amount of alarm. No amount of commitment, they would argue, should lock the partners into lifelong misery or the demeaning of one of them. Who would argue with that principle today? But where I lived, I saw no prolonged misery resulting from the marriage-for-keeps, nor many dysfunctional children who emerged from it.

But in the three or four times a year when my father had more than a few drinks, he was scary. Toward my mother he was hostile and menacing although she'd done nothing to provoke him. It wasn't their relationship that set him off. It was the booze. He didn't drink often that way, but when he did, his behavior was predictable. He was going to come home and rage about something. He never approached the kids. He yelled and stormed at Mary about some imaginary grievance until, a few times, I walked into the living room in my underwear and tried to tell them to calm down, but really telling my father, in whatever body language I knew, to lay off.

I couldn't have realized then that years later, alcohol would lead me into the same interludes of insanity I saw when I was a boy, if not quite the same behavior.

Those were hours when it was impossible for me to recognize this angry, drunken man as the same ordered and sensible man who gave us our daily bread and sheltered us. He was the same man who, for all of the imprisonment of his feelings, would take me walking in the woods with him when I was a boy, to witness something simple yet marvelous, signs of spring returning to the northern woods. I preserve the memory of those hours wistfully today. They create a posthumous bond, and I imagine a relationship we never quite had as father and son. I was five or six. I held his hand and we walked for hours in the snow, which squished in my tennis shoes. The snow mischievously worked its way into my toes, seeming to apologize for the long hard winter. And suddenly, without any doubt in my mind, I was an Explorer and my father was the guide.

Sometime in his forties, my father returned to church. My brother told me later that his personality in the household lightened up. He'd tease our mother and he'd roll out those old deer drive stories, now without the additive of drinks at the tavern. He drank a few beers now and then, but he never again went over the edge. Although he didn't it express it that way, he valued dignity, his own and that of those around him. His bouts with liquor poisoned it. He must have seen that. He changed.

Reflecting today on that picture of my boyhood, it strikes me that our household in the mining town may sound like some kind of purgatory to those unfamiliar with the mining country. It wasn't. My mother was an unquenchable and efficient nag and an advocate. In a thousand ways she reinforced the ambitions she thought she saw gaining a foothold in her sons' otherwise unexceptional behavior. She hugged us and sermonized and insisted we were undoubtedly going to hell if we didn't make our confession every Saturday. When my father dragged an old upright piano into the house one Saturday afternoon in the middle of the Depression, she looked at the invading instrument and then at my father with a notable lack of jubilation. This clearly came under the heading of finance, which was her turf.

"Where did you get the piano?"

"One of the guys at work said he and his wife didn't want it anymore and he asked if we wanted to buy it."

"You mean if *you* wanted to buy it?"

"That's right."

"What did it cost?"

"Fifteen dollars."

My mother made a silent assessment. She knew nothing about playing the piano. My father claimed he could play from the time he experimented with an accordion owned by a miner's wife in Chandler Location just past the Oliver Mining Company's A shaft. He installed the piano in a little room we called the den and brought in a chair from the kitchen. My father's left thumb was stiff from a mining accident that cut the nerves. The disability was not nearly as damaging to Mike's pianistic skills as his fundamental ignorance of the keyboard. He did get an aggressive bass going by rolling his fingers over C, E, and G, in endless repetitions. The melody was a dimly recognizable rendering of a Slovenian folk tune, "Moya Dekla."

My mother's evaluation was spare.

"It needs work," she said. But her attitude was abruptly transformed. Here was a piano. Here was her oldest son, a first grader at Pioneer School and the only child within three blocks who had not signed up for the school's Teenie Weenie Band. Culturally he was already deprived. "Mrs. DiNino gives lessons," she said. "You can be a piano player. I never thought I'd live to see the day."

At that moment, my mother was five million other mothers. She had a vision of the future, and the future was a great chandeliered hall in New York, and her son, Jimmy Klobuchar, in black tux and glistening fingernails, sat at the piano and played the music from heaven while the audience sat transfixed.

I never quite got there. But I learned to read music. In my second year's recital I mounted the stage of the community center in my white pants and my bow tie. I played Beethoven's "Für Elise." We pronounced it Fyur Eleece. I had no idea what Fyur Eleece meant, but I figured it for some kind of flower. What Beethoven had in mind, I learned later, was a piece for somebody named Elise, and when I heard it played professionally for the first time, I nearly dropped. The professionals took it at four times my speed and did subtleties with the arpeggios that Mrs. DiNino didn't have the heart to put into my program. But when it was over my mother and father escorted me to Buffalo's, next door to the Forest Hotel. Buffalo's was owned by a Greek who made banana splits that even Slovenians said were a treat better than blood sausage. That was our celebration of my passage to the concert stage, double banana splits at the sweet shop.

It didn't last. I quit after four years, having at least made it to Schubert's "March Militaire." I didn't touch the piano for nearly ten years, and then I began buying music. In later years, after I left home, I piled piano music on all available tables, and I played at any provocation, mostly with no one else in earshot. I played very amateurishly but earnestly, and a few years ago I finally blurted the truth to my mother.

"I want to tell you," I said, "that of all of the thousands of things you've done for Dick and me, introducing us to great music was one of the best treasures of them all. I've thanked God a hundred times for that."

She cried. She might have been thinking about that old upright, but I was thinking of the hundreds of hours of wonder and repose that came into my life listening to the music of some of those old dreadnoughts of my childhood: Mozart, Brahms, Schubert. My knowledge has never pierced much below the surface, but music has become priceless in my life, for which I can only thank the illusions of a little woman the day the upright came into our house. Listening to the music of Rachmaninoff and Tchaikovsky, the music of Russia, has in a very private and startling way explained some of my feelings and moods that I never seriously plumbed nor understood before. Russia is the land from which my ancestors migrated to Slovenia seven hundred years ago, and its music as expressed by Rachmaninoff and Glazunov and later by Shostakovich puts me in touch with a time and mood that seems to reach back into the centuries. One day in 1985 the Minnesota Orchestra and its conductor, Sir Neville Marriner, as part of a promotional pitch, put Mayor George Latimer, of St. Paul, University of Minnesota football coach Lou Holtz, and me in front of the musicians to rotate as the conductors of the overture to Mozart's *The Marriage of Figaro*. Holtz and Latimer gagged it up becomingly. No way was I going to follow suit. I remembered the banana split at Buffalo's and my mother's insistence that I would someday reach the concert hall. I took the baton from Marriner and plowed into *Figaro* with boutonniere flying, ignited by all of these great musicians responding to my cues. I was in flames.

When it was over, Marriner shook my hand. "How did it go?" I asked.

"It went and it's gone and that thank God it is," Marriner said with that impenetrable British suaveness. "I gave you a strong D plus because they did finish together."

Why should I have been deflated? That fifteen dollars we paid for our piano, it should be noted, was about right for the Depression economy. The normal rules of the market never impressed the Range mentality very much, because one way to make it through the bad times was to build communal networks—not much different from the circle-the-wagons strategies of the prairie in the 1870s. The house in which I grew up was towed eighteen miles from the then-abandoned taconite settlement in Babbitt in 1935. The house cost my mother and father one hundred dollars. They got the tow free in exchange for some deer meat my father had shared with the trucker the year before. Babbitt died in the 1920s (to be reincarnated years later) because the engineers lacked a practical system for extracting iron particles from the hard rock. Eventually a process of magnetic separation was perfected. It saved every town on the Iron Range from the ghosts after the ore ran out in the pits. But a dozen houses came onto the market in Babbitt in the 1920s and 1930s. The small wood frame house my father and the trucker dragged eighteen miles more than sixty years ago is still standing. My mother, now ninety, has kept it immaculate. The steel rail my father found on a deserted track is still there as the support for the living room ceiling, hidden by the stuccoed arch he built under it. The house had to be torn down on its arrival from Babbitt; a basement was poured, and the house was rebuilt. The basement was done in eight hours on a summer Sunday. It cost my parents a dozen ham sandwiches and two cases of beer. Practically nobody hired contractors to build a house on the Range in the 1930s. The biggest resources in town always were the relatives.

Sometime before the men went underground to work, or when they got there, they became amateur plumbers, electricians, carpenters, and masons. On the appointed Sunday morning, my uncles showed up with wheelbarrows, trowels, hammers, carpenter's levels, and large appetites. Most of them went to Father Mike's 6:00 A.M. service at St. Anthony's Church, the one he gave in the Slovenian language. If they were going to pour the basement they had to show up at St. Anthony's before dawn or risk hellfire until next Sunday. That was the unequivocal proposition the Reverend Frank J. Mihelcic put to his flock. Father Mike was born in the Yugoslavian province of Herzegovina. His mission of saving souls in our town was enhanced by his deftness with the Slovenian language, which most of the church veterans spoke. But he was handicapped by the fact that most of the undergrounders did not pursue salvation very zealously. Father Mike ignored these discouragements. He was a heavyset guy with a red, fleshy face and a pug nose that spread comfortably from cheek to cheek. He was hardly the only clergyman in town. The Lutherans and Methodists and Presbyterians all had spiritual shelter. There was even a period when the Holy Rollers established a foothold in Ely. The Iron Range was that kind of outland. Communists rang doorbells in the middle of the Depression, candidly recruiting. On the Mesabi Range, they even found a candidate who got elected to Congress for one term wearing a hammer and sickle in his lapel. The attempt to socialize the Range didn't last long. The mining companies represented a powerful, offstage political force because of the influence they exerted on school financing and, of course, on jobs. They conducted their own kind of jungle war against radical politics and eventually so did the unions.

While the Range politics of the midcentury were freewheeling and the beer joints were boisterous, the churches were oases of order and stability. But the call process in the Protestant churches meant that their pastors came and went. Frank J. Mihelcic stayed with the obstinacy of the Rock of Ages. This was his home, the impregnable seal of his stewardship. It was also his barony. He ran the church and terrorized some of the politicians. He rarely agonized over the doctrine of separation of church and state. If a priest was going to be a power broker as well as an apostle of redemption on the Iron Range, he didn't bury himself in the parsonage. He went into the street and a few times into the bars. He did it out of generosity of spirit and a lively interest in keeping the pews filled on Sunday mornings. More than one stoned parishioner found himself being lifted out of a snowbank on Saturday night by the ham hands of Frank Mihelcic, making one of his periodic winter rounds. The reverend usually had the chivalry to leave his shaky ward at the gate after walking him home, assuming the parishioner had regained his bearings well enough to find his way to the front door.

Frank Mihelcic's roaring pulpit style camouflaged a pastoral gentleness and compassion that often startled his parishioners when they came to him with personal grief. At those hours he was friend and consoler. But nobody messed with him when he got into the full flight of one of his Sunday-morning condemnations of the collection-plate slackers. The consuming vow of his life was to build a new church, high on the hill where the parish house stood, overlooking Shagawa Lake. He created a budget and a timetable. When they faltered, there were no urgent congregational meetings. Father Mike stood behind the altar and thundered his indictments. He invoked God, St. Michael, the souls of the deceased, and the evidence from his Saturday-night patrols. He threatened damnation and promised to take no prisoners the next time the laggards showed up in the confession box.

"You spend twenty dough-lar in the bars," he shouted, "but you don't have a dime for choorch." Scores of nervous hands could then be seen sliding into pockets.

On the day the new church was formally opened and dedicated, he opened the books.

There was no mortgage.

The new church was free and clear the day it opened. Father Mike could have committed himself to the saints and died fulfilled right there. He didn't. The next Sunday he was roasting some female tourists for desecrating the church by showing up in flimsy clothes. He's gone now, but there's hardly a doubt that Frank Mihelcic is flourishing with the saints. One exposure to his Sunday sermons and the devil would have run up the flag on the spot.

Father Mike and his autocracy aside, the real political leverage in town came from the usual Iron Range powerhouses: the mining companies, the merchants, and later the unions and the Democratic-Farmer-Labor Party. One way or another their interests merged in times of stress. And when those interests combined with the legitimate strivings of the mixed nationalities, an earthy kind of democracy began to settle over the Range before World War II, replacing the old enmities. Common problems outweighed conflicts and suspicions. Recognizing one another's strengths and struggles came slowly among the ethnic clans. Each had its own acreage. The Finns staked out the heights near the big lake, Shagawa, early in the immigration, and inevitably the place became known as Finn Hill. Woodland lovers who could afford it moved to the highland in the pines on the south edge of town up the Moose Lake road. There was space for spreading out. In fact, there was need for it. This was no hamlet sitting above the ore veins. When all four of the underground mines were working full shifts—especially during the war, when they unearthed millions of tons for the defense factories, round the clock—the town supported more than five thousand people.

The Slavs congregated in more communal quarters, which in the early immigration had the look of dingy Balkan ghettos transported to the mining frontier. But they worked their way out of them and built or bought their own homes with money they saved or borrowed from the bank. The banks eventually learned the wisdom of liberal loan policies. The immigrants had come to work and to stay. Most of their children lived by the same dogma. Almost nobody defaulted on a loan. Intermarriage between the ethnic clans gradually changed the town's social attitudes and made most of the prejudices obsolete, sped by the amorous hotbloods of the first and second generations who weren't much impressed by old-country feuds. So mutual esteem, while it often came grudgingly, came. It came in the tardy respect conferred on the Jewish merchants in Ely, the Gordons and the Rosenblooms. No point is served by dredging up the derogatory names they were called privately by some of the townspeople. The words were bad then and they're even worse today.

Mike Gordon and Phillip Rosenbloom were the proprietors of two of the clothing stores in town. They sold their clothes off simple racks, usually for a few bucks less than what their competitors were charging in the metropolis of Virginia, the Queen City of the Arrowhead, fifty miles down the highway. They were reserved and courteous to their customers but didn't feel comfortable addressing most of them by their first names, so when the lady of the house came in, it was usually, "Good afternoon, missus. How are you?"

Money for extra indoor clothes began running out in the middle 1930s. But if you walked to work in a northern Minnesota winter, or hung out the Monday-morning wash with bare fingers in twenty-below weather, you needed clothes.

No one carried plastic cards in their wallets or purses. Credit was extended if you didn't have enough cash. But something more than bookkeeping credit was needed to keep hundreds of families afloat on the Range during the Depression. Open pits shut down for months at a time on the Mesabi. In Ely, where winter offered no impediment to drilling for ore in the underground mines and therefore no excuse for closing them, the shafts stayed open, but the work hours were cut back. Miners would walk to the government employment offices and apply for a few days "for the city," or "for the county." They shoveled snow, drove trucks or cut the tall grass in the roadbeds with scythes. But eventually they would have to walk into a clothing store for a heavier coat or boots.

"I'm a little short this week," they might say.

"It's OK," the Gordons or the Rosenblooms would say.

"I might be a little short next week, too."

"It's OK."

"I don't know about next month."

At this point in the dialogue, as my relatives explained it, the proprietor would begin to smile with a mixture of hope and resignation.

"You are a customer here eight, nine years?"

"Right."

"You always pay?"

"Yes."

"Well, you pay when you can pay. I wait. Anytime is OK. Maybe you need some wool socks."

The democracy might have been too young and shallow to assimilate the Gordons and the Rosenblooms into the rough and tumble of a mining society that carried the old world prejudices to America. And here those prejudices were quickly layered into the new world prejudices. No all-nations love feast erupted among the immigrants on the Range until decades later, when festivals actually broke out with bands, picnics, and hundreds of people dancing under stars by a lakeshore. Chicago, Pittsburgh, Cleveland, Gary, Indiana, and dozens of other ethnic magnets would give the same testimony about the early years. And maybe the Gordons and the Rosenblooms were a little wary about what they might find out if they got too chummy with their customers. But hundreds in my hometown who lived through the Depression could not—and would not want to—deny the humanity they heard in the simple words from the Jewish merchant: "It's OK. I wait."

The Gordons and the Rosenblooms were hardly alone among the merchants who offered generous credit in those years. In my hometown the Lozars and Makis and Kovaches and Kangases and Zupanciches did it. Their sympathies were real, but so were their views of the world. There wasn't much choice. The government didn't give food stamps. The only welfare service available was called, in a gem of New Deal euphemism, "Relief." Most people avoided the Relief office. It seemed to be an admission of something unclean. Charity.

As though there is something unclean about charity.

But that was pride and stubbornness, which is why the merchant would say, "It's OK." Yet it wasn't a one-way street. Almost everybody worked a family vegetable garden or kept chickens, sometimes pigs. This was not then the north woods of nature-smitten dreamers. Roosters were more valuable than canoes. It was not uncommon to see a woman walking into a grocery store with bags of lettuce or eggs. The barter system was reborn. The Middle Ages weren't that far behind.

Yet I can't honestly recall any true horror stories about the hardship inflicted on the people in my hometown during that national trauma. The mines cut back, but they put food on the shelves. What the mines didn't provide for the table, the green grass did. Dandelion salad never went out of style. There were millions of dandelion plants to be picked, and on any given day in summer the grandmothers were out in their babushkas with their water pails, gathering dandelions until they overflowed the pails. Dandelion salad probably wouldn't get top billing today as the pièce de résistance at your average five-star restaurant, but the women figured out a way to give it a verve that raised it above the level of chewable grass. Beans, vinegar and oil, and warm bacon chunks spruced it up. Hot bread from the oven rescued almost any meal from mediocrity. Corn mush in milk (or coffee) at breakfast ushered hundred of kids on the Iron Range to school. So did grilled blood sausage with its stomach-sinking freight of hot rice and pork chunks.

Which meant that while it didn't take much encouragement to eat breakfast on the Range, it did take some character. At night the queen of desserts was blueberry pie, invariably made from blueberries picked by the whole family the previous summer, when we had advanced through the moss swamps with lard cans boiled clean and outfitted with handles. Blueberry picking was the Sunday recreation of choice. The goal was to fill a wooden box the size of a beer case. The box had served earlier as a dynamite crate underground, where it was called a powder box. We usually picked from midmorning to nightfall. The family down the block had to break it off one Sunday when a black bear muscled into their patch.

Yet the ethnic colonies produced genuine gourmet cooking, given half the chance and enough uncluttered space in the living room. It took maneuvering to make *potica* in Slavic homes. Pronounce it *poh teet-sah*, but don't eat it if you're battling the scale. *Potica* in its pure, Balkan incarnation was and is a dark walnut bread rolled in thin layers and sliced like jelly roll. It harmonizes naturally with baked ham and, when it appeared in a miner's lunch pail in the underground eating shacks, it was always a sign that he had managed once more to achieve good terms with his wife. The *potica* most of us coveted, however, was actually a Balkanization of the Austro-German strudel, a suicidally rich pastry rolled in layers of dough as fragile as tissue paper and filled with nuts and apple butter. The rolling of enough dough to fill three or four cookie pans with coiled strudel required engineering skills. With faces caked in flour dust, the women usually rolled it on the large wooden ovals of their living room tables and draped it over the edges in translucent curtains that flirted with the rug. In that condition it not only held the promise of a rare weekend of feasting but also provided excellent cover for kids playing hide and seek.

The Finns concocted a fish soup that won plaudits from visiting chefs who came up from Chicago to fish on Basswood Lake. The Italians hoarded their recipes for porketta. And everybody made pasties and claimed to be the originators. Pasties—pronounced with a short *a*—are meat and vegetables pies. There are still a dozen places where you can buy them on the Range. A few diehard cafés and grocery stores in the Twin Cities whose proprietors are expatriates from the Range also try to nourish the ebbing memories. Pasties were the housewives' salvation when the refrigerator shelves started to empty. The women could always grab a bowlful of potatoes, chop some meat, throw in a few rutabaga slices and sprigs of parsley, roll some dough, and extract a half dozen pasties from the oven in a few minutes. If you ate one at a sitting, you were full. If you ate two, you were heroic. The Finns loudly claimed to have exported pasties from Upper Michigan mining towns to Minnesota. My mother always disputed that, believing pasties were native to Ribnica, where her mother was born in the woodcarving country of Slovenia. The Swedes and Norwegians usually stayed out of it; they were outnumbered on the Range and at supper time generally sought refuge around their walleyes and boiled potatoes. It took them years to figure out that when the southern Europeans yelled and screamed at each other about food, love, or heaven, it didn't mean they were mad. It was their natural speaking volume, a rolling din.

The actual credit for introducing pasties to the Range belonged to the Cornish families who provided most of the early mining captains on the Mesabi and Vermilion Ranges. They came out of the coal mining country of the British southwest. Whether they were Welsh or Cornish or demonstrably English didn't make much difference in the town's over-the-fence gossip. They all had to absorb the sting of yet one more ethnic harpoon dipped in ore pit bile. The other clans called them "cousinjacks," an uncharitable reference to the old English acceptance of marriage between cousins. In my family, all harpoons were dropped when Angela, my youngest aunt on my mother's side, married Billy Bunney and Hannah, my youngest aunt on my father's side, married Eddie Williams.

Both Billy and Eddy, of course, were, ah, well, Englishmen.

While the Iron Range was ore pits and tangled nationalities, it was still the USA, and as kids and young men and women we played the same games and flirted with sex just as hopefully as anybody else. I'll admit playing ball on the Range was different. We were outside the accepted trade routes and, although we played under the same rules, our scorekeeping was somewhat primitive. I played shortstop for the Ely community team while I attended the junior college. Our diamond was the grade school playground. It was all dirt and pebbles and it featured an impressive trough running between second base and third base. If it rained the day before the game, the field in front of the shortstop bristled with hundreds of unraked small stones and a few miscellaneous washers and screws that flowed down from the industrial arts building. We played Virginia on a Sunday afternoon after a rain shower. It was the first year after the war and the baseballs were live, official-issue hardballs. The Virginia slugger Johnny Eaton hit a dirt cutter to short. It came like a bullet, skidding and swerving. Just before it reached me it took a homicidal hop. I threw up my glove and got my thumb on it. The ball ricocheted into my nose and from there into short left field. Blood spilled over my uniform shirt. I retrieved the ball and held Eaton to what I thought was a single. When the inning was over I came into the dugout, wiped off more blood and looked at Neecho Marjerle's score book. Neecho was a squat dark-haired guy with huge eyes and a literal mind. Next to Eaton's name in the fifth inning he'd penciled E-6, safe on the shortstop's error. I groaned miserably.

"Neecho," I said, "how can you call that an error? The ball takes a bad hop, I'm bleeding all over, and you say it's an error."

Neecho's big eyes were sympathetic but implacable. "Did you touch the ball?"

"Yah, but . . ."

"Then you shoulda had it."

The day was a wipeout. I finished it with eleven stitches and an error in the fifth.

Most people who have seen mining towns in films think of them as places of grinding ugliness, disheveled and plastered around buttes of slag and tailings. The earth is scarred and nature itself seems beaten into a hunkering exile. There was some of that dirt and slag in my hometown. But you could climb a hill and see the sweep of Shagawa Lake and the blue green of its bays shaded by the stands of Norway pine and white pine that escorted the Echo Trail up the slope to the north and from there to the edge of Canada.

What made my hometown more than a mining town—not that it had to apologize for being a mining town—was a treasure that will outlast its iron ore and all the other mineral riches. The people in Ely called it "the woods." Today, we call part of those woods the Boundary Waters Canoe Area. Another tract of them is preserved as Superior National Forest. Much of it, of course, is not woods at all. Its waters stream in hundreds of rivers and cascades, linking themselves with thousands of lakes where Indians once hunted and fished and where today residents and promoters quarrel with conservationists over who or what has prior claim and how much is silence worth, after all. For a long time that struggle was waged almost privately, between naturalists and protectionists like Sigurd Olson and Bud Heinselmann on one hand, and resort operators and a few developers on the other. But the politics of it has escalated over the years, bringing in special pleaders and congressional lobbyists in droves, exploiting the antigovernment attitudes of the time. Laws and policies once thought to be a sensible truce in the wrangling now are under fresh attack. For this there is no comprehensible reason other than the fact that a handful of people who called themselves losers twenty years ago—when sensible and protective Boundary Waters legislation was enacted—want to get even in a new political climate. There is enough water, enough woods, and enough silence for everyone if we can survive the clamor for changing it.

Until I began going back into the northeastern Minnesota woods regularly in middle age, I wasn't truly aware of what an extraordinary nature this is. It was a playground when we were kids, but it seemed utterly normal. Didn't everybody have a hundred lakes they could bike to or fish in, pine forests where they could walk for miles in the fall and feel and smell the coppery needles carpeting the forest floor? And didn't they have to confess to their parents one day, as we did, that the awful smell in our mouths was from the dry pine needles that we'd rolled into a strip of newspaper and smoked as our first cigarette? And didn't the subsequent soap in our mouths actually taste better than the pine needles?

The rowboat was our magic carpet when we were young. We would climb into the boat from a relative's cabin on Farm Lake or from the boat dock on Shagawa or Burntside, and we headed for the islands with bags of wieners and marshmallows. Not many of the islands had names. We gave them names that seemed to strike the right chord to harmonize with an adventure into "the unknown." We called one Mystery Point, another Lost Pines. It was the first and the last day anybody ever called them that. They're probably still unnamed. It may be a virtue. There is a chain of lovely lakes east of Ely not far from Snowbank Lake. An inspired cartographer decided to call them Lake One, Lake Two, Lake Three, and Lake Four, which they remain today. One more lake and he could have had a straight flush.

We rowed for hours and then deliberately steered into the shallows between islands to hear the boat swishing through the rushes. We didn't see ourselves as jackpine Huckleberry Finns. No, we were explorers, Magellan and Columbus, and right here and now I'll add Leif Eriksson so as not to get into any ex post facto squabbles with the wardens of political correctness.

These were the north woods and the lakes of our childhood and our adolescence. They were in our backyard. The men in the community hunted and fished in them. We walked in them in winter, my father and brother and I, to cut a Christmas tree. I can't tell you whether it was legal. Nobody asked very loudly, and the U.S. Forest Service didn't come charging into the balsam and spruce stands when a man and his sons were walking in there with an ax.

Does this history, of local residents living for decades in the midst of the forest and waters, drawing game and recreation from them, give the settlers a proprietary right to them? Does this history give them that right even when the woods and waters theoretically belong to all Americans equally?

There is certainly a human investment and a union there that can't be ignored by courts and legislators. But after those considerations have been made, after the snowmobile trails have been allowed, after compromises with the motorboats have been negotiated, somebody has to ask: Why do we have to keep fighting this draining, silly war, when nobody is being truly deprived, least of all the local motorboater who has hundreds of lakes at his disposal? The macho urge for revenge, roiling up since the last fight, is not enough reason.

The Boundary Waters represent a magnificent but fragile nature, unique and precious the way they are.

Leave them alone.

I first met Sig Olson, who lived in my hometown, when he was hurrying across the fifth floor of the stockade of a school building that housed what was then Ely Junior College, which has now become stylishly territorial under its new name, Vermilion Community College. The lower floors then housed the seventh grade. Sig was in his last year as dean of the junior college. He was hurrying because he was on his way to Washington to testify in one of those endless hissing matches between the resort and development lobby and the advocates of a roadless area in the northeastern Minnesota waters. Within ten years, he was filling a half dozen conservationist roles ranging from strategist to public conscience. He was tall and dignified, a virile man with ash hair, an articulate and stubborn man but rarely belligerent and never personal in his disputes. On behalf of the wilderness country he was warrior, evangelist, poet, lobbyist, and scholar. As much as any man in public life in the years from the 1940s to the 1970s, he brought the idyll of the woods to the written page. Through his books he aroused in thousands of people who had never seen the Boundary Waters a realization of their priceless quality and their place in our glands and our souls. But he was also a trained naturalist and, when he had to be scientific in his arguments, he had everybody else outpointed cold. His opponents in town vilified him because he had once been an outfitter, making money off the wilderness, and they called him a hypocrite. He defended himself amiably, saying that was true, but this was today and the wilderness was in danger of being destroyed.

But in his guts Sig was the reconstituted voyageur. On a canoe trip he was a laughing, storytelling gypsy, enjoying the escape and the restoration like any greenhorn. What he felt in his craving to be there, what he saw in others' need to be there, was that undefinable peace almost all of us feel when we are walking in the woods or gliding through the water and the sounds are the simplest and purest ones— the rippling, the birds, and then the silence. What we're experiencing, he believed, reaches deep into our genes, back to a time when we lived in the forest and on the water, and needed them to survive. We are at peace because we have rediscovered ourselves and the earth and the water from which we came.

Sig pictured a man coming into a place like the Boundary Waters and experiencing that sensation and perhaps asking why. The answer, Sig said, is that "he must feel old rhythms, the cycling change of seasons, see the miracles of growth and sense the issues of life and death. He is, in spite of himself, still a creature of forests and open meadows, of rivers, lakes and seashores. He needs to look at sunsets and sunrises and the coming of the full moon."

This man can still stand on an island in the middle of the Boundary Waters today and hear that uncanny yodeling of the loon. Or he can watch the aurora borealis shimmering in the north sky in its greens and ambers like some great, benign ghost of the universe, tantalizing us with yet one more mystery of our origins, entrancing us but evading us. He can do that partly because Sigurd Olson, while he was an unblushing poet, was an even more passionate warrior in defense of wilderness.

Each time I go back, when I camp alone in winter north of the Echo Trail or walk the Kekakabic Trail from the Gunflint, I think gratefully of Sig and, for that matter, of my father and of Tyne Souja, my high school English teacher. My father was not, strictly speaking, an environmentalist, although in his last years he supported Sig Olson and his confederates. But in hindsight I know how "the woods" captivated him. He could never go to sea, but he could go into the fir forests and the lake country, to hunt and fish but also to experience the freedom and the quiet bounty. I remember that miners and farmers, who brought wealth and widely divergent cultures to Minnesota, looked at the earth through different lenses. The farmer cultivated it and nourished it. For him it was tomorrow and the harvest, it was something good, to be revered. The miner fought the earth. He drilled into and dynamited it, and sometimes he was buried in it. The earth then was his adversary. To live, the miner had to claw his way into it and dig out its wealth.

My father may have realized that, although he'd never have philosophized about it. When he got into the woods and the waters, this was liberation for him. He could feel and enjoy the gifts of an earth he did not have to battle. It might explain why he would tend his tomatoes so generously when he planted his boxes indoors in the middle of the long winter. It might explain why his infrequent moments of tenderness with his children, when they were young, were likely to occur in the woods, as in the time when we walked in the snow to meet the spring. The day hummed with the sound of small birds and woodpeckers and snow plopping from the tree branches, emancipated by the sun, falling like confetti to greet the visitors. My father told me how to recognize the sound of the woods coming to life. The reserve had left his face, replaced by the excitement of rediscovery. He picked me up and threw me on his shoulders, and we moved deeper into the forest.

Years later, Tyne Souja would look out toward those woods and toward Shagawa when she recited from Wordsworth. She seemed electrified. She shook and turned her head in an unconscious body language aroused by the poet's thoughts. Her hair was askew and her eyes flashed; they seemed to take in the whole horizon. Wordsworth was writing about his reverence for the silence of the night from a bridge in London, where, "dear God, the very houses seem asleep." It was almost a song with her. I caught her fervor and I wanted to write like Wordsworth. Thank God I never tried. But Tyne on that day moved me in a direction from which I never drifted much. Each time that I go back, I offer a dutiful nod to the inevitable changes. Mining in the town vanished years ago along with most of the immigrants. The pungent ethnic flavor is thinning. Trim boutiques, pubs, and cafés smartly dressed in a wildwood motif stand today where the family grocery and clothing stores once stood. My good friend Si Bourgin of Washington, D.C., long a distinguished writer with the national newsmagazines and a fellow native of Ely, believes with some regret that the town is now on its way to being gentrified. Si is a wise observer, but that may be a reach. The town telephone book remains a jumble of chaotic syllables, and you can still hear the accordions on Saturday night—if you're persistent. But apart from the old head frame of the Oliver Mining Company, still standing, there is little evidence of the mining years that gave the town its guts and its music. The population has shrunk to under four thousand but the town seems stable, buttressed by the grants arranged over the years by its DFL political patrons. That is some comfort to the returning native. The political wrangling over the Boundary Waters seems never to end, which is not so comforting.

My recollections of the hometown I knew as a boy and young man expand as the years advance: Tyne and Sig, the Gordons and the

Rosenblooms and the Kovaches and the Makis; my mother flipping the word cards of my first grade homework; sitting on the cold and unfinished floor of our new house while my father built the house; the bachelor eating his godawful bear meat "bruinburgers" next to me in the eating shack fifteen hundred feet underground; time creating my wiser love of Mike and Mary, whose greatest gift to me was wanting me to discover; the days and nights in the Boundary Waters; and Grandma Rose's hug at Christmas.

It was my hometown, of another time.

3/ Jocks: Making Millions in a Sandbox

A few hundred yards from Metropolitan Stadium on a hot September Sunday in 1961, cornfields surfed in the breeze on the horizons of Bloomington, Minnesota. It was a lovely rustic scene, but old George Halas of the Chicago Bears didn't have the artist's eye or the farmer's cornpicker. What George Halas had was misery in his heart and black thoughts in his brain.

This was the day on which pro football came to the Minnesota prairie, a day that later was to be consecrated as more or less historic. It did not have that appearance to George Halas, the man who all but created pro football. He was the owner and coach of the Chicago Bears of the National Football League, for years pro football's most visible creatures. Halas was the person most responsible for the very existence of the Minnesota Vikings in 1961. George's fondness for dollar bills was so acute that he could not bear to see another football team just four hundred miles away from Chicago playing in the rival American Football League, so he arranged the birth of the Vikings into the National Football League to put one more competitor where he could keep an eye on it. With luck, he could nourish it to some-day fatten the Bears' cash flow. And now, playing their first football game ever—against their benevolent patron, George Halas, and his renowned football team—the Minnesota Vikings squashed the Bears 37–13.

Halas fumed in silence for an hour in the Bears dressing room. When all of the disgraced warriors had boarded the team bus for the ride to the airport, Halas got on, stared at his assembled wretches, and snarled his contempt in a postgame speech of only two words.

"You pussies," he said.

No rebuttal was heard. I recount the story here because Halas and the Vikings opened the gate on that day to what became for me a daily romp through the wildest zoological gardens on the continent, professional football of the 1960s in all of its slapstick and trench warfare. Money and endless television have changed its face today. Nobody's face, however, compared with George Halas's on that bus in 1961. Or, in fact, Sid Hartman's.

This can be explained. The snorting combat of the ball field has flavored my life as it has the lives of hordes of people around the world. But I'm not sure my immersion in it would have been as deep if Sid hadn't materialized in the *Star* and *Tribune* dining room in the early winter of 1961 as I was reaching for the parmesan.

I'd been working my way through a plate of spaghetti when Sid appeared at the table. Sid was then both a sports columnist and the sports editor of the morning *Minneapolis Tribune*. He had not yet become the institutionalized, multimedia legend of later years. In 1961 he was a candidate legend. Sid asked about my health. The question pleasantly surprised me. It revealed a Sid of growing social awareness. My answer might have sounded ambivalent, but it had nothing to do with blood pressure. I was preoccupied, undecided about where I was going to work for the next five or ten years.

Much as I respected the organization and the diversity of work it gave me, my career with the Associated Press in Minneapolis seemed to me to have run the course. At thirty-four, I was looking for something beyond the basic office work I'd been doing for eight years. I thought about applying to be an AP foreign correspondent, or to work with the AP in New York. Both might have been available. But now it was a Sunday evening in Minneapolis in the late winter of 1961 and Sid sat down at the table, carrying three editions of the morning paper. He offered an invitation.

"We need a guy to cover pro football," he said. "Why don't you come over? You're good at this and you'd never regret it. It would get you out of my hair."

Sid had a flair for delivering personal endearments of that sort. I told him that getting out of his hair seemed to be a useful service. I agreed to consider it. Both then and in the years to follow, Sid and I never quite managed to fall in love with each other. For this, both sides probably should take credit. We'd competed against each other a few months earlier at the Rose Bowl, in which the University of Minnesota made its first appearance. Minnesota in the Rose Bowl was your fundamentally gigantic story back home. The Twins and the Vikings were not yet in the field. Gopher football was the only significant game in town and the team had just been voted the national championship, which in those years could not be revoked by a loss in a postseason game. The coach was Murray Warmath, a man who had lived through the crudity of a campaign to remove him a few years before. Sandy Stephens was the backfield star, one of the few black quarterbacks in college football at the time. The opponent was the University of Washington. It was a marvelous story all around, but the two weeks of practice in California were endless and just about insufferable for the reporters covering them. They stumbled over each other trying to find something new, milking the earnest gibberish of the coaches' press conferences for an angle, retreading personality stories ad nauseam, and treating the starting fullback's nosebleed as potentially life-threatening. By the time the teams were ready to play the game, the writers were more exhausted than the fullback and maybe had a more legitimate need for professional help.

Sid, of course, was in the middle of the stew every day. It was the first time I'd worked with or against him, and it was an astonishing experience. He was on the field, in the dressing room, in the chow line, in the coaches' hotel rooms, riding the team bus, and on the telephone round the clock. Even then, Sid had a Rolodex the size of a bass drum. You could also find him at the second urinal to the left in the locker room, fortuitously standing next to a star linebacker. That was one of my more riveting memories of Sid's virtuoso performance in the Rose Bowl coverage. It was a scene that predated Sid's imperishable feat in the Yale Bowl ten years later, when Joe Namath of the Jets refused to talk to reporters and stalked into the shower room. All reporters except Sid were cowed and went off to interview somebody else. Hartman, however, advanced into the shower room with his tape recorder and interviewed Namath for five minutes in the middle of a cascade, without so much as an umbrella or a Dramamine tablet.

It was easier at the Rose Bowl. The coaches and players were accommodating. Although only a few years before he had been badgering Warmath and the university's athletic department about the team's futility on the field, Sid was now an unblushing confidant of the coaches, privy to their strategies for the game. I've never seen a man work as supernaturally hard covering a story. This is a trait that has not diminished, despite Sid's later visibility and wealth and the cartoons he inspired with every obnoxious blurt on his radio shows. But at Pasadena and for twenty years before that—and for thirty-five years after that—Sid has had to pay the price for his compulsion to cover every story, every quote, every coach, and every urinal. In Pasadena he was wound up like a three-spring music box. It was actually one of his strengths. When a phone rang, a coach appeared, or a defensive tackle asked for a ticket to the wrestling match, Sid leaped. It was his way of staying connected and ready for a story. The beneficiaries of all of that frantic energy were his readers and listeners. For pure stamina spread over more than fifty years, for range of sources and contacts, Sid became a one-man epic. For actual scoops, even discounting his pure publicity puffs for his friends, Hartman has no parallel in American sports journalism. I doubt that the fundamental Sid has changed much from the 1950s.

The tendency is to call Sid, when he's at work, overwhelming, rude, annoying, and intrusive. None of these claims is totally inaccurate. I speak with some assurance because I have harbored of few of those attributes myself. This being true, our competition in Pasadena was almost guaranteed to be brisk and largely unfriendly. Sid wrote daily columns for the *Tribune* and also pieces that supplemented the stories of the paper's beat reporter. I wrote for the Associated Press, giving the nonmetropolitan Minnesota daily papers and the broadcast stations direct coverage from Pasadena. Through no dereliction of Sid's, there were days when I drove him nuts. His problem was that he had to cram all of his production into the morning newspaper. He had more than he could print, and it depressed him. To avoid insolvency, the newspaper had to set limits on Sid's breathless exclusives. I had the advantage because I wrote for both afternoon and morning newspapers. This meant that I had two news cycles every day to spread the daily Gopher sagas, and Sid had only one.

Day to day at home, though, we didn't normally compete. Sid was a sports columnist. I did the grab-bag fare you handle daily in the wire services. When the *Tribune*'s managing editor, Daryle Feldmeir, formally offered me a job, I accepted without qualms. Pro football was coming to town with a menagerie of characters. The *Tribune* had a strong sports department and a prestigious place among American metropolitan dailies. My new colleagues on the sports desk included Sid; Dick Cullum, a highly admired columnist whose career reached back into the 1920s; Bill McGrane, then a college football writer; golf writer Dwayne Netland; and a half dozen more whose writing, editing, and photographic skills were part of a productive mix. These *plus* Lou Greene, the sports department's slotman, in charge of assigning copy to be edited and making up the sports page. He was also the head of disaster control on deadlines. He was a squat, bald-headed autocrat who'd handled the same job on the city news desk until his staff got depleted because of Lou's roaring demands for better editing and absolute obedience.

He was a dictator. No doubt. He was also one of Sid's private demons. Lou couldn't understand Hartman's spelling delinquencies, which drove him to the edge of delirium. The old Minneapolis Millers of the minor leagues had a catcher named Ray Katt. When the Twins came to town, Jim Kaat was pitching for them. Please note that Katt is not Kaat. Two years into major league baseball in Minnesota, Sid was still referring in his column to Jim Katt. It happened once too often. Greene the perfectionist lost control. Somewhere between tears and apoplexy, he threw his pencil down the copy chute and screamed, "Hartman, goddamn it, you're the only guy in this newspaper who can't spell *cat*."

It took me three or four years to find the other side of Lou Greene. Away from the newspaper, at a dinner or another social event, Lou was the gentlest, most deferring conversational partner imaginable. He was practically gallant. He did, however, preserve his nervous habit of looking up at the clock as the night wore on. You got the impression that Lou was ever vigilant for cats creeping into the copy.

Within a week, I was reintroduced to the coach of the Minnesota Vikings, Norman Van Brocklin. We had met a few months before when I covered for the AP when he was hired. We didn't have our first argument until five minutes into our third meeting. I can't remember what ignited it, but any excuse would do. We battled randomly for the next five years. We also prowled honky-tonks together. We confided in ways no reporter and coach would seriously entertain now, or find allowable by today's ethic. We liked each other most of the time but detested each other often enough to absolve ourselves of any guilt for the times when we got along. Our relationship was not much different from those Dutch had with a dozen people who knew him well. He had a hard time sustaining trust in anybody apart from his family. Dutch was a working paranoid. It's a symptom common to many football coaches, refined to a remarkable level by Van Brocklin. Incredibly, he once accused me of tipping off Halas and the Bears to a trick play with which the Vikings opened the game. It was supposed to be a deep reverse to Tommy Mason. The teams lined up. Mason was poised to take off with the snap but tried to look inconspicuous. "Watch Mason on a reverse," yelled the Bears' middle linebacker, Bill George. Mason was buried twelve yards behind the line of scrimmage. The Vikings lost and Van Brocklin came seething into the coach's office for his press conference. In front of all my peers, Van Brocklin's first words were, "What the hell did you tell Halas about that reverse?"

I told Van Brocklin he was full of manure. I said the trombone player in the Vikings band could have spotted the play coming. This would have taken a fair amount of acrobatics, since the trombone player was sitting behind a hibachi cooker in the parking lot. He still could have read it. It was that obvious. I said it was too bad the Bears seemed to have a better handle on the play than the Vikings did. Van Brocklin blew up and the press conference ended in a flood of f-words.

Two days later Van Brocklin and I split a beer. It was that kind of liaison. I have some bittersweet reminiscences of it now. We didn't speak during the last ten years of his life, the result of some misinterpreted remarks that sound silly today. I'm drawn to those years not only because of Van Brocklin's personality and his excesses, but also because the first years of the Vikings were an absolute Alice in Loonyland. They could not recur today. God help us if they could. I always thought the early Vikings were closer to a wildlife refuge than a professional football team. The team was made up of football orphans and derelicts, a handful of once-esteemed veterans set adrift by their former employers and a few authentic stars of the future—Francis Tarkenton, Tommy Mason, Rip Hawkins, Ed Sharockman, Grady Alderman. They were eventually joined by enough good young players to create a competitive team by the mid-1960s. But they all revolved around Van Brocklin, who was their bilious truant cop and zookeeper. He had been a great player, the best quarterback in the league the year before he became the Vikings coach. He began coaching predictably, with a snarling assessment of his new football team: he had inherited, he said, thirty-six stiffs. It was Van Brocklin's description of the players chosen by the team's management from a pool created by the league. He may have been right. In two years, practically all of the stiffs were gone, which may have been the break of their lives.

No matter what their previous football habitats, none of them was fully prepared for Van Brocklin's mercurial furies. He was not just tenacious about embarrassing a player who had blundered; he was absolutely creative about it. After an exhibition game in Portland, Oregon, in which the veteran quarterback, George Shaw, played badly, Van Brocklin might simply have said that Shaw played badly and left it at that. It would have been a professional courtesy to an established player—Shaw—returning to his home state, but Van Brocklin was incapable of temperance. He called Shaw inept and inadequate and generally tore him apart to reporters writing for an Oregon audience, and a few days later he cut him. It was more than unsightly; it was cruel.

And yet this man, here and there, was capable of something close to tenderness at the sight of a mediocre player struggling to hang on. Big-time athletics is a sandbox of novel characters. It is the best laboratory I know for the study of abnormal behavior. It makes demands on performance and ego, and in return offers big money and intense visibility. It also forces a dilemma on the athlete: personal glory versus team success. There is room for exhibitionists, screwballs, bionic supermen, decent guys who are stars, decent guys who are mediocrities, and scores of ordinary, muddled dudes who happen to be endowed with uncommon strength or skill. In the years I mingled with them, I found nobody quite as extraordinary as Van Brocklin.

There was only one person comparable to the Dutchman. They might have been twins, Van Brocklin and Billy Martin, the late baseball manager. Van Brocklin and Martin were alike in one unshrinking belief: their will and nerve and brains could win a game even when their athletes were inferior. In this they were uncompromising and crude. They drove and abused, swore and schemed. For most of their careers, that rampaging style didn't do much to lower their credibility with most of their players, who either tuned them out when it got gross or grew new layers of skin as the season moved on. Both knew how to win. Players respect that. Both were smart and resourceful. Players appreciate that, too. What they don't appreciate after a while is the relentless grinding of a domineering coach or manager who demeans them. They are also offended by aimless explosions in the clubhouse that seem to them to reflect more on the coach's growing neurosis than on any particular sins of the ballplayers. Both eventually became caricatures in the locker room, which is sure death for a manager or a coach.

Did Martin's alcoholism aggravate his behavior on the field? It's only a guess. There's not much doubt that it affected his behavior away from the field. Why else would anybody want to pound on a hapless marshmallow salesman in a bar? In the years I knew him, when he worked for the Twins, I found Martin companionable as long as he wasn't drumming on alleged conspirators or picking a fight with a Shriner from Dubuque. His social habits weren't the most admirable. This hardly made him unique in the jock lodge or among the people who covered it, but Billy's behavior was more loutish than most. As he got older he got meaner. Although he had an incisive mind, his conduct revealed an animalistic competitor and a vengeful streak. His disposition couldn't have been improved by his longtime association with an ego even larger and probably more destructive than his own, that of George Steinbrenner in New York. Billy Martin died when a recreational vehicle he was riding in left the road. He was popular with the crowds because he was defiant, independent, and willing to risk—a maverick. If he had tempered some of his resentments, got rid of some of his poisons, he might still be alive. But if he had, I suppose, he wouldn't have been the Billy Martin he chose to be and chose not to change.

Van Brocklin's drinking was less public and probably less volatile, but it did plow him into smoldering moods that seemed to enhance his natural vindictiveness. Sometimes, though, it put him into scenes of priceless hilarity. There was the night under a full moon among the northern Minnesota pines, a night touched with the soft glow of tranquility. In the midst of this idyllic forestland, Van Brocklin got out of the car and decided to duke it out with one of his coaches in the middle of the highway coming back from a roadhouse outside Bemidji. The assistant coach was stunned. He was also scared, but not by the prospect of absorbing one of Van Brocklin's wandering left hooks; he was worried that he might land one of his own hooks and lose his job. He settled the dispute by putting his arm around the Dutchman and telling him that it might be a good idea to get the car off the road because that looked like a police car coming from the north.

The Dutchman's pugilistic skills never came close to his ability to throw a football. In a lounge in Bemidji the next year, he swung a right intended for the belly of a salesman who was annoying him at the bar. The punch had strong motivation but erratic aim. It missed the salesman and landed in the midsection of Bernie Ridder, one of the Vikings owners who was standing innocently at the bar. The Dutchman was horrified. Ridder was gasping. The salesman was relieved. Ridder's fondness for the Dutchman precluded any hard feelings but didn't immediately restore him to normal breathing.

In Birmingham, Alabama, the night before an exhibition game a few years later, the Dutchman encountered a half-stoned reporter from Texas who probably said something snide, such as "How's it going in Minnesota, Dutch?" More inflammatory words followed. Van Brocklin again swung a misdirected right. The next morning he called a press conference in his hotel bedroom, evidently worried that word of the incident might have reached the two Twin Cities reporters on the scene, St. Paul's Roger Rosenblum and me. He was right. We had both seen it but had no intention to write it, since it was pretty normal fare for the weekend scene with Van Brocklin's Vikings. Van Brocklin's right hand was bandaged.

"I don't know what you saw," Van Brocklin said, "but it wasn't a fight and I don't see how it rates any kind of story. I didn't try to hit the jerk."

"So how did you hurt your hand?"

He said he had made contact with one of the pillars in front of the hotel.

"But you didn't swing a punch?"

"No."

Van Brocklin decided the ends of truth had been satisfied and closed the press conference, leaving the unmistakable impression that he was the victim of an unprovoked attack by a concrete post.

Somewhere in the middle of this slaphappy era, the Dutchman invited me up to his hotel room in Detroit to settle it man to man. I still don't know what it was we were supposed to settle. Our midnight argument in the hotel lobby seemed pretty pedestrian. He demanded satisfaction. I told him he was nuts. He said he never met a reporter yet who wasn't gutless. I rolled my eyes and we took the elevator to his room. When we got there we grappled for a few moments without much enthusiasm until we fell on the bed and capsized the television set, which crashed and splintered and ended the fight.

These things happened. They happened fairly often, in fact—the dippy wrangling, not necessarily the fights. Today's reporter will look at a burlesque relationship like that and say it couldn't happen now. Right. It couldn't. The game, the personalities are a thousand times more visible. The accountability codes of the newspapers would demand a public airing. What happened between you and the coach? Does our lawyer know? Were there any witnesses? The public deserves to know. So does the editor. So do your next of kin.

This is not to downrate today's more rigorous standards, which insist on or encourage arms-length relationships between reporter and coach or player. The Vikings beat reporter today, for example, is probably not going to drive around with the Vikings coach on a Monday morning listening to Ray Charles music in a tavern in St. Louis Park. If he did, there wouldn't be room in the car for all of the requisite lawyers on both sides. But today's standards do make sense. And they are stronger protection for the reading public, which ought to be able to read a piece, whether it is sympathetic or hostile, and be reasonably confident that the writer is more in tune with the readers' interests than with his own or the coach's or the player's or the club management's. I don't know of many reporters who don't accept that absolute now, or didn't accept it then. But covering pro football and baseball in the earlier years came with vastly different atmospherics. There weren't many people covering the teams in those years. It was more or less one on one, the newspaper reporter and the coach. The games weren't the fishbowls they are today. Television, especially local television, hung around the edges thirty years ago. It didn't have the resources or the competitive verve it has today in major league athletics. It didn't have cable. It didn't have the vast commercial interest in football it has today. The newspapers didn't have ten columnists and analysts, and they didn't have investigatory beagles examining the financial balance sheets of the athletes and their bedrooms. But these are the 1990s. Keyhole journalism is in. So is police-blotter journalism, unavoidable today when felonies and first downs are equally common in the pro game. Also prevalent today is some legitimate dig-out-the-news journalism that surpasses much of what preceded it thirty years ago. But it might be argued that a lot of the juicier and jazzier stuff isn't necessary. Mounting numbers of today's athletes are more than willing to reveal all there is in their personal lives, and some that isn't. They call it marketing.

This is not to say the pro game is better or worse now, but it's different. Familiarity between writer and coach was inevitable in the earlier years. It worked both ways. Vulnerable coaches often tried to cultivate the goodwill of guys who wrote about them, exercising the normal cover-your-behind instinct. That strategy is not entirely dead today, incidentally. Bud Grant never much bothered with it, though he was accessible, except on afternoons when he broke up press sessions to go home and feed his dogs—a priority he sometimes advanced above football. Grant would talk football in an offhand but informative way for hours if you wanted. He had a sizable closet of villains he liked to shoot at: officials, the pro football administration, television intruders. Grant nurtured streaks of malice, which he acted on at convenient times and might explain why he won so much. But when he got hostile he usually did it on the record and didn't enlist newspaper people as surrogates. Athletes won for him because they saw him as a coach who had his life under control, lived by a value system, and didn't need headlines but made winning a quieter crusade, shrewdly and cold-bloodedly pursued. The Vikings' Jim Marshall used to say that if it was ever his fate to get lost in a jungle full of man-eating crocodiles and he could choose one man to save his neck, it would be Grant. Grant would figure out a way to beat the crocodiles, Marshall maintained, and it wouldn't matter to Grant (and certainly not to Marshall) whether he strangled them or ate them. He was, in other words, the ultimate survivor.

Van Brocklin, conversely, had a bulldozer personality that demanded the right of way and all available lanes. If you were covering Van Brocklin with any kind of integrity, you could deal with that hazard by not letting him hog the right of way. This usually meant we went two or three weeks without talking during the season. It's an uncomfortable way to cover a football team on which the coach is the pope and issues all the doctrines. In between the macho games, we talked football and kids. We understood that some of the things we talked about were off the record, and that is a concept that has never really gone out of date. Assessing his football players privately, he was tart and sardonic, and he wasn't much better publicly. Still, he was capable of generosity and familial devotion. After raising their own children, he and his wife adopted two others. But professionally he never quelled the demons inside him. Much of the time he looked at his coaching world with an anger and a stridency that made him a jockstrap parody of Captain Bligh. As coach of a team of young players and castaways trying to hang on, he was capable of lifting them—at least for a few games or a few seasons—beyond their abilities. He could do that with his ferocities and his profound knowledge of football offense and his threats. In the culture of his time, he had bursts of bigotry. So did millions of other Americans. One difference was that Dutch's bigotry may have affected the lives and earning power of some of the athletes who were its victims. In later years I reported some of his racism. I didn't earlier, nor did other reporters I knew around the country when they were confronted with the same kind of racism. Most of the times I saw it or heard it were in private, off-the-cuff conversations that didn't seem reportable. That doesn't mean they had to be ignored.

For this, an apology is due. I apologize.

We learn.

We learned enough in thirty years so that in one year in the 1990s African-Americans were coaching the Vikings, coaching the University of Minnesota basketball team, and overseeing the university's athletics departments. That has to do with something more than white America's conscience. It has to do with recognizing ability. It also has something to do with wanting to win.

Distance tends to heal some of the sores and the abuses of that earlier time in pro football in Minnesota. In fact, the game of the 1960s may have taken on a charm and romantic quality it doesn't deserve. There wasn't much charm in the heavy drinking and sex parties in hotel rooms; or in three grown men rolling up and down the football field vomiting in exhaustion on a hot Sunday morning in punishment for coming in at 3:00 A.M., while Van Brocklin bellowed his retribution behind them; or in an overweight rookie tackle resigning from pro football after fourteen minutes in camp, lying prostrate in the middle of the agility ropes and appealing to the trainer, "Take me to the church. I'm dying." He avoided that fate but did manage to make the next flight out of Bemidji.

The ballplayers of that age didn't necessarily play harder. If anything, today's game is more violent. The players are bigger, compulsively well conditioned (except for some of the fatter-than-thou offensive linemen), and faster. When they hit each other, more things are likely to break. But there was a place in the game in the 1960s for the Huckleberry Finns, for scamps and hobos like Mike Mercer. Mike was a Vikings kicker who had played for a half dozen colleges, roaming the campuses of America with his flat-front kicking shoe and his kicking tee. His field goals had strength but unpredictable direction, which inevitably put Mike on Van Brocklin's pits list. He got a reprieve by kicking four field goals in Baltimore, but Van Brocklin's fondness for shaky field-goal kickers was marginal. Against the Lions, Mike missed a thirty-five-yard field goal and then one of twenty-one yards, which is almost impossible for a man with two legs and unimpaired vision. Mike tried to avoid eye contact with Van Brocklin as he returned to the bench. An oncoming hurricane would have been easier to avoid. "Mercer," Van Brocklin screamed, "you couldn't kick a whore off a piss pot."

That is creative language. Maybe it's a reason why those crinkled old rotogravures of pro football of the 1960s are hard for older fans and writers to erase. I wouldn't want to erase the picture of, for example, Hugh McElhenny running in the open field. McElhenny was one athlete who aroused the kid in me, a player I would have paid to watch every day of his career. I admired and envied him in the same way the ticket buyers and the television watchers did. Like most reporters, I looked at the game without the pain that most devotees insist is part of the privilege of being a fan. If you're sitting in the media stalls, you really shouldn't be a fan, although you usually want your own athletes to win because you know them and know their struggles and goals. It's the human thing. Today, though, you'll find some bizarre reverse bounces in the relationship of reporters and columnists and the teams they cover. Some folks in the news clan hate writing the fan magazine puff stories about the local heroes. I don't necessarily blame them. It means catering to the herd. The problem is, they have to keep writing those daily pieces if the local heroes insist on winning. One way for the sore-headed Shakespeares to escape is for the local heroes to lose. It feels better on the nerve ends (and looks flashier) to write venom than to spread roses. Be kind to the local author whose mind works that way. It can happen to you in the business if you listen to too many talk shows.

But you do have to watch and write the game with a sensible amount of professional detachment in the press box. For most of the years I covered Vikings football, first in the early 1960s and again during the Bud Grant and Fran Tarkenton second-coming years in the 1970s, I sat two seats away from the one uproarious exception to this traditional rule of the working journalist.

Sid Hartman was an unreformable fan. For two years I wore ear plugs, a defense that was pitiably inadequate. Sid was unstoppable. He agonized and erupted from the kickoff to the last drip of beer from the upper-deck customers at Metropolitan Stadium. When the game was going badly for the Vikings, Sid was beyond consolation. He delivered thunderbolts of bitterness and excoriation directed impartially at the Vikings defensive backs, the Vikings pass rush, the National Football League, and the officials. The officials were mentally disordered or card-carrying members of a conspiracy. But never, ever were any harsh words lodged against Grant or against Tarkenton, both of whom long ago had entered Sid's personal Valhalla, Grant with his hunting dogs and Tarkenton with his stock coupons.

I have to admit that in maundering through the days of the Met, I don't miss Sid's howls of anguish quite as much as I miss McElhenny's art. I can still hear Hartman's howls, but McElhenny was just one of those irreplaceables. He met the classic definitions of what the great halfback was supposed to be in those years. He glided and then burst; his movements were sinuous and intuitive. He ran with grace and speed, with changes of direction and tempo, but always under control. He brought with him to the field and its homicidal tacklers what the matador brings to the bull ring, the same kind of finesse, measured doses of bravado, a little showmanship, and, when it is needed, nerve. McElhenny was a likable guy with a bronzed face, curling black hair, and no special airs about being a football star. He was filling out his last years as a professional football player when he got to Minnesota, an aging virtuoso athlete who had a balanced view of the world but was hardly immune to the usefulness of the dollar bill. In Seattle, where he played his final two collegiate seasons at the University of Washington, they still remember McElhenny's grinning observation that he had to take a pay cut to go from collegiate football into the NFL. But he wasn't a wise guy and he wasn't around Minnesota football nearly long enough. In the two years he played for the Vikings, I was fascinated by the effect he had on crowds in the arenas away from home. It was very close to the reaction of a music hall audience to a performer in recital. A McElhenny run might have damaged the local forces on the scoreboard, but it was a performance that was pure concert, that seemed to suspend partisanship and to wring admiration from crowds wherever he played. It was the kind of status achieved only by those athletes who play with such art or such strength that they become everyone's star, honored by all audiences, whether friend or foe.

Beside McElhenny in the Vikings huddle stood Francis Tarkenton, a saucy young man from Georgia. In the years that followed, Tarkenton acquired the kind of wealth that made McElhenny's highest one-year salary, $25,000, look like tip money at the barbershop. Even so, Francis was modestly paid compared with the Pentagon-scale budget numbers now going to anybody capable of lining up onside. Tarkenton eventually also acquired a broad unpopularity that may have resulted both from the absence of a Super Bowl flag floating above the snowdrifts of Minnesota and from his perceived arrogance and selfishness as his career wound down.

Tarkenton never argued with the arrogance charge. In fact, he embraced it. Francis was a player of competitive creeds and axioms. Most of them made sense because he played incredibly long at a high level of performance. Some of the time he did it with bad teams, and in his later years with a stress-weakened arm. One of his maxims was that quarterbacks have to be chesty, have to be superconfident, worried about neither enemy torpedoes nor lousy press reviews. If the passes were off that day, the quarterback had to brazen it out. If he took a hard lick from the linebacker after the whistle, he didn't cry about it or look to the bench. To support their egos, he said, quarterbacks had to be able to deliver, and he was willing to be judged on that. The fairest judgment of Tarkenton was that he delivered.

But he didn't deliver a Super Bowl championship. That is supposed to be the final verdict of the quarterback's leadership and his entrée to the halls of the mighty. Every quarterback whose team has failed to win a Super Bowl has enthusiastically rejected this doctrine. Harry P. Grant, who himself coincidentally never won a Super Bowl, also rejected it. A casual stroll through the pro football Hall of Fame at Canton, Ohio, will reveal the names of Francis Tarkenton and Harry P. Grant, prominently displayed. Which means what? It means that Tarkenton was one of the best quarterbacks to play the game and Bud Grant was one of the best coaches. Does this then clear Francis of the lurking charges that he was a selfish football player?

Ron Yary, an all-pro offensive lineman who himself belongs in the Hall of Fame, is preachy on the subject and partly responsible for the notion that Tarkenton's self-interest dominated his game and his conduct in the locker room. Those qualities were not exactly invisible later in the corporate boardrooms, where Tarkenton first flourished and then stumbled. It was typical boardroom conduct in the 1980s, 1990s, or any decade. Most of the men with whom Tarkenton played didn't see him as being unusually twisted by ego and greed as a player.

Was he looking for bigger bucks? Of course he was. Not many of his teammates emulated Mother Teresa themselves. There isn't much doubt that Tarkenton was partial to players who made Tarkenton's kind of offense shine. Once he got himself surrounded with strong offensive linemen and versatile runners and receivers, his style was to toss the ball here and there, distribute it to a half dozen guys, turn little passes into long runs, and let his team come at the other guys from every direction on the compass. Nobody juiced up the Tarkenton offense the way Chuck Foreman did. Foreman ran with power and speed. He ran resourcefully. And when he caught the ball, he ran even better. Needless to say, Tarkenton loved him. He talked him up to the writers: "Best running back in football. There's nothing this man can't do. He's more versatile than O. J." Tarkenton gave him the ball on the slightest provocation.

Wouldn't you?

We were close acquaintances for all of the years Tarkenton played in Minnesota, and we wrote a book together. I remember him as one of those athletes who undergo a transformation in lifestyle and temperament as they mature. He came into professional football with the wide eyes of a campus hero and a preacher's boy. He had a cheerful naïveté that seemed startled, although not necessarily offended, by the dockwalloper language and spectacular bedroom stories that flavor the football locker room. Eventually he built a harder crust and spouted four-letter words with a gusto that such earthy characters as Boom Boom Brown and Mick Tingelhoff could hardly match, and with a vulgarity that startled even his coaches. In short, he developed a permanent new skin of worldliness. He became an entrepreneur and a conglomerate while it was still early in his career, and he acquired high-roller friends from the business and entertainment worlds during his five years in New York. Tarkenton juggled time, events, and people. Some of his earlier friends tended to get lost in his swift rise to celebrity. He might have mourned that, but he also might have shrugged it off with another one of his creeds, this one convenient: sometimes a man who is moving higher and higher has to make choices about where to direct his energies. What that means is he tossed some of his old friends. There wasn't enough time in the express lane. It's probably what Ron Yary meant by selfishness. You could make that case. Francis's popularity in his later years wasn't improved by his response to the occasional booing he took at Met Stadium. He reacted by lecturing the fans in his postgame dialogue with the press. He was personally offended, he said, because performance over the long term, like that of a Bart Starr or a John Unitas—or a Fran Tarkenton—ought to reap something more dignified than boos and sneers when the star had an off day. "In other places," he said, "they revere the veteran players. Here they boo."

Right about there, Francis's reputation as the thinking man's jock disappeared in a morass of self-conferred martyrdom. Minnesota crowds have no special history of cutthroat behavior. The sound of their boos, in fact, might be compared with the gurgle of Bassett Creek in contrast to the Niagaras of Philadelphia, Boston, and Detroit. How is a football player earning $400,000 then ($4 million now) entitled to reverence? He is entitled to courtesy, what the rest of humanity is entitled to at the checkout counter. If he blows a game while he's earning $4 million, you may want to reconsider courtesy. Revering jocks—or presidents, generals, or tap dancers—doesn't usually come until the funeral. A notable exception was the outpouring of affection and grief that accompanied Kirby Puckett's 1996 retirement from the Minnesota Twins in the face of an eye disorder. That was close to reverence, and it may have set a television record for longest-orchestrated reverence.

Tarkenton's struggles to establish his credentials to greatness in later years were strung with irony. Most of the men who played with and against him were sold on him. Reporters, in his later years, weren't, despite his numbers and his longevity. He was slick at public relations, but as his career lengthened so did the underground hostility in the press boxes. The oddity there was that he played the game not only shrewdly but with uncompromising fire. He deserved the warrior label when a lot of his muscular peers didn't. He rarely acknowledged injury. His game depended largely on wit and inventiveness, but when they were inadequate, he fell back on guts. That was Tarkenton the football player. Tarkenton the self-constructed dynamo of the corporate world and television was something else, but that had nothing much to do with the kind of quarterback you wanted in the huddle on third and eight. Tarkenton handled that as well as anybody who ever played.

Yet it was another Vikings quarterback, Joe Kapp, whose personality and raw values as a ballplayer I'll cherish. His was the gruff ideal of what the game is about when it draws the best that is in the athletes and the goals they set for themselves. Joe was a sourdough of a football player. He trudged where others ran. He bellowed and snorted and laughed in the mud. He had big muscles and scars all over his face from a beer bottle fight in Canada. When he lined up behind center it looked as though the personnel office had made a mistake and picked a bartender to play quarterback. Even on windless days, his passes fought the air as though they were trying to deal with an alien element. They usually lost all semblance of a spiral after five yards of struggle. But Joe Kapp was one of those studs who never had an identity problem on the field. There was a man named Kapp and there were eleven named the Team, and the eleven were the ones who counted first, last, and forever. He played with a primeval drive, attacking when he ran, flinging jocular insults at the other guy. It was the playground all over again, every play. And because his accomplices included Jim Marshall and Bill Brown and Dale Hackbart, who played the same way, the sourdough quarterback was utterly believable. The team treasured him, droopy passes, homely codes of team play, and all. And when they won a National Football League championship on the green ice of Met Stadium one Sunday afternoon and they charged into the locker room to yell and cry and drink champagne, Carl Eller, the great black lineman, held up a fizzing bottle and pointed it at Joe Kapp, the Hispanic quarterback. "Joe," Eller shouted, "you're my brother, and I love you."

Those rotogravures out of the past can be downright haunting. One sight I'm not likely to forget is bulbous, grumpy old Twins owner Calvin Griffith throwing up his breakfast as we talked at his desk, a few days away from a decision he had to make on Billy Martin. Griffith was going to fire him, in the midst of Martin's enormous popularity with the crowd. The stress of it was tearing Griffith apart, and he couldn't control his stomach. It was a homely and unsightly scene, but it might have described the collision of personalities and turf in the big leagues better than the drama on the field. He was Calvin, plodding, standing guard over the vaults, butchering the English language, fighting hopelessly to avoid the twentieth century and the fast lanes of corporate baseball. He was a semicomic, semitragic, but still romantic character of his time. He never received the credit he deserved for knowing the game and creating a World Series team. It was left to the Kirby Pucketts and Harmon Killebrews and Frank Violas to reveal how much he knew.

Maybe it's appropriate that Calvin is a kind of baggy but dimly noble embodiment of big league ball's transformation in Minnesota from that day of Halas's croaking disbelief in the Met Stadium parking lot to the ritz and glitz of the 1990s. Calvin belonged with Halas. Both were nickel-squeezing patriarchs who owned their teams and clung to them like misers protecting the strongbox, and they never imagined $100,000 luxury seats for fat cat customers. Halas was so cheap he actually sold seats at the end of the players' bench for a couple of years. But he was a poleaxer out of the Neanderthal days of big league ball. He observed some rules when it was convenient and ignored others with gusto and impunity. He grabbed and held and built pro football. Griffith, in his fashion, was a builder, not domineering or very smart, but a baseball man from his jowls to his fat toes. In the end he didn't have the money or the finesse to live with baseball in today's cutthroat corporate lifestyle or the survivor's wiliness to give in to the millionaire gypsies who are its ballplayers. So the Griffiths are now extinct. Ball today is huge and powerful and essentially out of control.

There can still be beauty in it. In fact there is a tidy, thirty-year symmetry, a closing of the circle, that unites that first game of pro football at the Met with a climactic day in 1991 eight miles away. Taken together, the events reveal much about what has happened in Minnesota since the big leagues arrived in the cornfields.

By the fall of 1991, the creaky little stadium that brought big league ball to Minnesota was gone, its abandoned asphalt and lingering ghosts about to be reincarnated as the marketing circus of the Mall of America. Met Stadium's successor, the Metrodome, enjoyed less public esteem but attracted a lot more duffs in the seats on the autumn night when Jack Morris and the Twins went for the 1991 World Series championship against Atlanta.

The Vikings' victory thirty years before had been a freaky little prologue to Minnesota's adventures in big time sports. But Morris and the Twins that night represented professional ball lifted to its highest plane of skill and theater. They were the most compelling three hours I've ever spent in a sports arena. There was Morris, an old, unrepentant gutfighter, vowing with each pitch that the Braves could keep swinging into next month and they were never going to score on Jack Morris. He was intimidating and obsessed. He had few illusions about his character stains. People called him selfish and a hard man to befriend, self-centered and likely to be rude without a lot of provocation. Nobody said, though, that Morris was ever scared on a baseball mound. Pitch for pitch, he went eight innings against the scorching fastball of a much younger John Smoltz, who had kept Jack Morris posters when he was a kid and Morris was a star with the Detroit Tigers. Neither buckled. It was baseball out of the fantasies of the tens of millions who watched. But Smoltz left before the ninth with the teams still scoreless in the seventh game of the World Series. In the tenth, Dan Gladden crossed the plate to win the game and the series for the Twins. The game and Morris and the Twins had brought a jubilation day to Minnesota. They had redeemed the groans of disillusionment and aborted frenzies of the fans spread over thirty years in Minnesota, the promise and the flops of the baseball teams, the football teams, hockey and all the rest that came in the wake of pro sports' discovery of Minnesota. The Twins had won a World Series before, in 1987, but that was essentially a team of hackers and derelicts held together by Puckett, Kent Hrbek, Frank Viola, Bert Blyleven, and the inane bounces and fluky ceiling of the Metrodome. What happened in 1991 was a kind of coronation. It validated a vow made thirty years before. The hawkers of big league ball for Minnesota said there would be a night like this, when great ballplayers would take Minnesota's 4 million people to the moon and the celebration that followed would almost never end.

It was not a bad prediction. I've looked at this phenomenon, the big leagues in Minnesota, with two sets of eyes for years. Whatever else is arguable, this is pretty hard to deny: the public's absorption with a ball team, the prestige and the sense of ownership the fan feels for the team, are real. The passion is real. The pride is real, as is the high of winning and the misery of nursing a loser. Fun at the ballpark is real. So are the lopsided time and fervor (and money) that the truly iron-butt fan devotes to ball. What's offensive about professional sports today is the legalized form of corporate racketeering it's become, forcing taxpayers to finance the billions of dollars in players' salaries and the vanities and greed of the people who own the ball clubs. The agent of this extortion is the New Stadium, scores of new stadiums being built or schemed, being built needlessly and in some towns being built in bunches—side by side, a new stadium for football, a new stadium for baseball, just ten or fifteen years after the stadium to end all stadiums was built in that town. Now it's being razed to appease the superrich mercenaries who play the game and the superrich owners who blackmail the public to make themselves richer.

The scam works this way: Because of the ineptness of ownership in big league sports today, and its refusal to confer real power on its commissioners, the ballplayers—through free agency—actually hold the balance of power. They are protected aggressively by what they call their "union." It is the only union in America that represents multi-million-dollar wage earners who work part time and can pretty much dictate where they work after their apprenticeship. But what they have isn't a union and they're not union members. What they are is wealthy independent contractors operating a "union" the way cartels operate in international finance. The club owners, in spite of net worths up to a billion dollars each, describe themselves as helpless to shut off the annual free agent auctions that keep escalating the salaries. They need millions more in revenue each year, they say, to keep feeding the monster of player salaries. Television and tickets alone can't do it. They need creative revenue, esoteric revenue. Where they get it is from the pockets of the taxpayers, millions of whom may have never seen a major league ball game because they're not interested or can't afford it. The taxpayers build a new stadium, into which the ball clubs engineer millions of dollars worth of luxury seating for corporate customers, who pay for it partially with tax write-offs. And that makes one more abuse of the taxpayer who has built the stadium. The promoter-hustlers jack up the price of the seat and then, particularly in new franchise cities where the pro ball mania is insatiable, they extort a license fee for the privilege of paying for a seat. And finally they escalate the price of brats and nachos into realms in which only Kuwaiti sheiks could pay for them without asking what in the hell is going on.

What's going on is the systematic mugging of the public through the jawboning of its politicians, who actually vote the scam into legality.

Billions of words have decried it and defended it, and the words continue and so does the mugging. A growing segment of the public is offended by it, but eventually submits. It's taken a while for the once-gullibles to see how they're being undressed, but the scene somehow seems to escape the legislators, who turn out to be the muggers' enablers and accomplices. Each time the citizens are bulldozed into underwriting another Hanging Gardens stadium, they are directly subsidizing the stratospheric salaries of ballplayers who are part of the heist.

The other half of this broad-daylight skinning of the taxpayer is the overblown claim made by the jock industry's bagmen about the economic benefits of big league ball. Some of these benefits can be considerable. Most of them are grossly and deliberately overestimated as part of the coercion of the politicians. "Build it or we're going to Nashville," the politicians are told. "You're going to lose big league ball. We're making money here but we want to make more money. It's our God-given right. Do you want to move with the times or move back into the Middle Ages?" And then the politicians are told, "Do it because everybody else is doing it."

Doing what?

Caving in to the pressure by forking over millions of public dollars that should more decently be spent on saving or improving lives. There's an economic truth here that is usually ignored. Those millions of dollars could be produced by the manipulators and promoters themselves if their willingness to risk their own money matched their willingness to risk the money of people who can't afford to go to the ballpark.

Does this mean no case can be made for spending public money to keep a ball club in town?

Of course a case can be made. It was how the Metrodome was built and how (you may have to close your eyes here) the Twin Cities held onto the Timberwolves by agreeing to the ransom demanded by the former Timberwolves owners. The test for forcing the public to pay for a stadium that enriches wealthy people—and at the same time gives pleasure and satisfaction to a sizable part of the public—is fairness and reasonableness. It wasn't reasonable to guarantee a profit to the wealthy promoter who tried to bring a National Hockey League team to Minneapolis in the winter of 1995. The taxpayers and the politicians saw that. As a result, no hockey team came.

We should observe the aftermath of that. Bankruptcy didn't strike downtown Minneapolis. The sports crowd did not riot in the streets demanding hockey at any cost.

In fact, life proceeded normally in Minneapolis and in Minnesota without a National Hockey League team. Pro hockey is nice to have, but not in the face of that kind of shakedown. In the auctioning of professional sports franchises in America today, extortion is an acceptable and increasingly popular strategy. The public is routinely whipsawed between its desire to bring in or keep a bigtime ball club and its reluctance to be the patsy. The auctioneers have become so heavy-handed that practically all major cities in America with any integrity either have lost or will lose one or more teams. There's a limit to selling out the taxpayers to meet the comfort requirement of rich egos.

It comes down to building an understanding among sensible people—the promoters, their corporate allies, the politicians, and the citizens who are dying to root for a winner. If you really want a new stadium and think you need one, all of these people will probably have to pay. Each has an agenda. One or all of them might be a selfish agenda. But it's possible to accommodate each if the process is open and believable. What the public has to demand of the politicians is this: Are those who will make millions on this deal paying enough for it?

Now, if you can get that many sensible people in a room respecting one another's interests, you will probably have more than a coalition of reason. You might win the Super Bowl.

The escalating power of money in professional sports often obscures the other, often irresistible part: the game itself. The innocence of it may be gone. The hoary metaphors picturing the game either as a war without muskets or as a thumbnail of life have mercifully disappeared from most of American literature. But you don't have to love today's corporate takeovers of the franchises to understand what "our ball club" can mean in town if it's managed right and shows some symptoms of sticking around.

Minnesota has had that for more than thirty-five years now. I don't know that major league baseball and football are the most important community bonding agents in the Twin Cities and Minnesota, as a Twin Cities newspaper recently claimed. You might get a rebuttal from people who attended the Billy Graham appearances in 1996, when God decisively outdrew Chuck Knoblauch. But a popular football or baseball team, a genuine folk idol like Kirby Puckett, can bring thousands of people together in a solidarity of joy. If the hero strikes out, of course, or if the team goes into the tank in the ninth, the solidarity is not quite as tight. The Minnesota loyalty to the Twins and the Vikings is rooted not only in success on the field and in superstars. The public's need to see its loyalty recognized matters just as much. While the Vikings and the Twins both have threatened to move, and will threaten again, they have hung around for more than thirty years. It's generally understood by the fans that the management of the Twins and Vikings have loosely met the test of good corporate citizenship, and the relationship between the fans and the ball clubs has been spared the open warfare that has split the customers and their communities from the clubs elsewhere.

So if that sounds as though the ball clubs have built a community in Minnesota, I wouldn't argue about it too strenuously. I'm putting my nose into it because in one way or another I've mixed with the jocks and their games for most of those thirty-five years. No other species of human conflict or entertainment could produce an equally thick and wacky quilt of personalities and moments of drama and absurdity. For years the sportswriters wryly taunted their own business by calling the sports page the toy department of the newspaper. It was that, for sure, a place where make-believe came to life, the make-believe of grown men and women warring with each other on the playing field as though winning or losing were a matter of life and death. The players may or may not buy that today, when a guy can sit in the bull pen and make more than a million dollars a year throwing eight or nine pitches every other day. But there's not much doubt that hordes of people who squat in the stadium galleries and in front of their television sets see the game as something larger than prosperous athletes romping around and yakking with the guys in the other uniform in the middle of the game. For many of these people, probably too many, the game—especially the game of collision and violence—is stirred into their identities. And if the local gladiators lose or disgrace themselves in other ways, the fan's psyche hits the wall. Sociologists sometimes deplore that primitive connection between fan and ball team. Why should they, when you think about it? It's an old and universal attitude. It could be worse. In this country, at least, we ought to be grateful that three thousand people don't get trampled after the game, although it could happen in Boston or Philadelphia.

In the face of the money hysteria and overexposure on television, it's possible to overlook the humanity in the game. You can also lose sight of the quality of some of the men who play the game. Bud Grant, for one, put huge stock in finding and holding on to players of character. I don't think it was a coincidence that the Vikings of the late 1960s and 1970s presented players like Alan Page, who became a state Supreme Court judge; Tarkenton; Jeff Siemon, who became a minister; Fred Cox, who built three chiropractic clinics; Chuck Foreman, who looked so rootless when his playing days ended but dug into himself and became a business executive; Ed Marinaro, who became a television star; and Ahmad Rashad, another television star in life after football. Ahmad was the jewel. He was one of those people whose very entrance into the locker room gave the room instant vitality and seemed to signal better times to come for everybody in the place. He was a player of high ability whose personality attracted players of all moods and colors. He had an instinct for the camaraderie of the game and a gift for mimicry and storytelling that sometimes overshadowed his brilliance as a player. I've never met another big-time athlete whose manner and intuitive goodwill so immediately cut across color lines in the locker room and made him equally accessible to black and white, and friend to both.

I usually find a buffer to the insufferable merchandising of shoes and marmalade hair on television by coming back to some of the basics of the game as entertainment. There is still a kind of core genius in competitive sports when they're played right. To define it, the best place to go is the locker room for the simple but eloquent language that ballplayers themselves speak to idealize their game. There's an expression some of the players use. "This guy brings it," they will say. "Brings it" means that here is a player of commitment. They mean a player coming into the line or running the bases or hitting the backboards with every muscle and gland and all the force of will. John Madden uses another term: "selling out." It expresses the same ideal, the pouring of all of the energy and fervor available to the athlete on that play, in that game, and delivering it without compromise. This is the athlete giving all there is to give. If you watch a game for the intensity of it as well as the skills, for the clash of wills, that is the most profound sight there is. The picture I remember from the Vikings locker room, Joe Kapp with mud smearing his face and Carl Eller with blood on his uniform, celebrating each other and the team, summarizes that ideal.

It still occurs in athletics today. The pity is that too often the player's sacrifice and commitment are obscured by the player's marketers.

4/ The Time They Stonewalled Hubert

The stars of the Democratic-Farmer-Labor Party campaign descended on an assembly of middle-agers and seniors sitting in a bus parked outside a lake resort in northern Minnesota. There were thirty or forty passengers in the bus, scarcely enough to require loaves and fishes or any related DFL miracles. But older folks do tend to vote, and the DFLers came in waves.

So here was the star of stars, U.S. Senator Hubert Horatio Humphrey, romping into the bus with a smile from the driver's wheel to the door and his arms stretched out in a greeting *cum* benediction.

The nasal voice twanged. "Howdy, folks. It's great day to be runnin' for election. I'm Hubert. I want you to know it's a privilege to speak for you in Washington."

Hubert leaned down to extend a hand to a lean old man wearing spectacles in the front row of the bus. His wife sat beside him. "I'd welcome your vote," Hubert said.

Nobody stirred in the front row. "I'm Senator Humphrey," Hubert said, on the chance that the folks had tuned their hearing aids to the wrong frequency. "And I'm Napoleon," a voice brayed from the rear of the bus. The fellow in the spectacles stared into the windshield, a stare so grim it might have ground down the glass. His wife displayed slightly more vitality. She squinted at the candidate with a look that Hubert would have sworn translated as "get lost."

But here was a candidate who could put a cheerful construction on an avalanche. He switched to the other side of the front row, where another couple sat. Both ignored him and sat expressionless. The two old-timers behind them seemed bored. Neither took Hubert's eager hand.

It went that way from the front end of the bus to the back. More than thirty voters on that bus, and none of them so much as eyeballed the U.S. senator from Minnesota. A couple of them yawned and invited Humphrey to show his ID. The natural pink in his faced thickened into a sunset red. Somewhere before he got to the last row Humphrey noticed one of the passengers give him a furtive look. It fell short of saying welcome. It was closer to drop dead. When he ran out of aisle, the effervescent senator was in disarray, stunned and demoralized. He'd seen it all except this. In 1960, with more than twenty years in politics behind him, he could truthfully say that nobody had ever stonewalled him before. He'd been booed at the national convention in 1948 and uproariously applauded at a hundred DFL bean feeds. Either way was acceptable. Hubert could take a roasting and he could take adulation, but nothing in his political history or the gregarious blood running in his veins prepared him for being shunned. This was the kind of reception Henry the Eighth could expect in a health food store.

Finally he confronted a man sitting near the back.

"Let me ask you a question, my good man," Hubert said. "Is this a Republican caucus?"

The man said it was not.

"I can't understand what I've done wrong to the folks in this bus. Maybe you can help me."

The man finally gave Hubert his undivided attention. "Listen. We heard all about you. You got a lot of nerve and you're a phony. The young fella who was just in here said there'd be a guy coming on the bus impersonating Hubert Humphrey. He said to give this guy the cold shoulder. The young fella said his name is Miles Lord. In fact, that's him looking at us just outside the window. Real nice fella. I don't know who the hell *you* are."

Hubert followed the man's finger in the direction of his scurvy persecutor. He found himself looking straight into the gleeful eyes of Miles Lord, U.S. attorney for the state of Minnesota and champion horseplayer of the DFL Party. Humphrey gathered the recoverable parts of his aplomb and walked outside. "Miles," he said, "you ought to be impeached."

He may have been right. But if you wrote news in Minnesota in that age, you wanted to burn a candle each time Miles Lord opened his mouth, which was often and generally without provocation. Like most people in the craft, I lusted for political creatures like Miles. It was one reason—apart from the fact that we shared bloodlines and our early habitat on the Iron Range—why I usually found a way to examine the latest amazements of Governor Rudy Perpich in my column. And those of Charlie Stenvig, the silver-haired police politician who got himself elected mayor of Minneapolis and promptly announced that he was one politician who was going to speak his mind, which appeared to limit his conversation considerably.

But Charlie was a man to be cherished. A problem for newspaper folk in Minnesota in the 1960s and 1970s was the stability of its politics. There were people like Harold LeVander and Walter Mondale and Elmer Andersen and Wendell Anderson and Donald Fraser and Arthur Naftalin and the joyous kingfish himself, Hubert. Now, these were people of uncommon achievement and exemplary character who, individually and in concert, were largely responsible for Minnesota's reputation for good and progressive government. Editorialists loved them. They could explore Harold LeVander's fiscal policies and Wendy's Minnesota Miracle and Fraser's latest breakthrough blueprint for a seven-county sanitary sewer district. The material for these and related explorations was unlimited. I didn't mind exploring sewer blueprints, but I found an afternoon in Miles's courtroom a lot more suspenseful.

By the time they installed Miles on the federal bench, confounding all predictions made in his yearbooks, I'd become a newspaper columnist. My work covering professional football and writing Sunday-morning travelogues in the *Minneapolis Tribune*, the morning paper, had ended in the mid-1960s. There was a personality issue involving one of the *Tribune* sports executives. No good ends are met by saying more, apart from the fact that both parties eventually experienced immense relief. What happened at the end is that I got sick of it and telephoned Bernie Ridder, publisher of the *St. Paul Dispatch* and *Pioneer Press* and one of the owners of the Minnesota Vikings. We were acquainted from my coverage of the team. I found him trustworthy and perceptive. I told him I was leaving my situation and making myself available to write pro football for the St. Paul newspaper if he was willing. He called back to say he was, and the necessary documents—my signature on the payroll forms—were executed.

I rarely saw the interior of the St. Paul operation. Although I enjoyed bantering with Don Riley and Ken Murphy, I spent most of my time in training camp or at practice or on the road or squabbling with

Norm Van Brocklin, and I usually filed by phone. Still, I found the interlude satisfying. Ridder never involved himself in the Vikings coverage. If I wrote a piece critical of some Vikings management policy, I didn't expect to hear from him either way, and I prized that independence. I was gone, though, in three months. In Minneapolis, the daily columnist for the afternoon *Star*, Bob Murphy, had died. He'd been the successor to Twin Cities media institution Cedric Adams. The newspaper's hierarchs decided their readers needed a change of pace, twin columnists, a man and a woman alternating in the space formerly occupied by Adams and Murphy. They chose the woman early: Barbara Flanagan, an effervescent name-dropper and civic bloodhound who became one of the two or three best friends I had in thirty-five years of Minneapolis newspapering. Her columns breezed and flitted this way and that, but she showed an immense amount of common sense in plotting how the town could and should be upgraded and how some of the dragons in power could be nudged or dynamited into action. She rarely peddled idle gossip because, well, it just wasn't done then.

The search was on for her columnist partner. One of the hierarchs said, "What about our man who went to St. Paul?"

The way it turned out, the Minneapolis newspaper was interested not only in finding a male columnist but also in mounting a recovery mission to liberate a former employee who had been dragooned in the dead of night to work in St. Paul. That was the construction, a little bit paranoid, that the Minneapolis editors put on my switch to St. Paul. Danny Upham, one of the senior editors, and John Cowles Jr., also a senior editor and the son of the newspaper's publisher, talked to me briefly. Upham and I met at the Leamington Hotel, where he outlined the specifications of the job. "Write what you want to," Danny said. "Our only requirements are that it should be interesting and free from actual libel."

It seemed to be a reasonable request. I walked into Bernie Ridder's office to apologize. I said he'd given me a job when I'd needed one, and now I was asking to be relieved of that commitment after just a few months. I had had no idea of the column possibility when I moved to St. Paul.

"You'd be foolish not to take it," Ridder said. "If I were in your shoes, I'd do the same. You have no reason to feel badly about it, and good luck."

I've never said millionaires couldn't be square guys. Most of them take a little longer. Years later, when I was gathering material for a book on the Vikings, I called Ridder and asked for an hour in the middle of his busy week. He gave four. I still read the St. Paul newspaper with more than average warmth—most of the time.

Barbara and I became twins with the shortest half-life in genetics. We'd grown up in the same era, sang the same songs, remembered the same radio skits, and enjoyed each other generally. The idea was for the two of us to produce some kind of synergy that would pair us as two peas in a pod in the public mind. The idea dissolved in a couple of months. Barbara waxed the city council for not cleaning up what she called Dirty Old Third Avenue. She made a living off that for a half dozen years. She lobbied for flower stalls on Nicollet Mall and sidewalk cafés all over town. We were going to be the Paris of the subarctic.

By and large, she succeeded. Much of the strolling and the relaxed ambience of downtown Minneapolis in summer today is the legacy of Barbara's scolding and tenacity.

I went in other directions, none of which I tried to define when I started writing the column. Upham said "write what you want," and ultimately you have to do that if you're going to hold the franchise. The direction you want to avoid, I discovered soon enough, was a chronic self-indulgent airing of personal passions and whims. I did that at times. But the biggest satisfactions came in probing community needs and interests, the fears and fixations, why it laughs and when it cries. The columnist discovers, or creates, rules of thumb. What are people talking about today? A glimpse of the ten o'clock news will usually give you the answer. But you will be shallow more often than timely or profound if you confine yourself to what's topical. Addressing the public's anger in the wake of another murder, or its puzzlement in the wake of a respected politician's confession of deceit, may be the obvious choice. It may not be the best one.

There are times when a kid's struggle with ostracism on the playground is what you had decided on for that day, and it's worth writing despite the murder. In other words, columnists, like mothers and harassed politicians, usually find intuition to be a better tool than the book of percentages in making decisions on what's best today. Those decisions for the columnist ought not to be cavalier. Selection of material and the credibility of the writing rather than any rhetorical bravura are what separate most good columnists from ordinary ones. I decided fairly early that I had enough curiosities and appetites and enough energy to give the readers something different day to day. It might not always be entertaining. It might not always bristle with insight or incitement to think, but it would be a switch from yesterday's gore or yesterday's filibuster.

I'm in no position to say whether this was the right outlook, but it did keep me moving. It kept my telephones ringing and, thank God, it ended my battles with Van Brocklin.

Barbara and I sat at adjacent desks. Trying to survive her telephone conversations dropped me into the first minefields of the job. She was a compulsive, flying-down-the-backstretch talker, whether the prey on the other end of the phone was Louise Saunders of Charlie's Cafe Exceptionale or the veterinarian who was taking care of her cat. Yet she was a strategist behind all of her nonstop verbiage. Fifteen or twenty minutes into a conversation with an important source, Barbara would ask the question that all of her sweet talk was meant to camouflage. The conversation was now so friendly and guileless that it was almost impossible for the source to duck the question without sounding like a social hypocrite. On the other hand, she declined to appease bores or nonentities, whom she would blow off without a spasm of conscience. She did this by suddenly giving out sounds that suggested she was enormously stressed and facing imminent cardiac arrest. "I can't," she'd say, "I'm on a deadline." The tenth time I heard that I couldn't hold off my curiosity. "Barbara," I said, "understanding the urgencies of your job, I have to ask how in God's name can you tell that caller you're on a deadline. This is an afternoon paper. It's three o'clock. The next deadline for this newspaper doesn't come until 8:30 A.M."

Barbara pretended to pout, as though it was going to be hard to snow two people in a row. She decided on a stage line, cribbed from Hollywood and one of her imitations of Katharine Hepburn. "Jimmy John," she said, "in this business there's a deadline every minute. Really there is."

Really there wasn't. But Barbara was one of those I-love-reporting newspaper folk whose first impressions of the news business had come wafting into her teenage mind and fantasies via the sound tracks of B movies. Chester Morris or James Cagney would grab a telephone and wisecrack his way through the switchboard operator and invariably demand to be put through to rewrite. Barbara memorized whole swatches of dialogue from those movies. Until she came to Minneapolis, she was torn between two visions, each impossible to abandon. Should she become an actress and fill the screens of America, or should she become a newspaper reporter and fill its front pages? Unerringly, she chose the job that allowed her (if I were to believe half of those phone conversations) to be both. It's true that newsrooms are generously laced with people who find a way to romanticize a business that digs deep beneath their skin. I probably was among them. But Barbara was the only one I've ever met who actually acted it out every working hour, loved both the reporting and the posturing, and did both persuasively.

The *Star* staff consisted mostly of unchained individualists who contrasted with the earnest professionalism of the bulk of the crew of the morning paper, the *Tribune*. That's a generalization I might have to sweat to defend because at various times over the next few years the *Tribune* itself housed a few of the notably unchained, among them Molly Ivins and the lovably manic but well-respected city editor Frank Premack. But we had people like Paul Presbrey, a photographer who wore a middle-aged crew cut and moved around the newsroom and on his beats at a sprint, shirttails flying and belt unbuckled. I'm not sure what state of readiness the unbuckled belt was supposed to convey, but that was Presbrey. He outshone the movie set by five hundred watts. He kept a police dispatcher's radio under his pillow and once shot a picture of the victim of a building collapse, lying under the fallen beams, cut and groaning. The photo was sensational. It appeared in a national newsmagazine whose editor asked Paul why he didn't help the bleeding victim instead of taking a picture. Presbrey seemed baffled by the question. He said he didn't work for the ambulance service and he had to hurry to get back to the darkroom.

Bob Beebe was a crusty old sportswriter who nonetheless observed the codes of the lodge. A few years earlier, when I was writing for the morning paper, Bob covered pro football for the afternoon *Star*. Since I was trapped in the press box writing immediately after the game, Beebe volunteered to provide me with a few quotes from the Vikings dressing room, stuff he didn't plan to feature the next day. He came back to the press box after a game in Detroit, where the Lions had beaten Van Brocklin's Vikings on a day so bad and so cold the Lions fans lit fires in the stands to keep warm and nearly burned down the stadium. The score, the quality of the day, and his general biorhythms did nothing to appease Van Brocklin's disposition. "What do you have,"

I asked old Beeben on his return from the locker room. Beeben looked pale and demoralized. Finally he spoke. "James," he said, "I don't have a thing for you. Worse, I don't have a thing for me. Van Brocklin talked nonstop for forty-five minutes and he didn't give me one damn word that's printable."

Don Morrison sat a few feet away from my desk. He wrote entertainment as elegantly and sometimes as dyspeptically as anybody I've read. He could have written politics or gardening the same way. It was Morrison who happened to be struck by one of the first identity crises of the hippie revolution. He walked into the restroom of a crowded restaurant one day, stood at the urinal, and was flabbergasted to find himself stationed next to a person with hair hanging down to the shoulders. It got to be commonplace later, but at the time Morrison was so disoriented that he tried to finish his business prematurely and admitted badly fumbling it.

In a tiny cubicle not far away sat John K. Sherman, a vaguely absentminded but highly civilized man, a critic who in a lifetime of concert reviews could not bring himself to write a paragraph that might wound one of the musicians or conductors who made the music he revered so much. He would have been run out of the lodge by today's standards of criticism. But that was yesterday, and the newspaper and its audience, to say nothing of the relieved performers, seemed to work their way through all of John's generosity without permanent damage.

Roy Swan swam in the paper's pond of rare ducks. He was a highly competent photographer who walked around with the intuitive frown that most photographers in those days wore like a uniform. You couldn't shoot a hundred frames with fast-firing cameras in those years. If you blew the picture, no backup camera could rescue you. Swan was about to wrap it up one day after shooting a fire. Providentially, he appeared on the scene just as a mongrel dog, possibly belonging to the house owners, came into view. The dog looked totally distraught and began whimpering as the building burned behind it. Swan's camera took in the scene with the mournful dog prominently in the foreground. As he was about to step into his car, a St. Paul photographer, late on the premises, asked him what had happened to the dog and could Swan help find it. Swan's response was not overwhelmed with compassion.

"Go get your own goddamned dog," he said.

Maybe because I worked in an environment of originals like that, I coveted the same qualities in the political bozos that were stitched into the workaday quilt of the newspaper columnist. But there was no avoiding the stars, whether they were high octane or mush. Humphrey was high octane. He'd become an international figure at about the time I'd settled into the job, and his stature and fizzing personality made him hard to resist. I've wondered often in the years since his death how much of the genuine Humphrey we really knew and how much of his fund-raising creativity would have survived the x-ray scrutiny that media agencies fix on the candidates today. Hubert had angels who preferred the shadows in bankrolling him. But for all of the ridicule he absorbed early in his career on the national scene, as a blabbermouth who could afford to talk a great liberal game because he had no minority problems in his backyard, Humphrey rarely temporized in that crusade. He was a natural and a pure politician. He was so good as a politician that the Jim Crow southern oligarchs of the U.S. Senate eventually befriended him and liked him. He was so good a politician that he could make himself popular with political enemies without giving up any crucial ground on his social principles. He was so good that he could serve as an architect of historic legislation like the civil rights bills of the 1960s and creation of the Peace Corps and still keep the constituents dazzled with his us-folks talks at the bean feeds while he was planning a talkathon in the Kremlin.

And yet while he was driven by the need to be in front of the crowds, at ground zero of the political action, Humphrey's obsession to move his agendas didn't seem to reach the pathological level that characterizes others whose lives are dominated by politics. His glad-handing was as much a part of his day as the morning editorials. Maybe what he needed to become president was a streak of ferocity—the hunger to win that lifted John Kennedy and Richard Nixon and Jimmy Carter into the White House. Hubert wanted to win, had things to say and the will to act, but he was always much more the dolphin than the shark. That may be better for his legacy than a victory in 1968. People at the heart of his presidential campaign, with nothing to gain by pushing sour grapes now, insist that Humphrey would have won given the benefit of a few more days in the campaign. They say he was gaining on Nixon at an extraordinary speed, that the polls reflected this, and that Humphrey would have become president if the election had been held four days later.

It wasn't and he didn't. In 1968 the *Star* thought it might be instructive to its readers if I covered four or five days of each campaign: Humphrey's, Nixon's, and Governor George Wallace's. It might have been more instructive to the columnist. I followed Wallace in New Jersey and Ohio. He campaigned with a scowling pugnacity that was more amusing than scary and reached a slaphappy summit in Cleveland, where the Wallace-hating hippies almost outnumbered Wallace's liberal-hating supporters. The hippies came with the intention of disrupting, not to be muscular. They came mostly to have a great time. Toward that end they organized a chant around an appointment Wallace had just announced. The governor had selected as his choice for vice president the retired head of the U.S. Air Forces, a broad-chested nuclear character who could have come directly out of *Dr. Strangelove*. He was on the stage when Wallace started his speech. Thousands of hippies began their mocking chant directed at both Wallace and the bomber general: "All the way with Curtis LeMay. All the way with Curtis LeMay."

His microphone overpowered, Wallace stopped talking. The hippies sent up a triumphant cheer. Wallace gave them his most photogenic sneer of disdain and took a few steps backward to a table. From the table he picked up a bullhorn. It was the biggest, most implacable bullhorn I've ever seen. It was so big it could have swallowed a tuba. The candidate needed two hands to hold it. He began talking. The sound made hash out of the hippies and everybody in earshot. The bullhorn made Wallace's voice sound like Victoria Falls. No eardrums in the auditorium could prevail before it. The hippies tried to recycle their chant, but nobody heard them. Wallace was blasting pointy-headed administrators in Washington, and he did it until the hippies shut up in futility. The bullhorn didn't get Wallace elected, but it did clear the hall.

Nixon's campaign was joyless to watch. His entry into each town was preceded by cadres of campaign workers who hustled thousands of balloons into the hands of schoolchildren to create a festive atmosphere intended to convey to America's television watchers: Dick Nixon is America. This is a scene in which Americans show their trust in a man who stands up for America and loves its people.

It was one of the first campaigns in which the glitzy humbug of stagecraft and imagery had begun to pervert the election process. It would get worse. Nixon's was bad enough, and it created the paradigm. Friendly guests on phony panel shows lobbed marshmallow questions at the smiling candidate, after which he would disappear, off limits to the professional interrogators. Nixon's campaign had the synchronization of a Rose Bowl card show. It was so good that the cheering, flower-throwing receptions for Nixon actually looked spontaneous.

In the five days I watched it, the Humphrey campaign had the general order of a pie-throwing contest. In Salt Lake City the Humphrey forces scheduled a news conference on a Monday morning to preview a major speech Hubert was going to make that night on ending the war in Vietnam. The speech would be a centerpiece of his campaign, and television and the afternoon newspapers were certain to play the candidate's advance remarks heavily. The news conference was scheduled for a big convention room in the hotel where Humphrey was staying. At 8:00 A.M., the campaign manager, Larry O'Brien, advised the journalists that Vice President Humphey was working on campaign matters and would be a few minutes late. Nobody complained. The candidate normally ran fifteen or twenty minutes behind schedule on whatever was on the agenda, handshakes with Ford workers or photo ops in a baseball cap. O'Brien looked unbothered. He was decked out in a chic and becoming navy blue suit, diplomatic striped tie with gardenia in place, his waved hair impeccable.

At 8:30, Larry returned to the microphone with a graceful apology, giving assurances that the candidate's itinerary was under control and announcing that the candidate would appear momentarily. O'Brien's gardenia looked slightly askew.

At 9:00 A.M., O'Brien announced that serious matters, unscheduled, were under discussion in the candidate's suite and his best information was that Vice President Humphrey would arrive sometime in the next few minutes. A television reporter from Chicago wanted to know whether the candidate would show up in time to make next Sunday morning's religious show. O'Brien's composure had wilted in concert with the vanishing crease in his navy pants. At 9:30 A.M., ninety minutes late, the vice president swept in to begin the news conference. If there was any explanation for the unconscionable delay, I don't remember it. If there was any doubt that every reporter in that room was going to leave with an impression of a campaign in comic disorder—and would write it—that doubt had pretty much evaporated with Larry O'Brien's serenity. Alongside Nixon's parade-ground precision and

George Wallace's ear-busting bullhorns, Humphrey's campaign bore a striking resemblance to a Boy Scout troop whose scoutmaster remembered to bring to camp a hundred rolls of toilet paper but forgot the canoe paddles.

It said much for Humphrey's personal resilience and the stubborn although fading coalition of the Democratic Party's power base—the workers in the industrial states, the South, and the minorities—that Hubert came as close to the presidency as he did. Consider. The country was split violently by the issues of Vietnam. The incumbent president, Lyndon Johnson, was virtually under siege in the White House. Hubert was popular in Minnesota but not especially esteemed around the country, which generally saw him as a robust, decent kind but still too gabby and inclined to be weepy. The Republicans were efficiently organized behind a candidate who looked plausible if not lovable to the country. The Democrats' convention in Chicago left a residue of chaos. And yet—

I remember Humphrey's postconvention return to the streets of Waverly, Minnesota, where he lived. It was a radiant late summer afternoon and this day, more intimately than his nomination and acceptance speech in Chicago, harvested the sweetest fruit of Hubert Humphrey's political evangelism. All his friends and neighbors were there, joined by thousands of Humphrey's Minnesota supporters from the Twin Cities, the grain fields, and the ore pits. If the presidential nomination had been a political ascension for Humphrey, it was a tentative one because the election lay ahead and his chances were thin. But Waverly on a Sunday afternoon on the eve of the campaign was a celebration and a thanksgiving. It was all that had been good and personal in Humphrey's politics. It was the hoedowns and the caucuses and the rubber chicken dinners and the big DFL blowouts at the Minneapolis Auditorium.

I knew him in the same way a dozen other reporters knew him, well enough to ramble around in politics for a half hour or more when he had time. I approached him through the exuberant crowd and shook his hand in congratulation. He delivered all the right words and the right grip, but I don't think he really saw half of the faces he looked into on the street that afternoon. His eyes were fixed and crystalline yet watery, the eyes of a man nearly in a trance. Here was the look of a man who'd seen a vision. He flung his hand over this well-wisher's shoulder and under that elbow, pumping hands, his soft pink face lit by a congenital smile of elation. He listened, and because he was a politician who knew all of the responses, he seemed to hear. But I don't know how he could have heard much. This was the transforming day, from the South Dakota prairie to the drugstore to the rough-and-tumble of Minneapolis city politics. From there, creating the DFL with Art Naftalin and Bill Kubicek and all the others, vaulting into the mayor's office, setting off a near riot in the Democratic convention with his call for racial justice, outtalking Republican Joe Ball in the Senate campaign, being lifted into the vice presidency (and sometimes embarrassed there) by Lyndon Johnson. Finally, coming before America, and on this day before his friends and neighbors, as a man who would be president of a nation that needed healing so desperately.

I think Hubert might have healed. He certainly would have healed beyond the capability of the man who beat him. He would have taken sizable ripping and baiting from his critics. But the qualities that raised him from his beginnings as a windy political innovator to the presidential nomination essentially were qualities of character and mind. He had ideas that were bedrock strong, not ideas advanced as political stunts but ones that had a chance to make a difference in thousands or millions of lives, and often did. The causes and goals he pursued often matched the greatness or the potential greatness of the country. Within five or ten years, some of them were derided as obsolete and expensive liberalism. In time, the country's politics shunned some of them. But in the years of the street revolution and while the country was anguishing over its deepening disparities, it needed a believable appeal both to its conscience and to the impatient urges of its widening middle class for more security and more prosperity.

Humphrey would have made those appeals to what was better in the American nature. Who knows whether it would have worked? Or whether the nation eventually was stronger or weaker for his defeat? I do remember watching him disappear into the crowd in Waverly and asking rhetorically, "Hubert, with all the baggage you're carrying into the campaign, how are you going to do it?"

The night of the election, sifting through the settling gloom of the Humphrey party in the Leamington Hotel in downtown Minneapolis, I indulged in a second-guess. Humphrey was losing, but it was closer than forecast. His handlers might have been right. A few days more might have been enough. If that was correct, the place where he lost it seemed to me beyond any argument. He made one of his first major campaign speeches in Seattle, a few days before the debacle of that tardy news conference. The hall was jammed with thousands of Democrats. A half dozen bands jazzed them up. People danced in the lobbies. In its political colors and ethnic spectrum, Seattle was an ocean-front version of Minneapolis: a labor town, lots of Scandinavians, progressive politics, lots of Democrats. Humphrey wheeled around the stage before the program, shaking hands and slapping backs. It was the old bean feed politics multiplied by huge stakes, and the place exploded when the feature band rolled into Franklin Roosevelt's campaign anthem of the 1930s, "Happy Days Are Here Again." But before they introduced Hubert, the hippie war protesters turned the night into one of the calamities of his political life.

They occupied two or three hundred seats in the second deck. They came with scruffy clothes, pot fumes, and a blunt objective. They were going to break up the rally of the warmonger Humphrey, Lyndon Johnson's vice president and, they said, his toady. They pretended to conduct a trial. They accused Humphrey of high crimes. The crowd booed, but finally Humphrey stood before his speech and said to the crowd, "Friends, this is the Democratic Party. We'll listen to these people if they don't get too offensive." It might not have been bad philosophy, but it was atrocious strategy. The hippies screamed and hooted and got offensive. Humphrey tried to stop them. He said, "All right, let one of you speak and we can talk." One of them spoke. But when Humphrey replied, none of them listened. They set off another din. The Democratic candidate for president glared at them, helpless to manage a couple of hundred stoned troublemakers at his own rally. Security people finally muscled them out of the building, but the mood was shattered. Humphrey's talk was mechanical, and it took his campaign a week to regain momentum.

You had the feeling that what Hubert needed most that night was not his willingness to listen, but George Wallace's bullhorn.

But the hybrid political party Humphrey and his accomplices created in Minnesota during the war years, the DFL, had a vitality that survived Hubert's defeat. That quality declared itself in the elevation of another DFLer, Walter Mondale, into the vice presidency just eight years after Humphrey occupied it. And eight years after that, Mondale was running for president.

He didn't run very well or very far. Aside from a squeaky victory in Minnesota and in the District of Columbia, Fritz Mondale was smoked.

Ronald Reagan won from Long Island to Maui island. Hurricanes have been kinder than America's voters were to Fritz. He had to be numbed by his wipeout in the electoral college, but he couldn't have been surprised by the defeat itself. Polls gave him no chance, especially after Fritz announced in his best Norwegian earnestness in the middle of the campaign that he would probably have to raise taxes if he got elected.

Republican brainstormers sent him a congratulatory telegram.

Mondale's tax increase was never anything more than an academic promise or threat. Running for a second term, Reagan was unbeatable. Mondale was more a sacrifice than a serious candidate. Reagan was popular, untouched by the national economic muddling his first victory had produced, and almost hypnotic in his effortless charm. He did have trouble staying awake, but he could have won the 1984 election in bed, and he practically did. Of all Mondale's political and personal achievements, though, his response to this defeat always characterized him most memorably for me. The temptation was to call the 1984 loss humiliating because of its raw magnitude. I don't think Fritz felt humiliated. What he probably felt most acutely was dumb for letting his ego, practically always under control, suck him into the race.

What I liked about Mondale was the relatively modest weight he gave to Walter Mondale's political success in the overall scheme of the universe. Most of what he got in politics he lucked into. He was appointed Minnesota attorney general when Miles Lord left to be district attorney for Minnesota, and he was appointed to the Senate when Humphrey became vice president. He justified those appointments, though, and served well. At practically all levels of politics he attracted kingmakers who liked his package of unhurried competence, goodwill that seemed to reach the public, and a mind that put most events in perspective. You never quite got the impression that here was a guy gored with the ambition to be president. He dropped out of the 1976 campaign because he just wasn't inflamed by the idea of running every day for two years, raising money every day for two years, and getting beat out by Jimmy Carter. So when he was buried in the 1984 election, Mondale resurrected the essential Fritz Mondale. He produced no outpouring of mea culpas. He did not set fire to himself in front of the Library of Congress. He came back to Minnesota to be a lawyer and to melt quickly into the fraternity of lawyers and the society of private citizens. Others in the same place have torn themselves apart with second-guessing and bitterness over the betrayal of political friends or the voters. "It was a fair fight," Mondale said. "It's over. Life doesn't begin and end with running for president, or any office, for that matter."

That is a truth many professional politicians accept only under duress, especially those who have suffered defeat after years of success. Defeat can change their personalities. It can turn them into recluses or cranks bent on revenge in the next election, and the one after that. Donald Dwight was publisher of the *Star* and *Tribune* for a few years before the intramural slaughter of its incumbent executives in the early 1980s. Before coming to Minnesota, he'd been the lieutenant governor of Massachusetts. We talked once about the dicey quality of the political career. "I know one thing I've seen about defeat in an election," he said. "It can be absolutely devastating, particularly if that person has been popular or in power. It can destroy the man or woman because it's a repudiation, a rejection more painful than almost any other kind of loss. It is a rejection by people who once thought you were great and wonderful and applauded your every act, and now they're saying, 'you're dirt,' or 'you're too old.'"

In 1990, still popular and electable in Minnesota, Mondale considered running for his old seat in the U.S. Senate against Republican Rudy Boschwitz, a man famed for his prowess at attracting campaign money. Mondale pondered for several months. He had access to resources and a positive reputation in every corner of Minnesota. But Boschwitz seemed entrenched, capable of raising vast funds. He could, in fact, as a sitting senator conceivably beat Fritz Mondale in Minnesota, which not even Reagan had done. Mondale weighed the allure of returning to the electricity of politics in Washington against the real hazard of spending the next twenty years as a political corpse. He held a news conference in which he made the obligatory statements about spending time with family and living a rounded life. But what the practical Norwegian had probably done was to take a long look down an uncertain road and decide life was too comfortable at this stage to risk turning himself into a cartoon.

He deferred and walked away—and into the ambassador's mansion in Japan a few years later, still getting the good political jobs the old-fashioned way, by appointment.

They were substantial public people, Hubert and Fritz. But they did not tweak the newspaper columnist's antennae as abruptly as some of the more inspired nonconformists, a Eugene McCarthy on one side of the pole and a Charlie Stenvig on the other side. McCarthy and Humphrey served together in the Senate for several years. Remarkably, both were potential vice presidential nominees in 1964, when Lyndon Johnson was headed for a landslide. McCarthy admired Humphrey's political savvy but was never quite sure about his intelligence. For a few years, McCarthy was a genuine heavyweight in American politics. He might have been vice president. As a long shot, when he led the youth rebellion against Lyndon Johnson in 1968, he might even have been president. His ultimate political fate was to dwindle off in his later years as a kind of intellectual Don Quixote, futilely declaring his candidacy in this election or that. For a while it made him a Democratic version of Harold Stassen.

I always regretted that, although in a few years McCarthy exerted the good sense he was born with and stopped running. No one of depth that I've met in Minnesota politics, or politics generally, brought into the dialogue the same kind of off-the-wall aptitude for the satirist's quick stab to the groin. In his later years, when nobody was paying much attention to him, McCarthy amused himself by lobbing his barbs whenever the mood struck him, ambushing the hypocrisies of windbags of both Democratic and Republican stripes. Or he read his poetry in little bookstores with a pure Irish gift for self-disparagement that was never quite self-disparagement but always reminded you that here was a very bright guy who should have been listened to. I always thought in reaching his own particular pinnacles in politics, McCarthy overcame a lot of temptations to compromise. But he might have been president if he had overcome an even higher temptation, the one to be lazy. Still, he might have done himself a favor by not getting there. As president he couldn't have burned the windbags as exquisitely as he did. No one—with the exception of Winston Churchill—did it much better. I never heard much malice from McCarthy. This is why, three or four times I year, I'd call him at his place in rural Virginia or in his book dens in Washington and ask what he thought of the news.

"What news?'

"How do I know? Your old sparring partners in Minnesota miss you. Tell me what's wrong with American politics."

It wasn't usually my intention to goad McCarthy into tossing some of his better shafts for a newspaper column, although when I called he'd often say, "Give me a couple of minutes to bring in the groceries," which meant he was organizing his ad libs for the audience back home. Mostly, I called just to talk to him and to enjoy his nimble mind. For McCarthy, the joy of doing political parody was basically the joy of manipulating the language to score points in a mock war. It wasn't mock war back in his 1960 battles, but it was as he got older. It's not easy to be outrageous and wise in the same sentence. Especially if you want to throw in a quotation from Aristotle in the middle of it. But Eugene McCarthy, poet, former senator, former amateur baseball player, and aging, unappreciated critic of the times, usually managed.

I'm not sure where you'd put a fellow like Charlie Stenvig in the Minnesota political firmament of the 1960s and 1970s. Charlie might have been a loose meteor before he burned out. He was one of those triumphs of the silent majority movement, the middle-class and laboring-class resentment against the generous grants to the poor and minorities by the federal government, a.k.a. the Democrats. Dick Nixon popularized the term "silent majority" on television. It got to be code not only for the genuine insecurity felt by millions of Americans but also for racism. Although Charlie preached no racism, he said he was running as a cop who knew how to keep our streets and homes safe. He may or may not have known how, but he got elected mayor of Minneapolis. He was a blue-eyed, white-haired Scandinavian who made an attractive appearance but had a genius for the social gaffe.

Jim Shoop, a *Star* city hall reporter, remembers Charlie's phone presentation to the general manager of the Minnesota Vikings, Jim Finks. The question was the possible construction of a stadium in Minneapolis. The two had never been introduced. Stenvig picked up the phone and said, "Hello, Fink. This is Chuck."

The general manager of the Minnesota Vikings was an urbane and civilized man. He preferred to be addressed as Finks instead of Fink, and he had no idea who Chuck was.

It was the misfortune, also, of the king of Norway not to have been previously introduced to Mayor Stenvig when they met in the royal palace in Oslo. A member of the Minnesota entourage later described the meeting with some pain: "There aren't many rules that govern introductions like that. Mostly common sense prevails. The only thing you have to avoid is making any kind of physical contact with the king. The only other courtesy is to address him in a reasonably respectful way. 'Your majesty' is usually OK."

Introductions were made. Mayor Stenvig was affable and smiled a greeting. He also gave his majesty a sociable clap on the shoulder and said, "Hiya, king."

The rest of the entourage melted perceptibly.

I have to admit that there is some nonconformism that pushes the margins too far, even for the columnist attracted to it. Rudy Perpich's, though, was pure cream.

He might have been my brother. Our blood and genes had a common source, the Balkan hills of what was once called Yugoslavia. We were the same age, lived though the same childhood experiences of the mining country, his near Hibbing, mine in Ely. To help pay the college bills, we both worked in the mines for a year or two. By the time I met him he'd become lieutenant governor of Minnesota. He'd been in office for five days, presiding over the Senate, when he threatened to quit on a point of honor or procedure, or maybe it was the sniping of a Republican from Rochester. Rudy. He reconsidered the next morning when he found himself in the middle of some other crisis that demanded his instant energies.

I've always tried to separate my views of Rudy from our common bloodlines and the peculiar environment we shared in our childhood and adolescence, with the nationality mishmash that shaped our attitudes.

I gave up the attempt several years ago.

I once drew a two-week suspension from the newspaper for writing the introduction to an inaugural speech he delivered in the Hibbing high school. In hindsight, I'd say it was an act of innocence, but it was dumb. Still, we were a long way from being inseparable pals. When his media feuds steered him into some especially air-headed pronouncement or melodramatic pout (he wanted two portraits in the capitol rotunda, recognizing his split terms as governor), I took my rips along with the others. How could you avoid it? I thought he was foolish and vindictive.

But it was part of being Rudy. And when he tried to overstretch his governorship into one more term—"to finish my business," he said— I thought he was falling into the old political manhole of the once-popular public servant trying to hold onto power for the sake of holding onto power.

We ignored each other for months at a time. That wasn't hard to do because he was juggling a thousand people and some strange events as the governor, and I had other and often better things to do at the newspaper plant, and we had people enough covering the governor of Minnesota.

The last time I talked to him was a few months before he died. He and his wife, Lola, came to lunch in what I think was their Peugeot, although it could have been a Jaguar. From the time they'd lived in Austria during one of Rudy's reluctant exiles from Minnesota politics, they were unblushing continentals. Rudy had rushed back into one of his campaigns with a hot proposal to establish a branch of the University of Minnesota in an abandoned Austrian castle. The school's board of regents examined this idea with solemn eyes and a silent plea for relief from Rudy's latest creative stroke. Someone, possibly Lola, decided that the University Minnesota did not have a space problem that urgent.

The idea slowly retreated into the political twilight zone reserved for some of Rudy's other inspirations—for example, the one to expand Minnesota's tourist appeal by advertising to the nation's ailing. The campaign would focus on Minnesota's world-class reputation as both a health center and a wonderland of nature. In other words, come to Minnesota to get your lumbago treated at Mayo and then spend two weeks of rehabilitation on the shores of Leech Lake. To Rudy, the idea looked unbeatable. The problem was that it had to compete with Rudy's other ideas, the ones that seemed to make immediate sense, such as the Center for Victims of Torture and the Super Bowl at the Metrodome, and ones that didn't, such as the factory in northern Minnesota making chopsticks to ship to the Japanese.

On the day of our last lunch, I'm not sure he'd abandoned the idea of a comeback, even though he surely knew about his cancer by then. He looked strong and full of drive. He wanted somebody to write a piece in the newspaper about the awful mistakes being made by the American government in dealing with the Bosnian crisis. But I didn't come with a notebook. Mostly we talked about the Range and families. Finally I told him of the pride I'd felt in what he'd done in Minnesota politics. An immigrant's kid from the ore mines had become governor. It wasn't done every day. People used to hear the words *Croatian* and *Slovenian* and look blank. Is that some kind of social disease? Now they knew something about that part of the world, about the rich flavor of the nationality stew on the Iron Range, and about the Range's undeniable quirkiness. And if they looked on our part of the world with some new understanding and even with some fugitive affection, it was mostly because of the impressions they drew from Rudy Perpich.

But becoming governor was only an invitation at the door. It was saying, all right, he looks good and sounds OK, but what is he and who is he?

With the people of Minnesota, he went the full 360 degrees, from his inauguration to his death. He was welcomed as an odd confection of Minnesota politics when he arrived, was jeered and laughed at later, and was loved on the day of his death.

He began as a dentist but soon decided that political and civic affairs in Hibbing were much too important to be left to political mediocrities. He decided that one person with the energy and imagination to run politics in Hibbing was Rudy Perpich. He became a citizen-politician on the school board. He decided that one problem with citizen-politicians was that their creativity did not have a large enough canvas. So he became a professional politician. He reached the legislature, the lieutenant governor's office, and was been maneuvered deftly into the governor's office because Wendy Anderson, the governor, wanted to go to the Senate as an appointee and he needed a governor to appoint him. Rudy became the governor in 1976. His inaugural made all previous inaugurals look like reviewals at the mortuary. They held it in the Cathedral of St. Paul, where Father Frank Perkovich of Gilbert conducted a polka mass. I remember it because the place was jammed and I was the only journalist there who covered it from a confession box. When it was over, Perkovich sold his polka mass records at a discount in the narthex.

So Rudy came in as a sudden new resource of the people, a governor who danced the polka and took solitary rides at night to drop in on his constituents in the country. He started talking about Minnesota as though there were no horizons it couldn't reach if it thought boldly and acted aggressively. Meaning now. He was a big guy with a robust presence, black wavy hair and an open, pliant face that made him instantly appealing. If every election put the candidate out in the towns and country to meet voters and to listen to them, Perpich never would have lost. To the end, face to face, he was an immensely likable guy. When he talked family, he talked family and not the cue-carded Family Values. He was believable when he talked that way because from his childhood to his death, family was the one unbending truth of his life. All right, he got slugged by the old man, Anton, one day when he brought home a tie for the old man's birthday. Rudy, the six-foot high schooler, blinked as though asking the logical question. What the hell's going on, pa? He knew a few minutes later. The old man was giving him an economics lesson. Money is serious business. Don't waste it on foolishness.

Was that a pretty barbaric homily? Well, probably. I told Rudy years later that I had God to thank for the fact that my own father took a different educational approach when I brought him an Arrow shirt for his birthday. He said "thanks," which I was glad to settle for in view of the alternatives. But Anton and his wife raised remarkable kids—Rudy, George, Anton, and Joe. All of them graduated from college and succeeded. All of them worked through school, in the mines, at tables, wherever they could earn a buck. The old man and his wife provided what they could. And when Rudy and Lola got married, they paused en route to their first honeymoon destination in Duluth to have their wedding lunch at—where?

"Every time you wrote that it was at a Burger King I cringed," Perpich said.

"Why? That's the way one of your brothers told it."

"It wasn't a Burger King. It was a Dairy Queen."

They made a magnetic couple, Rudy and Lola. His energy and physical presence and easy self-confidence, her dark-haired loveliness and composure. She was never quite "the first lady," but closer to a working partner. He trusted her instincts and her judgment, although all the evidence suggests that she didn't intrude often on the purely political matters. In later years, partly in bitterness over the mounting media ridicule of her husband and the sharpshooting at her own efforts to refine the governor's residence, she withdrew as a public figure. Her grief at the time of his death was private, her memories unspoken. As the wife of the governor she carried herself with an unshowy elegance that never subdued the girl from the Range in her. In the middle of his stewardship, Rudy gave a party for Twin Cities newspeople. It was a walk-around kind of dinner in which the main event was a serving of *sarma,* a traditional Croatian and Serbian sausage roll often anglicized as pigs-in-a-blanket. The journalists revealed no enthusiasm for the Yugoslavian plum brandy called slivovitz that Rudy kept in the house for the connoisseurs. They were enthralled, however, by the *sarma.* When the party ended and the guests trooped out, the wife of the governor of Minnesota stood at the doorway, handing out pigs-in-a-blanket to take home. It may have been the first time in Minnesota social affairs when the guests left the governor's mansion carrying doggy bags.

When all of the loops of his behavior and brainstorms are ironed out, what Perpich brought to Minnesota politics was a rollicking gospel that grew out of his fundamental belief that Minnesota was practically heaven on earth for people with ideas and energy. He looked at his own beginnings, and those of his brothers, poor kids emerging from the ore mines with an education to become dentists, politicians, and doers. Yes, it was the sweat of their parents and their own thirst to succeed that moved them in front of audiences, he said. But it was more. It was the environment where they lived, the schools of the Range and of Minnesota, the level of life in Minnesota, its business and medicine, its trailblazing politics and its generosity. This might be an appraisal of Minnesota too sanguine for cynics, but it's a picture Rudy Perpich grew up with. The governorship, he realized, had limited political power. But there was nothing in sight to limit the governor's schemes, so he flung them out like rice at a wedding. Let's bid for the Saturn plant. Let's shoot for the Olympics. Put a soccer stadium in Blaine. How about a Minnesota version of the world-class ski jump in Oslo?

How about a great international trade center in St. Paul, where Minnesota and the world will come together in a marketplace unique to America? Let's go after the Super Bowl; we can entertain the visiting notables with sled dog races and ice fishing. That would be a mind-stretching switch from the Super Bowl beaches of Florida and San Diego for the visiting notables. But the Super Bowl happened. So did Mikhail Gorbachev, wheeling through the streets of Minneapolis and St. Paul at a time when he was the international megastar of the decade. So did the Mall of America in Bloomington, for better or for worse, a retail marketing attraction unmatched in America.

None of these bombshells were Rudy Perpich's exclusively. But none of them would have happened without Perpich's impulses and his gall. He actually believed that no dream of the politician or the civic promoter was beyond fulfillment in Minnesota if he or she harnessed the right resources and enlisted the right people. His enduring political strength was his willingness to take risks. The risks usually involved getting past the predictable ridicule that met some of the more esoteric schemes of the wild man from the Range. What do you mean, Gorby coming to Nicollet Avenue? Why would the chic, glamour-conscious National Football League put its showcase extravaganza in a dump like the Metrodome?

Some of his notions deserved the horse laughs they got. Some of them will survive in concrete and dollar signs for decades into the future. He was one of those politicians who went for the fences, connected sometimes and dribbled out to the infield other times. That didn't mean he neglected more powerful priorities. The day he died, a person who was disabled called my office.

"I don't think anybody before Rudy had seriously put the problems of disabled people on their agenda," she said. "He did that. He gave us dignity, and he took us seriously."

He also took the gender disparity in government seriously. His appointments of women to the Minnesota Supreme Court set national precedents in their scope and aggressiveness. His appointments were uneven. A few looked almost inspired. More of them came off the wall. He put in reasonable numbers of qualified people, but he was a political freelancer who leaned on his hunches and personal ties more than he listened to the headhunters. It didn't penalize a candidate for appointment to have bloodlines reaching back to the ore pits. A few days after he was elected governor in 1982, reversing his loss to Al Quie of four years before, Rudy called and offered me the job of director of the Department of Economic Development. It was like asking a Quaker to run the Pentagon.

"Rudy," I said, "what do I know about the Department of Economic Development?"

"You don't have to know; you don't have to be one of those technocrats," he said. "You can put in experts to do the technical work. You can look over the broad picture."

I declined with relief and much-warranted modesty. It was an outlandish idea, but it was Rudy. He was out of the blue and all over the place. The latest idea that came to him was always the best, the most irresistible. His popularity, while it was strong through six or seven years of his governorship, started to limp when his acts got more bizarre and when his feuds with Twin Cities columnists and reporters turned him cranky and defensive. When he didn't think he was being accorded proper respect at the dedication ceremonies of the World Trade Building he had fostered, he just didn't show up. It was an act of huffiness with which most people who grew up on the Range are familiar—a to-hell-with-you reaction to a personal slight, a reaction straight from the ore pits. But it isn't what you'd normally expect from an experienced politician. The Republicans peddled him as Governor Goofy, and that portrait overpowered the public's earlier perceptions of his achievements and the core decency he brought to public office.

His final mistake was getting proprietary about the governor's office. He deserved it more than the opponents who made jokes about him. But the ease he had felt as a campaigner ten years before disappeared in his last campaign. He almost disappeared himself, confining his electioneering to small-town coffee klatches. The public derision got so thick that he lost an election that normally would have been impossible to lose. The Republican right put up Jon Grunseth, a corporate executive. Two weeks before the election, Grunseth was forced to withdraw because of embarrassing disclosures about his private life. Arne Carlson, the state auditor who'd been rejected by the Republican convention, came in as the Perpich opponent practically in the dead of night.

Carlson won handily. That was Rudy's political finish, but it wasn't the end of his will-o'-the-wisp politicking. In the early 1990s, the government of Croatia made Rudy Perpich of Minnesota the foreign minister of Croatia. It was an improbable act, naturally, but it looked legal and it was vintage Perpich. It also looked a little silly, and it didn't last.

And yet for all of his public scrambles and causes and brave new ideas—and his public blunders—Rudy Perpich at the end was a private family man of an intensity his friends found painful. No one outside his immediate family knew he was dying. Three weeks before his death, one of his closest financial advisers went ahead with a fundraising plan for Rudy's next campaign—confident that there would be a campaign.

Something extraordinary happened at his death, which produced a genuine grief without parallel in Minnesota since the death of Hubert Humphrey, and perhaps exceeding that. Thousands remembered personal encounters with him. The affection felt for him from border to border was real. The cantankerous last years of his governorship were overridden by an outpouring of goodwill that remembered his frolicking and unpredictable personality, his willingness to take chances and his decent impulses. He was seen finally as a public man of substance and personal honor. He was seen as a man who lived a private principle to the end by turning down the brief martyrdom he could have gained by going public with his approaching death.

He went instead in the arms of his family.

He was somebody to remember, whether he was polka dancing or going for the fences.

5/ The Muppets of the City Room

In the 1960s and 1970s, the *Minneapolis Star* harbored an editor, Lee Canning, who ran the newsroom like a circus barker.

I mourn the disappearance of the Cannings of journalism and their times. Lovers of peace and quiet might not.

It was the time before word processors and, you would have sworn, before simple interoffice telephones. Canning stood in the middle of the city room an hour before deadline in the morning, making the sounds of a man about to activate an elephant stampede. About deadline, Canning was a noisy paranoid, worried that some of his warriors would blow it and expose his forces to the humiliation of getting skunked by the *St. Paul Dispatch*. He was also never confident that he had the best story of the day in hand. In time he would start stalking and yelling. "Any late ones? Anybody with copy coming? Identify yourselves."

The newsroom stirred. Nervous feet cantered to the city desk. Copy dribbled in. Canning exhorted and hustled the troops. He was never sure about their sense of direction. A few times he sent scouts into the men's room. Once every few weeks Canning would swing around in the direction of my desk and bellow, "You got anything for page one?"

This was usually fifteen or twenty minutes after I finished my column, which was my normal allotment of creativity for the day. I didn't usually stash backup stuff for page one. Still, writing and editing for the *Star* in that age always gave us the same loose turn-on you feel choosing up sides for a touch football game. You never knew quite how it was going turn out, but there was a fighting chance that some identifiable order would eventually emerge from the chaos. Not always, but often.

Plus, I liked Canning's manic MO.

"How much time to deadline?" I'd yell to Canning.

"About forty-five minutes."

"All right, I'll have something."

"About what?"

"What do you want on short notice, the Magna Carta?"

Canning would schedule this phantom story for page one. I dredged through my source list, made some telephone calls, and produced a story. It usually made the deadline sliding, and the *Star*'s newsroom once more was spared the scourge of calm and normalcy.

The country's afternoon newspapers began their death rattles in the 1970s. Some of the newspapers were relatively viable economically, the *Star* among them. But the nation's reading habits and its leisure-time choices—in fact, the basic trends of the economy and marketing—all conspired to doom the afternoon paper. The catalyst in much of this was television. For more than a hundred years, working people came home from the factory or the office in the late afternoon and read the newspaper before or after dinner. It was their primary source of news.

Television changed that. The waning of heavy industry in America changed it. So did the speed of the times. People began to acquire more recreational time. They got home earlier. But when they got home now they rushed to the golf course, or they stopped at the athletic club before getting home, or they turned on television. One thing they did considerably less than they did before was to read the afternoon newspaper. Aggressive, free-circulation city weeklies added to the competition for the reader's time and loyalties. This was no particular agony for the publishers of many afternoon newspapers, since they also published the morning newspaper in the same plant. The number of major American cities where actual competition occurred on the newspaper stands, publisher against publisher, had been dwindling for years. The more successful ones gobbled up their competition. It had happened in both Minneapolis and St. Paul, where the two surviving publishers operated sister newspapers under the same roof.

I wrote for the afternoon *Star* for eighteen years, much of that time when it was running against the tide and trying to make itself relevant and entertaining. It didn't take an oracle to see the crisis. Local television news was expanding its audiences and its resources, legitimately competing with the newspapers on some types of coverage and swamping them in getting to the audience first. It was bad enough for the morning newspaper, which still could bring in strong overnight breaking news—ball games and news from the world capitals plus its own enterprise. In other words, it came in fresh every morning. The afternoon paper either came in with old laundry sudsed up to look new, or it poured its major resources into investigative stories, extended personality profiles, and a whole gingerbread oven of feature stories. The idea was to give the readers recycled news that still belonged in a daily journal no matter how tardy, and stories and twists they weren't getting in the morning paper. Most of those television didn't have the resources to tell or had no interest in telling in the twenty seconds available between the weather, auto crashes, and commercials.

The *Star* retaliated against fate and its media tormentors by trying to be inventive. It also tried to be compelling. Often it succeeded, but that was a parlay certain to send the newspaper over the brink from time to time, sometimes willingly. This it did in hiring Steve Isaacs as managing editor to be the *Star*'s salvation heading into the 1980s. He came in with the reputation of being a hothouse innovator and one free-wheeling, unpredictable citizen. One of Isaacs's first acts of citizenship when he got to town was to take a chain saw to a small acreage of trees on the boulevard in front of his house across the street from Lake Harriet in Minneapolis. His premise was that he'd bought the house largely to look at the lake and the trees were plain intrusive. The amalgamated nature lovers of Minneapolis nearly choked, to say nothing of the guardians of the parkland.

To be fair about it, the *Star* by then was pretty much an unshackled leprechaun of metropolitan journalism, ready to battle potential reader boredom in all sections including the editorial page. The editorial page was reconstructed as a sanctuary for some of the exhibitionist ax grinders in town, many of whom had been deservedly ignored until then.

There weren't many limits. "We've got a guy coming into town," an editor said. "He claims he can shoot a cigarette out of your lips with a revolver 100 times out of 100."

"Out of whose lips?" I asked.

"Yours. You can talk to him tomorrow morning if you want. Looks like it'd make a great photo layout for page one."

I have no idea what the newspaper's legal liability rules were in those days. I'm mortally sure it wouldn't have happened today. Moreover, it wasn't really an assignment. Nobody ordered this screwball story. But it was available, and I thought it was a piece that could put pepper into the day. The gunman showed up with his armament. He said this project was a piece of cake. He had a little platform with a holder in which he propped the gun. He said the holder acted as a kind of vise, and the gun was fixed and secure in there, without "play" or deviation that could throw the bullet's flight out of line. "All it takes," he said, "is a metal backstop where the slug goes. We could even do it in your house."

It was afternoon. My wife was teaching school and the kids were in class. I noticed with some relief that none of the neighbors was at large. We set up in the basement, where, as a courtesy, the sharp-shooter said he would give a demonstration. He lined up the gun and fired four or five .22 slugs into the backstop, all of them in the identical place.

"As you'll note, this is live ammunition," he said.

I said that was plain for anyone to see.

"What I usually do is substitute a length of white writing chalk for the cigarette," he said. "Photographers prefer that because the explosion of the pieces when the bullet hits is more vivid and comes across in print, whereas a cigarette just sort gets clipped on the end."

I don't remember the photographer. It might have been Russ Bull. I asked if he had any preference. He stared, a reasonable facsimile of a man aghast. He said he didn't have a preference but he didn't have any chalk, either. He said he was dying to see how this was going to come out. I told him that personally, I would have used a different metaphor. I asked the sharpshooter for the longest piece of chalk he had. He said he had standard school chalk, about three inches long. It seemed dismally inadequate. We set up. I put the chalk in my lips and the sharpshooter fired the revolver.

All available lead hit the chalk and the backstop. It never laid a glove on me. The chalk was still in my mouth after he fired. On second examination, only half of it was. This means the lead passed within an inch and a half of my lips. Momentarily, I was at a loss. Finally I said, "Nice shot." It was the best I could think of. The next day, the exploding chalk in my pursed lips made a sensational photo on page one.

My wife, however, didn't talk to me for a week.

The gunshot episode had the effect of loosely launching a phase of special-effects journalism that seemed to match my impulses with the *Star*'s restless hunt for off-angle material. I went scuba diving under the three feet of ice in Lake Minnetonka with no special inducement other than the fact that it isn't done every day and probably beats shoveling for suspense in winter. One day Jim Marshall, a Vikings football player lit by similar impulses, agreed to meet me at an airstrip in East Bethel. We were going to do a photo story on Jim's parachuting passions. Marshall was a gifted athlete and a generally captivating human being who seemed to be singled out by fate as the subject of strange events. Early in his career he accidentally shot himself with his revolver. He explained that he owned the weapon because he frequently carried large sums of cash. This was a revelation that surprised his friends; Marshall and cash rarely had a long association in those years. Another year, Marshall was hospitalized for five days because he incorrectly swallowed a grape. Still another time, he and teammate Paul Dickson joined a snowmobile caravan I organized in the Beartooth Mountains that came to grief and tragedy in an overnight blizzard. Jim later revealed that he survived by lighting a fire with hundred-dollar bills. On review, they could have been check blanks, although I would be the first to admit that blizzards do tend to affect the eyesight.

On the day at East Bethel, Marshall failed to show. He may have had the wrong day or he might have driven south instead of north. Either explanation I would have bought. And either way, I was stuck with a photographer, two planes—one for the parachutist and one for the photographer—and two pilots. A skydiving instructor also happened to be on the premises.

"Marshall isn't going to show," I told the disappointed photographer.

"Too bad," he said. "I've never photographed a skydive up close. It's a shame to waste these two planes."

It was, and that was a fact.

It was coming up on twilight. There was still enough sun for good photography. I asked the skydiving instructor how long it would take to learn to land if I jumped myself.

"Have you done this before?" he asked.

"No."

He said life was a constant source of valuable new experience.

I said this was so, but as a practical matter, what was his opinion of the parachute I'd wear?

"You shouldn't have any trouble," he said. "You climb out on a step near the wing to prepare the jump. You then put your hands over the leading edge of the wing. And then you push off and assume the aerodynamic position, arms and legs flung out. The chute will open in a few seconds. It's automatic because you'll be hooked up to a static line. It's a tremendously neat experience. Incidentally, you've got a backup chute on your chest in case anything goes wrong. I've got some boots for you, and you can do a little workup here jumping off that table nine or ten times. We use it for students. You ought to be just fine."

I jumped off the table a few times and said OK. The photographer went up in the other plane and ours leveled off at around three thousand feet. The drill was for the instructor to tap me on the butt each time it was necessary to move to another stage in my departure into space. He connected my chute to the static wire inside the light plane and helped ease me out onto the open step.

The effect, literally and truly, was the same as stepping into the middle of a hurricane. The plane was flying at about a hundred miles an hour, which is well within the parameters of a hurricane. Standing on the step in the tempest, I hung on to the wing struts for balance, a procedure the instructor interrupted by batting me on the tush again. This meant that I should wrap my hands around the leading edge of the wing. I found it almost impossible to do that in view of the air resistance. But the drop zone was just a few seconds away, and my hands crept up to and around the wing's edge. A moment later he was swatting me again. I wasn't sure whether this was the second or third swat, but I grasped the general idea that right about here is where I should fling myself backward into space. I performed that step with much reluctance. If something went truly amiss here there was nothing left to hang onto, nothing to go back to, and three thousand feet of air in which to consider the wages of rash acts.

But I remembered to throw out my arms and legs into the spread-eagle position, and I was flying. More correctly, I was dropping. The farm fields and the islands of woods between them spun violently and wind screamed in my ears. And then my shoulders jerked and I was embraced by silence. I looked up into the sun, and there was no sun. What there was, was a huge and wonderful striped canopy, the parachute gently turning, bearing me to earth. I tried to remember how to work the control cords, having little success but not worried because this was euphoric, twisting pleasantly in the breeze, floating toward the ground and the approaching trees and utility wires—

Oh, wait a minute. These were the hazards I was instructed to avoid. I worked the controls, irrelevantly as it turned out, because the danger was past. Here was a meadow, right now, and I thumped down into it, upright and exuberant. The wind was forcing me to trot along the ground while I tried to bring the parachute under control. And then I realized it wasn't the wind so much because there were *two* parachutes trailing behind me, the main chute and the emergency chute, which somehow had popped open when I hit the ground.

I came to a stop harmlessly, wrapped around a friendly cottonwood.

The subsequent photos of my leap and descent were passably dramatic. The accompanying story was not bad. My wife had been out of town the day of the jump, and I neglected to tell her about it. She read about it in the Sunday newspaper, which meant four more days of silence in the house.

While I suppose the traditionalists would call some of these exercises stunts, and while I wouldn't argue very strenuously with them, I found myself genuinely charged by these little odysseys into the unknown. Why? I asked myself. I couldn't truthfully say I was doing this to shock or titillate the reader; fundamentally, it was because I was turned on by it. And I found that some of the episodes gave readers a few minutes of either entertainment or befuddlement. The exact reaction was hard to predict. I learned to fly and shared the experience. I rode with a professional race driver in downtown Minneapolis traffic and shared his view that life seemed more hazardous there than it did in the safari races in Africa, where the obstacles were merely elephants strolling on the highway. I organized bicycle rides and tried to bring the reader onto the pavement and into the rainstorms with us. Later, I began to share some of my sensations and summit moments from a part of my life that was more serious and important to me, the mountain experience.

Much of that was drawn from my private life. My sagas from the mountains grew out of the newspaper's interest in them and the readers' perceived curiosity about people who like dangling from cliffs. The theory must have been sound. During most of my later years as a columnist, I found that the readers' strongest single identification with me grew out of my experiences in the outdoors.

So I became a personal columnist, with whims and attitudes that got to be recognizable to the reader as time went on. The *Star* as it was constructed then welcomed that kind of writer-reader relationship, although it wasn't always sure it approved some of the plots. Neither did the management of the Minnesota Orchestra one year in the early 1970s.

Most of the conventional stars of our society don't arouse immediate thrills for me. Generals and knuckleball pitchers and reform candidates may be OK and even powerful personalities, but in the news business they become part of the landscape. People with the art and skills to make beautiful music, however, attract my awe. It may be because the Mozart and Rachmaninoff I play is scarcely recognizable on my bad days. I can't imagine people with the virtuosity to actually play the music as it was written. Which means that sooner or later I was bound to meet the conductors of the Minnesota Orchestra: Stanislaw Skrowaczewski, Edo de Waart, Sir Neville Marriner, Eiji Oue. In the 1970s I lunched with Skrowaczewski, who had the look of a Polish patrician but was and is a pretty cordial guy who happened to have climbed mountains. We lunched at Bennie Berger's old continental restaurant, Schiek's. At Skrowaczewski's insistence I was calling him Stosh after fifteen minutes. Stosh the patrician maestro. I wanted to talk Chopin and Dvořák. The maestro wanted to talk about the Teton mountains and climbing. Mount McKinley came up. I said I hoped to climb it. Climbers of average ability and sensible stamina, I said, could manage it with a professional guide or with someone in the group familiar with the mountain.

I asked the conductor if he was interested.

He needed no prompter. He said, "Let's do it. Let's pick a time and start planning."

My telephone rang at 7:30 the next morning, the first call of the day. It was Dick Cisek, the symphony orchestra's general manager and den mother to conductors. He said he'd run into the maestro and understood we'd talked about climbing Mount McKinley. I said this was correct. He asked what the elevation of Mount McKinley is. I said about twenty thousand feet. He asked if it had glacial crevasses, avalanches, and high-altitude blizzards. I said these could be over-dramatized, but they were not unknown on Mount McKinley. Cisek said he thought it was an exciting concept but he'd been looking over the maestro's conducting schedule and his guest appearances; after an earnest conference with the maestro, he'd reached the conclusion that Mr. Skrowaczewski was booked solid for at least the next ten years.

It was a pity. On the summit, Stosh could have conducted a few bars of the Antarctic Symphony in pantomime in the middle of a blizzard.

The character of the *Star* and my yens for the off-the-wall experience combined to put me into many strange settings during my labors with the afternoon newspaper. For this, I have to say now, thank heavens. Lee Canning read a wire service story about a major change in life in Sweden, the ancestral home of scores of thousands of the newspaper's readers. Since the invention of the automobile, the Swedes were part of that throng of traditionalists who insisted on driving on the left side of the road. In the late 1960s, the government decided they should move to the right side, thus catching up with most of civilization. "They're going to do this next weekend," one of the editors said. "It could be traumatic. We should be there to tell our good Swedish-American readers what the damage comes to."

I resisted briefly. I told the editor I thought there were more Swedes driving on the left side of the road in Minneapolis than there were in Stockholm. Nonetheless, I flew to Sweden for the weekend. What I found was a gripping study in thought control. It was every bit as scary as the sight of 8 million Swedes changing direction overnight. Before the driving change, the Swedish government, which was promoting the plan, had polled the people and found they were overwhelmingly opposed to changing their driving habits, something like 85 percent. Undeterred by the small impediment of a public opinion landslide, the government launched a saturation brainwashing campaign on national television. It went on for several years. The government cited safety. It invoked the convenience and logic of driving on the side of the street where most of the rest of the world drives.

Before the changeover day, the government took another poll. Nearly 85 percent of the people said they approved moving to the right side of the street.

My dispatches recorded this phenomenon along with the results. On changeover Sunday, the Swedish government enlisted hundreds of thousands of block workers. There was somebody on every street corner, reminding the Swedish drivers which side of the road was right. The change went brilliantly. No violations in Stockholm were reported, no injuries. The only police incident occurred just inside Sweden, along the Norwegian border. A truck driver was stopped for driving on the left side of the highway. He said he was a Norwegian from Stavanger and hadn't heard the news.

About then a story idea reached my desk from John Cowles Jr., the son of the publisher and, not surprisingly, a man rapidly rising in the organization. John was an agreeable and serious young man who was destined to make powerful contributions to the culture and viability of downtown Minneapolis. But he was also touched by a few eccentric ideas and some plain bad luck in his years in power and was forced out in a board rebellion in the 1980s. Before he became an executive with the newspaper, John had acquired passing notoriety for an incident during his days as a reporter. Emerging from his home near Lake of the Isles one morning on his way to work at the state capitol, John noticed an unusual object under a nearby hedge. Investigating, he found a woman's body. It turned out to be that of a patient of a Minneapolis dentist, A. Arnold Axilrod, who was convicted of murder a year later.

John was a man committed to rigid good citizenship. He immediately called the police to report the body. He neglected, however, to inform the city desk of his newspaper. The critique and second-guessing by the newspaper's editors the next day were understandably muted.

John was an idea man and also an amateur student of the enigmas of the mountains. He suggested to the *Star*'s editor that the readers might benefit from a series on the possible existence of an Abominable Snowman type of creature in the wilds of northern California. He suggested that I was singularly suited to lead an expedition and write the series.

I admit to not being much impressed by the lingering stories of a Yeti in the Himalayas or a Sasquatch in the British Columbia mountains or a Bigfoot in the hills of the California rain forest north of the Klamath River. I had traveled in the Himalayas, and I still do. Prints in the snow have been found, of dubious origin. Sherpa tales are told, usually after the third bottle of *chang*, the local brew. Skulls have been displayed, arrayed with hair, which usually turns out to be that of a deceased goat. I examined one of the skulls in a Himalayan monastery through the courtesy of a Buddhist monk, who managed a tasteful wink as he was displaying it, meaning that it was still worth thirty rupees to the monastery to show it. Not one shred of acceptable physical evidence has ever been found to suggest the existence of such creatures. But speculation heated up in the late 1960s when a national magazine published a photo from California showing what appeared to be a gorilla-like creature with sinuous movements. The photo later proved to be a fraud, a creation of the photo lab. But at the time it thickened the speculation. Maybe Bigfoot was female. All of this fueled the shaggiest of all mysterious creature stories: a prospector had been kidnapped years ago by a Sasquatch family in British Columbia for the purpose of becoming the spouse of their daughter, five hundred pounds, seven feet tall with long hair. The prospector was said to have escaped before the projected consummation, but was so shaken he spent the rest of his life as a hermit.

My recruits were John Fletcher of the Como Park Zoo, who came with an anesthetic-loaded capture gun in case we actually encountered the creature; Monte Later, an Idaho businessman and outdoorsman with whom I'd climbed; and Jerry Singer, a Minneapolis criminal lawyer who came as a notary public with a record of having defended Mafia characters, which qualified him to deal with Bigfeet.

We scoured the rain forest and lonely creeks and ridges for a week. We found prints that looked promising until we found out they'd been fabricated by the local chamber of commerce. I filed my reports diligently but had to conclude that if there actually is or was a creature in California seven feet tall and five hundred pounds, with bad breath and shaggy hair, he would have been drafted on the first round by Al Davis of the Oakland Raiders.

The newspaper sent me to Italy expressly to drive in the traffic of Rome with Italian drivers (actually *against* Italian drivers, because it was every man for himself). It also sent me to Venice to haggle with the operators of the early-morning flea markets. It sent me to Moscow while the communists were still running the show and tapping hotel telephones. I attended the Bolshoi opera with a bulky female Intourist guide who as a teenage partisan during the war had shot twelve Germans. She was sociable and insisted on something stronger than Prokofiev, although the big band in the National Hotel, playing American pop music of the 1930s, was not quite in Prokofiev's league. Still, after forty-five minutes of vodkas, she insisted on dancing. I demurred. She started to taunt me: I was an inept capitalist. I said she was wrong, I was an inept dancer. She dragged me onto the floor, actually pulled me. She spotted me fifty-five pounds and four inches of reach, but I was dead game. I danced, and not badly at that. But when the evening was over and we had to ride to the apartment she shared with her husband in the Moscow suburbs, I asked her to call the cab. She did. It rolled through the steppes for an hour and a half and was halfway to Novosibirsk before we got to her apartment. The night cost me four hours of sleep and cost the *Star* ninety-five dollars in cab fare.

It was Steve Isaacs himself who got me mixed up with some genuinely murderous Reds. When he was brought in as the *Star*'s managing editor in the late 1970s, he decided what he needed to do immediately to give himself credibility as a stager of events and agendas was an International Impact Story. None such developed for weeks. Then, in the middle of the week, the wire services carried a big story out of Rome. Aldo Moro, the premier who had been the victim of an abduction by the violent Brigato Rosso, the Red Brigade, had been found murdered in a parked car on a street in Rome.

I was heading for Rapid City, South Dakota, to make a speech when Isaacs overtook me in a corridor. He was a large, overweight guy who had a distinctive waddle as he made his way through the hallway carrying a half-gallon water glass.

"Rearrange your schedule," he said. "Fly directly to Rome from Rapid City."

I wasn't sure that was possible, I said.

"Arrange it," he said.

Why?

You're going to cover the services for Aldo Moro Saturday.

OK. Why?

"It's a big story with global impact. You can cover it in a personal way, talk to the Romans, get stuff from the Trevi Fountain and the Coliseum." The way Isaacs talked, I wasn't sure whether it was a funeral or a Triple-A tour. There was one other small question. I tried to picture readers from Mound to Blooming Prairie hungering for a first-person report on the funeral of Aldo Moro in Rome, and I was getting very fuzzy images.

But I wired for credentials and flew to Rome after contacting a Minnesota resident familiar with the scene in Rome. He conscripted a friend to meet me at the airport outside of Rome. He said this man would produce contacts. He would identify the places to go for comment from both mainstream Italians and the communists. Because of the surprising procurement practices he revealed later in the weekend, I will call this Italian agent Vito. He was fabulous. I found people and scenes that turned what I thought was a contrived, journalistic side-show by the *Star* into a pretty thrilling mystery story about Moro's abduction and death, and the effect on the country.

I got into Rome late on a Saturday morning and plowed into the stuff without sleep. I worked my tail off all day and, after dinner with my confidant, walked to the hotel elevator to go to my room. At the elevator we were met by a young woman who was without question the most gorgeous blond I have ever seen, dressed expensively and totally gracious. Vito made introductions. I produced my mostly courtly smile, said goodnight, and pressed the elevator button.

He took me aside.

"What are you doing?" he said.

"I'm going to bed."

"Alone?"

"I had that in mind."

"But that is impossible. I have asked this lovely young lady to be your friend for the night. I think she would be terribly embarrassed and disappointed if you didn't accept."

As generously as I could, I told Vito that this was doubtful, but I did summarize my condition. "I'm married. I'm tired. I'm probably over-worked. I have to get up at six o'clock."

Vito's tossed shoulders suggested that he did not consider these to be persuasive obstacles. Nonetheless, that's how the conversation was left. I thanked Vito for his thoughtfulness and the young woman for her patience. Vito looked momentarily crestfallen but shook it off. He frankly enjoyed maneuvering the American around Rome and putting him in touch with his offbeat connections. "Tomorrow," he said, "I might bring you closer to people who know about the killing of Aldo Moro."

It was a suggestion that I might be getting closer to personal contact with the Red Brigade, the kneecap-shooters.

I have never met an Italian who can't act. I didn't know whether Vito was putting on a show or laying out an agenda. We met at six for dinner in the hotel, after which Vito drove me to a moldering tenement on one of the Seven Hills of Rome, the Esquilino, in a shabby part of the city. The building housed a fruit market and some non-descript offices above. It was a Sunday night and the building was apparently deserted. I asked Vito what our plans for the evening were.

"There are some young guys, radicals, who run an illegal radio station in this place," he said. "They have some connection with the Red Brigade. I don't know how close. I don't know what they know, but I have a drink sometimes with one of the guys. They've never been in the press. They put out their political stuff on the radio station an hour or two at a time and then they shut down and get out of there. They don't like the government. They want to make changes. They're right on the edge."

"Of what?"

"I don't know. I thought you might want to meet them. I told this guy I'd bring you up. He said OK but we should be brief."

We walked into a freight elevator. Vito clanked the doors behind us and pressed a button. The elevator groaned and refused to move because we needed a coin. Neither of us had one. The option was to walk up seven flights of stairs. We walked. Vito opened the door to two small, unswept offices with graffiti and news clippings on the wall and newspapers and paper towels strewn on the floor. We walked through them and Vito knocked on another door. A young man in headphones opened the door, nodded to Vito, and admitted us. Three other young men and a woman were standing around radio equipment—microphones, meters, scopes, and the rest of it. One of them spoke English well.

"You're from the USA?"

"Right."

"You want to know if we know anything about Aldo Moro."

I noticed an empty gun case under one of the chairs. I don't know if it meant anything sinister. Maybe they hunted ducks. I said yes, it would be helpful if he and his friends knew anything about Aldo Moro, but it certainly shouldn't mar a budding friendship if he didn't.

He apologized and said he would have to check me out, meaning frisk me. Fleetingly I thought about Isaacs and his big water glass and couldn't escape asking myself a private question: What in the hell are you doing here? The shakedown finished, we talked. He gave me an antigovernment tirade about working and living conditions. He expressed no deep sympathy for Aldo Moro but denied knowing anything about his death. He might have been lying, but it was no place to turn on a polygraph. About the Red Brigade and connections with it, he was murky. He said he didn't like some of their terrorist tactics. He didn't denounce the brigade. He was full of passion about the reasons for the rebellion. He explained how his people ran their underground radio operation. His story was good enough to report. We talked some more, and after a while I looked at the clock and at Vito.

"I suppose you've got work to do," I said to the young man.

"That's right. We'll take you to the elevator." The words sounded ominous for some reason. The hall was dark and echoed with our footsteps and distant sounds of doors and street traffic. Someplace I'd seen this set in a movie and I didn't bother trying to remember how it came out. But we got to the elevator. Somebody had a coin. The descent must have taken two months.

"Did you get a story?" Vito asked.

"Yes. I didn't think I ought to press them on Aldo Moro. I mean, they did have the home court advantage."

"My friend," he said, "you were smart tonight. But you were dumb last night."

The Italian perspective.

Predicaments like those didn't happen every day, although the *Star*'s needs and my peculiar juices produced the occasional hairy scene, like the one in Rome and another at the Republican National Convention in 1972. The Democrats and Republicans both held their presidential conventions that year in Florida, where the hippies, yippies, and assorted flower children and guitar pluckers had arrayed themselves in tent cities and the banyan trees. The Democrats' meeting wasn't a convention; it was the futility bowl. The splinter sects and the special pleaders in the party dominated prime-time television and drove off the viewers in herds. They made tiresome speeches that promised to dismember the Democratic Party—not the Republican Party, which never listened to them—unless every one of the fifty-five points in their manifestos was adopted. The one possible candidate who might have challenged Nixon, Ed Muskie, had been driven off by dirty commando tricks in the New England snows during the primaries. So the Democrats nominated the doomed George McGovern, who was introduced to the voters of America as the Democratic candidate at the original hour of 2:00 A.M.

Nixon's convention, on the other hand, wasn't a convention either. It was closer to an enthronement. But the disruptionists in the Miami streets when the Republicans were in town behaved just as bumptiously as they did when the Democrats were there. At about the time Spiro Agnew was to be swept in as the vice presidential nominee, I heard a report of a rumble in the street. It sounded better than another dose of Agnew, so I walked out of the convention hall, making sure that I had all seven of my identification badges and stamps to get back in through the Nixon security. The yippie protesters were advancing in the street, carrying banners and shouting the usual obscenities: "One, two, three, four, we don't want you're f_____ war." By then they had ripped into a delegate bus from South Carolina, tearing out the engine and smashing glass. From the opposite direction the troops and cops were coming down the street with their clubs and rifles and gas masks. The enforcers and the rebels came together, and it was a war. I ran up to get closer and heard something thud on the street. I know now it was a tear gas canister. I didn't then. In a minute or two I was lying in the street, trying to breathe. It wasn't going particularly well, but one of the yippies ran to me with a damp white cloth. He put it to my nose and mouth. "Breathe," he said. "Don't rub your eyes."

In my woozy condition I had to be sure I didn't get his directions reversed. A few moments later a guy wearing a white collar joined the yippie. "Father," the yippie said, "you know some Spanish? See if you can make this fellow understand."

The yippie thought I was Hispanic. "Hey," I said, "I can understand English. I'm one of the boys." Together, they got me more or less upright. By then a cop had joined the scene, obviously the only married man among them. "I got some advice," he said. "This happened to me. Be sure you take that suit jacket to the dry cleaners. I didn't, and I caught hell from my wife."

Gunships were flying overhead. Troops were marching in the street with rifles. The yippies were throwing garbage can covers over the barbed-wire fence into one of the command posts. And here was a cop giving me a laundry lecture.

Personal journalism often means functioning as a kind of agent for the readers, opening the antenna and letting events hit it and bounce around for the reporter or columnist to unscramble in his or her peculiar fashion. Personal journalism doesn't mean the events necessarily have a personal impact on the reporter. But some do. Dwight Eisenhower died in March of 1969. The world's leaders and his wartime friends and colleagues congregated in Washington the weekend he died: Charles de Gaulle, the shah of Iran, Omar Bradley, thousands of others.

Although I hadn't voted for him, I mourned him because here was a man who truly deserved the love and trust of the people he'd served as general and as president. He embodied qualities that Americans seem to value in their leaders. He was gregarious and decent. He was decisive when he had to be and harbored a useful spark of temper. He botched the English language routinely, a failing all but the most rigorous linguists had no trouble forgiving. He was a man of principle, but he was revered for another reason: he had commanded American forces at Normandy and through Europe in a war that stirred in Americans a pride and a national unity that we may never again experience.

Before the observance in the rotunda of the White House that Sunday, I walked to the National Cathedral to witness the silent lines of thousands of Americans paying their respects before his casket, which was draped with flags. I noticed a man taking a little more time than most. His lips moved uncertainly and his eyes were closed. When he walked away, I approached him, guessing that he'd served under the general.

"I did," he said. "I was a rifleman in the Ninetieth Division at Normandy. I saw him once when he came to inspect us at a training beach in England a month before D-Day."

Mike Eloff was now a lineman for a power company in Cleveland. At Normandy he had waded ashore in the second assault wave, through the floating bodies in surf roiled by the gale winds. He had survived German machine gun fire and later shrapnel wounds in the Battle of the Bulge. He had come to the National Cathedral, to stand behind the cordon of red velvet ropes with his teenage sons, to mourn his commander in chief but also to remember those who went to Normandy with him and didn't return. No remembrance could be more solemn. No one could personify the commitment of Normandy, the nation's unity, and the sanctity of that day in 1944 as Ike Eisenhower could, in life and in death.

"I tried to say something, standing there," the wartime rifleman said. "I just couldn't put the words together. What I wanted to say was that he was such an honest-to-God type of guy, the kind of guy you wanted to walk up to and shake hands with."

The rifleman considered what he'd just said.

"You know, I think that's what I was doing today."

It was a salute the general would have felt privileged to return, and one the recording journalist felt privileged to witness.

Other privileges for the recording journalist were slightly less gratifying. Someplace in this time scope I found myself invited to explore the black hole of talk radio, augmented by a weekly public affairs show on television. Walking the tightrope of time was one of the hazards of the rush-the-clock professional life that I found invigorating. I took stock. I was writing five columns a week. For seven years in the 1970s I also wrote pro football daily for the *Star*, in addition to my general column. I spoke here and there two or three times a week, published books in the odd-numbered years, performed two hours of late-afternoon talk radio five days a week after my chores at the newspaper, and acted as host of a weekly television panel show. This was frenetic juggling at an advanced level.

The question was this: Was I serving the best interests of the juggler, of the readers and viewers and listeners, or of the cardiac specialists at Abbott-Northwestern Hospital?

The final answer on the cardiac specialists may not have been delivered until fifteen years later, but the short-term verdict I settled on was this: I found all of this writing and talking and running about energizing. Sometimes I performed a service. Moreover, it was a huge amount of fun. Whatever benefits flowed to the readers and listeners and viewers I have to leave to them to judge.

Talk radio, even in the early 1970s, often left the host with only the narrowest escape hatches to sanity. I gave my two-hour segment the subtitle of "the revolving squirrel cage of radio journalism," explaining that it had the virtue of keeping eccentrics off the street and either listening to the radio or sitting behind the microphone. I did two years of talk for WLOL and four years of television for Channel 11 and then, years later, a couple of years of talk for KSTP-AM and two years of interview shows on Twin Cities public television. Talk on WLOL twenty-five years ago actually offered interludes of genuine public service. In those years, talk radio was not necessarily seen as a showcase for political screwballs and electronic molesters.

My late-afternoon assembly of guests over a month's time might include the president of the University of Minnesota, the governor of Minnesota, the university medical school's Dr. John Najarian, or a world-class mountain climber, Gaston Rebuffat. Baseball's Ted Williams would drop in for a chat, shepherded by Bob Short, the owner of the Washington team Ted managed in those years. Chet Huntley would telephone from the airport, or Muhammad Ali. The raunchiest off-mike guests might have been Germaine Greer, the feminist author, and

Tony Randall, the film sophisticate and lover of classical music who off the air told some of the most elegantly dirty stories I've ever heard. The talk was wide open, the questions from the listeners out there in the great void usually provocative. WLOL's share of the radio audience was large, although it was disproportionately made up of people who didn't buy cars or high-ticket clothes. This drove the station's accountants daffy because they had a big audience but couldn't sell.

You could never be sure about the next call. One of guys who called me often off the air hated my attitude on gun control. He said he had been tracking me, and he knew when I crossed Highway 55 and Winnetka Avenue on my way to work in the morning and when I got to Wirth Park. The fact that he had the time right was discomfiting. I'd ask him if this was a threat. He told me to draw my own conclusions. I did: He was going to call again in three days, and next week and next month, and he always did.

Howard Cosell showed up at 4:00 P.M. on the day of a Monday-night football game at Metropolitan Stadium. He said he had come partly at my request but mostly to express his heartfelt contempt. I'd written a column less than flattering about Howard's blatherings on television, although I liked parts of his work and later we actually got along. Cosell arrived at the station with a local representative of the network, who came along to make Cosell's excuses when he decided to leave. Cosell said he would take a few questions from the audience; he was going to give us fifteen minutes of his valuable time and no more. With this, he coughed. Moreover, he said, he was feeling miserable. I asked if I could get him some water. He looked hesitant. One of the station employees remembered that he had something stronger in his car for tailgating that night. He asked Howard if this might be more helpful. Howard said he was the last man to be discourteous and he would oblige with a sip. The guy went into the parking lot and came back with a quart of Johnnie Walker Red. A water glass was fetched from the restroom. Howard was asked to say when. He was gripped by a sudden loss of vocal power. Before he recovered the glass was full and, in a minute or so, it was gone. I'm not sure about the FCC regulations on all of this, but I do know that the local rep must have reached every friend he had in town, because Cosell was deluged with flattering calls. Cosell said he was touched by the erudition of the radio listeners of Minnesota. His fifteen minutes stretched into thirty, into sixty, and past ninety.

"Howard," I said, "I'm off the air at six and you have to go to the Met. We'll have to make this the last call."

He said that was a pity, but whatever happened to that little old water glass?

Television talk usually presented the same kind of test of logic and good order. Wrestler Verne Gagne, one of my very best friends, once put me under for fifteen seconds on live television—I was the moderator—by exercising the sleeper hold. He was not invited back. During the first outbursts over building a domed stadium, I scheduled an audience-participation show for a Tuesday taping at 7:00 P.M. The announcements got the date wrong, and at 7:00 P.M. Tuesday there wasn't a body in the studio. We had access to the taping crew for only ninety minutes. The producer went one way and I went another. We hit the Monte Carlo restaurant, Bob McNamara's Sports Lounge, and a joint on Hennepin Avenue. In thirty minutes we had rounded up twenty-five people for an audience debate. I don't know if it was the most influential debate of the season. I do know it was the rowdiest.

Talk radio was unsurpassable as a vehicle of instant communication. My wife had been trying one day to reach me to get me to bring home some groceries. My telephone line at the newspaper office was busy or I was en route someplace. Ten minutes before the end of the radio show I got a call from my wife, on the air. "I've got the shopping list for today," she said. "This is my only shot."

Exercising the privilege of any caller on talk radio, she read the list on the air. Thousands of people suddenly knew our favorite brand of mayonnaise.

The next day three listeners called in, quarreling with her choice of mayonnaise and insisting that she switch to Hellmann's.

6/ Walking on Thin Air

In the German-speaking countries of central Europe, there's a distinctive word that identifies a hiking trail. It appears on a small sign, typically in the shape of a yellow diamond posted on a tree beside the mountain trail. The word is: Wanderweg.

It's a pretty straightforward word in the German language. It means here is the way to walk, the trail. But just as the libretto of an opera in a foreign language arouses the imagination, coaxing the listener to read into the mysterious words what may not literally be there, seeing Wanderweg *in the mountains instantly evokes something more than a hiking trail for me. I see the sign, and the* wander *in it translates into a shifting screen of memories and anticipations, of a hundred trails and ridges where I've been or where I want to be. The* wander *in that little sign brings a rush of invitation: one more day to ramble on the mountain trail, one more day when the way goes up.*

An advertising man who lunches with me once a year spends half of the time telling me how he hates complexity. There is practically no side of human behavior, he maintains, that can't be reduced to a short and punchy diagnosis, preferably one word, exposing the meat of the behavior. It's a creed of his working life, so ingrained now that he tries to prove his thesis with parlor games at lunch.

"Use one word to describe how you define your life, how you look at it and what you draw from it," he said. "Don't argue with my premise. Give me a word."

To avoid wrecking my salad, I complied. I had an answer that I thought was truthful, but I told him straight out it was going to sound like cornmeal.

He was ruthless. "And the answer is . . . ," he said.

"I suppose the answer is *adventure.*"

He wanted to know why I was so reluctant to make the admission.

I said it sounded melodramatic, like something lifted out of Jack Armstrong. It also sounded slightly breathless and probably raised questions about how the adventurer viewed the larger purposes of life.

He wanted to know if I had answered all of those questions satisfactorily. I said I hadn't. But I thought it was possible to see life in part as a daily exploration for what was around the corner or beyond the hill. You can do that and still meet the basic tests of normalcy. You can do that and still find it possible to do useful things like earning a living and loving the in-laws. The conversation ended in disarray. He tried to wring a final admission from me: "So you put your newspaper work under the same heading?" No denials were necessary, I said.

The authority on this may be David Nimmer, former managing editor of the *Minneapolis Star,* former news reporter for WCCO-TV, former investigative hawkshaw, and now a journalism professor. In the years when he ran the *Star* newsroom, Nimmer had direct supervision over the news budget. He was and is a friend of mine and was an occasional confessor. Annually I'd go into his office to outline my schemes for the year. I'd explain the amazing collateral benefits that would come to the newspaper's readers, in terms of international understanding and cultural depth, from reading about a new journey through the Himalayas or the Alps. Nimmer usually acceded after drawing himself up to his full five feet one inch of corporate authority. He'd remind me that I was wearing out my credibility with that line. One day he turned me down flat on a climb in the Himalayas. "This is it," he said. "The answer is no. You gave me that same stuff about Nepal last year, how our readers were desperate for the latest news in Namche Bazaar. Write about Minnehaha Creek."

I had learned years before that the Nimmers of the world can be dealt with. Under his dictatorial patina was a desire to be loved. I had a fallback position staked out: a climb in the Andes. What the readers didn't know about Peru, I said, could hurt them.

Nimmer approved the budget for the Andes. I have to say this today about the years when I mixed my outdoor passions with the newspaper's bookkeeping: if my response from the readers was a valid argument, most of the time it was a fair exchange for the newspaper. The idea of the stories was not to cast the principals in heroic postures or in the traditional hair-raising drama of man against nature. The in-tent was to take readers into the crater of a dormant volcano or into a snow cave in Alaska, places where they probably had not spent a substantial amount of time but might be curious to know the feeling. Taking them there in credible ways meant removing some of the mythology from mountaineering or camping alone in the wilderness and to present these experiences as real and fallible people—not supercreatures— live them. The idea further was to show that when or if hazard actually developed, normal people acting rationally could usually handle it. And, finally, it was to suggest that a climb in the mountains can often produce more amusement than fright.

In later years, I took the newspaper's budget out of the equation. I did this by creating a private adventure travel club whose finances, properly managed, allowed me to underwrite my travels at no cost to the newspaper but with some continuing benefit to readers who liked an adventure story. I certainly wouldn't claim that *all* of the readers were enchanted by those sagas from the middle of a blizzard. On a quiet day in Lake Wobegon, Garrison Keillor once did a piece for the *Star* analyzing its content. He decided that Barbara Flanagan and I were probably the parts of the *Star* with which most of the readers identified. About me, he had two primary observations. He thought my pro football pieces over the years ranked with the better ones he'd read. But what he couldn't understand, he said, was what possessed me to (a) grapple with a mountain ridge two miles in the sky and (b) write about it. My explanation ran something like this: In that particular month, I shopped at Target four times. I filled my fuel tank five times and changed the oil in my car once. I bought two new pairs of pants and read about the Democrats and Republicans wrangling over tax reform eight times. During that period, I grappled with a mountain ridge two miles in the sky once.

It was my notion, possibly flawed, that most newspaper readers might find something more tangy in a man wrestling to stay upright two miles in the sky than they would in four trips to Target and a change of oil. Value judgments like this are treacherous, I admit, and I might have been wrong, which is why I limited those episodes of Jungle Jim Faces Life to two or three a year. In penance the rest of the year, I directed my unused energies to airing out the more mundane hazards posed by egomaniacs in the boardroom and mediocrities in city hall.

But while I tried to avoid the dicier parts of the outdoor experience when I wrote, I still couldn't resist putting myself in the wild and edgy places. It might have reached back to one of my first adventures, my weekly trudge to the public library in Ely when I was in grade school. Our teachers had been preaching the virtues of outside reading. Broaden yourselves, one of them said. Take a subject you like and learn more about it. Ask the librarian to help you.

The textbook that aroused me in my early grades was the geography book, a catalog of the faraway places of the earth. I'll never forget the photo credit under each picture, Ewing Galloway Photo. There was a picture of water pouring out of a giant new dam at Dnepropetrovsk in the Soviet Union. The Great Wall of China took up half a page. And maps. There were maps showing the trade routes and maps showing the effects of military conquest. Some of the maps still had large white spaces with the legend "unexplored" or "unmapped."

I appeared at the librarian's desk one night and said I was interested in books about geography and explorers. The librarian seemed pleased. She left her desk for a few minutes and returned with two lists, one long and one short. The short list named the author and title of one book: Richard Halliburton's *Book of Marvels*.

It was my first wish list of places I wanted to see. Richard Halliburton was a young man who tramped around the world, financing himself by writing stories of natural and human-created spectacles. The stories were unblushing testimonies to Unbelievable Things I Have Seen. The photos sent me rushing to the one-volume encyclopedia my parents bought in the Depression. I searched out maps and X'ed the locations of Victoria Falls, Egypt, the Golden Gate, Agra, the Himalayas, the Matterhorn, Yosemite Falls, and dozens more.

I kept the list for years. It had disappeared before I saw the first of Halliburton's marvels, the Empire State Building, and I made no actual vow to see the others. What Richard Halliburton's Arabian carpet did was to bring a stubborn genie into my life, one who would prod me to look around the bend in the road for the rest of my years, to go where I'd not been and to find what I'd not seen.

In my earlier years, that need translated itself into an urge to feel a sensation by courting a risk. It wasn't the noblest motivation. But in examining my reasons for going to mountaintops, I learned long ago to resist being needlessly harsh with myself. When they're boys and girls, kids climb trees. When they get older, some of them climb mountains or raft whitewater or drive through the potholes of Minnesota in

March. Risk. Getting to the top or to the end of some artificial obstacle we create for ourselves is a fairly common human aspiration. We make it a test of the resolve in our bodies and minds or the outlet of our curiosities, however we picture it. But I think it's a different matter to consciously put yourself in a place where you could die if you fail to reach that goal. It's one reason why most people are mystified by the mentality of the climbers killed in the storm on Mount Everest in 1996. It is also a reason many of them scorn that mentality.

It's harder for me to make that judgment. It can be hypocritical for one who's climbed to judge the decision of other climbers who guessed wrong or the motives of people rich enough to buy their way to Everest. It comes down to the difference between a defensible risk to achieve a goal and an absolute *insistence* on getting there whatever the weather, whatever the danger signals from the body. There's a difference, in other words, between desire and monomania.

Once I'd separated the thrill-chasing of my earlier years from the calmer satisfactions that came later, I found the mountain experience too good to allow much fanaticism. Much of that quieter outlook I drew from Glenn Exum, a man who made it one of his commandments of the high country. He was a mountain man for nearly sixty years and a music teacher in Idaho who'd come to the Tetons one day as a college student, wearing football shoes and carrying a length of clothesline. With those and a ham sandwich, he pioneered what is now the most popular route on Grand Teton mountain. For years after that he headed the climbing school and guide service at Jenny Lake in the Tetons. Scores of his professional protégés later climbed the world's highest mountains. Some of them died in the attempt. Glenn, though, was a man of harmony in his relationships and modesty when he entered the dominions of nature. Let the tigers climb in the Himalayas. His mountain climbs required no desperation or frozen toes. On a glorious day in July of 1981, a dozen of his friends joined him on the fiftieth anniversary of his first and solo ascent of what is now called Exum Ridge. He'd undergone a cancer operation a few months before. But here he was approaching his mid-seventies, dealing with the aftermath of a critical surgery, climbing at the head of the rope, his every movement singing one last song on his mountain. And, although the climbers behind him included some of the virtuosos of American climbing—Willi Unsoeld, Yvonne Chouinard, Al Read, Peter Lev, Dick Pownall, and others—Glenn Exum was more than their honorary leader; he was the actual leader, gliding up the cliffs and ridges as though he were an adolescent.

Before we rappelled down just below the summit, I asked Glenn if he remembered the advice he'd given the day I met him in the climbing school shack more than twenty-five years before.

"I do," he said. "You looked worried but eager, and I usually liked to give this talk to new climbers to put the whole business of amateur mountain climbing in perspective."

"And you said . . ."

"I said there are old climbers and there are bold climbers, but there aren't many old *and* bold climbers."

In other words, be sensible about where you climb, when you climb, and how you risk. Do that and you can take most of the risk out of climbing. You can enjoy it and you can probably grow to become a respected member of AARP.

But what about this psychological needle that propels people to run a risk that may expose them to injury or death or worse—as they might say—expose them to failure or looking silly? Because we're fascinated by peering into the dark side of human nature, we sometimes call that a "death wish." Is there something Wagnerian in there, a fatalism about life and a willingness to throw the dice to appease the ego?

To this, most climbers will roll their eyes and say, "Migawd, all I wanted to do was to get to the top."

You can't blame them for not wanting to get snared in the briars of self-analysis. The invitation to risk, the assertion of ego inevitably are hovering somewhere on the fringes at some stage of the mountain climber's experience. I've looked at mine. There *was* a time when risk was part of the stimulation of the climb, a spur to overcoming.

Overcoming what?

Overcoming fear. In the early 1950s, the French mountaineer Maurice Herzog wrote a book called *Annapurna*. It told of his team's now-or-never climb to the summit of the first eight-thousand-meter peak to be scaled in the Himalayas, the highest mountain that had then been climbed. Herzog wrote well and without sentimentality. He told candidly of the quarrels among the climbers, of the terrible beauty of the great mountain near the summit. He described human emotions under duress so powerfully that I found myself attracted to the idea of some day climbing. Hiking beneath the Matterhorn in my army days

Archives of the Minnesota state high school basketball tournament are largely silent on the exploits of a five-foot-eight-inch forward named Jim Klobuchar. No slam dunks or MVP awards. But there he was (*second from right*) with his Ely teammates reading the reviews of the 1945 tournament, in which his team lost in the finals to Patrick Henry of Minneapolis. Others pictured (*from left*) are Matt Banovetz, Brian Murn, and Frank Lozar. (*Minneapolis Tribune* photo)

It was a match between the legendary Minnesota Fats (Rudolph Wanderone, *left*) and a pudgy newspaper columnist who in 1964 didn't weigh much less than Fats. Fats ate better than he played pool, and he proved it by scratching on the eight ball in this less-than-historic match. (*Minneapolis Star* photo)

Into the thin air he goes: Jim leaps out of a light plane above Bethel in eastern Minnesota in 1964 as the unscheduled backup when the subject of a photo story failed to show up for the jump. The chute opened, and the story arrived on time. (*Minneapolis Tribune* photo)

Chalk exploding in Jim's mouth testifies to the accuracy of a commercial firearms expert who vowed he couldn't miss. The chalk holder, venturesome but less confident than the sharpshooter, decided not to open his eyes when the bullet was fired. (*Minneapolis Star* photo)

One of the world's renowned advice givers, Abigail Van Buren, offered some private counsel to a fellow columnist in 1967. The subject was how to stay out of trouble; he listened enthusiastically but managed to ignore the advice. (*Minneapolis Star* photo)

Their Christmas lists finished, Amy, age seven, and Meagan, four, did some fence-mending lobbying with Father Jim before the holidays in 1967. Amy became a lawyer, and Meagan is now attending college in Iowa. (Photo by Rose Klobuchar)

A baby gorilla named Donna, the object of research by a science class at the University of Minnesota, drew her own assignment from the scholars: greeting visitors to the project. The gorilla met the truth-seeking columnist at the laboratory door and appears to have made a disapproving evaluation. (*Minneapolis Star* photo)

Hubert Humphrey (*right*) and the master-of-ceremonies columnist worked out an Irish brogue skit at the St. Patrick's Day street party in Minneapolis in 1970. They got polite applause from the assembled Ryans, Mulligans, and O'Tooles, although neither was noticeably Irish. (*Minneapolis Star* photo)

His outfit was not exactly what the well-dressed young man would wear to the spring prom on his native Iron Range, but Jim managed it with reasonable aplomb escorting Jane Lundeen, Miss Downtown of Minneapolis, down the runway at the annual downtown style show in 1971. (*Minneapolis Star* photo)

The late Ginger Rogers and her resident jogging guide romped through the streets of downtown Minneapolis on a fall day in 1972, causing shoppers to blink. They blinked especially hard when the actress-dancer insisted on doing a couple of ballroom steps with the self-described most inept dancer in Minnesota. (*Minneapolis Star* photo)

As an overage admirer, Jim won cuddles and a tug on the hair from five-year-old Debbie Wresh of New Brighton, Minnesota, who in 1973 dazzled the judges of a national beauty contest for tots in New Orleans and came home the winner. (*Minneapolis Star* photo)

The star of athletic stars in Minnesota in the mid-1970s was quarterback Fran Tarkenton (*right*) of the Minnesota Vikings, with whom Jim wrote a book in 1975. They frequently appeared together at banquets and book autograph sessions. (*Minneapolis Star* photo)

The marquee of the old Ely Theater hung like a monument of another time when the native returned to his hometown in 1978 for a story on the Iron Range trauma of dealing with a world of declining steel. Jim worked in an underground mine to help pay his college tuition. (*Minneapolis Star* photo)

High on an ice wall of the twenty-two-thousand-foot Nevado Huascarán in the Peruvian Andes, Jim jams his ice ax into the slope to secure a stance. He and Minneapolis lawyer Rod Wilson, a longtime climbing friend, reached the summit a few hours later in a 1979 climb that nearly ended in disaster. (Photo by Rod Wilson)

More than eleven hundred miles—from Minneapolis to the Teton mountains in Wyoming—lay ahead of Amy Klobuchar and her father in 1981. Cartographers affirm that the altitude gain between Minneapolis and the Togwotee Pass en route is nine thousand feet, practically all of it into the wind. That fact prompted the younger Klobuchar, sharper in trigonometry, to ask her father, "Did we ever consider going west to east?" (*Minneapolis Star* photo)

The Himalayas of Nepal, the high and mighty of the world's mountains, have drawn the adventurer-columnist irresistibly. After climbing in the Himalayas, he organized an adventure travel club and has introduced scores of hikers to the Himalayas' quieter—although still lofty—trails. In 1994 he and Minneapolis computer wizard Tom Gray (*right*) trekked to the base camp beneath Mount Everest. (*Star Tribune* photo by Stormi Greener)

strengthened the idea. Exum's climbing school in the Tetons gave me some counseling in the mountaineering craft of rope management and climbing technique. I climbed the Grand when I was twenty-nine, a novice with no serious appreciation of what climbing involved nor any understanding that one could actually find pleasure in it, apart from the boost of standing on the summit. I did make one discovery not long afterward. I'd pumped so much romance and mystery into mountaineering that I hadn't really considered the fear factor.

It reached me on a ridge of a rock-climber's mountain in the Tetons called Symmetry Spire. It was a guide-and-one climb, two people on the rope. The guide was Al Read, later a Himalayan climber and still later Glenn's successor as director of the Teton climbing school. It was early summer and we had the range to ourselves. We climbed a moderate route called Durrance Ridge, which is airy and highly exposed but presents only two or three sections that demand sophisticated climbing technique. Read was young and eager to get down the mountain for a Saturday-night date. He moved us along quickly. Just below the summit, he disappeared to fix a belay point and then yelled for me to come up. He allowed three or four feet of slack as I advanced up a long, high-angled flake of rock. The rope is often held loosely by the climbing leader to give the second on the rope a chance to climb the mountain unencumbered by the rope's tension, but still secure. Not much harm can come with a slip of three or four feet. But I couldn't see the guide behind his big belay boulder, and I wasn't sure how much slack was in the rope, and my footing started to give way and—

I was terrified.

I imagined the protective pitons and snap rings pulling loose on the ridge separating Read and me, and I yelled. I tried to tell Read I was in a precarious place.

Nothing happened. I kept feeling tugs on the rope, Read nudging me to come up. Secure again, I resumed climbing and finally reached the guide.

"What happened back there?" he said. "I heard this banshee scream like somebody had seen a ghost. Anything happen?"

"No," I said truthfully. We walked together the final few feet to the summit and then, having descended to the snowfield below the Symmetry ridge, glissaded on our ice axes for hundreds of yards. It should have been pleasant, classic downhilling in the alpine style. I finished miserably, though, remembering my reaction to high exposure and almost funking it out.

For the next couple of years, climbing was no special recreation for me. It was subduing fear, the worst reason to climb. I'd been doing this love-hate act for a while now and fighting my way to the summit, not the sleekest way to get there. I felt some exhilaration on top, but it was closer to an exorcism, the aftermath of a hard competition with a bare-knuckle adversary. Not much fun. But in the process, I learned climbing. And I learned what my fear had been about, a pretty normal feeling most of us experience when we're thrust into the unknown. I'd been afraid because I didn't know the techniques to make climbing more comfortable. I didn't know how to deal with the body's tensions or about the body's resilience. I didn't know the equipment well enough to trust it. But over these years of relative stress, I learned the movements in climbing, the nuances of leverage and friction. I learned which rock or seam to look for, which to avoid, about controlling myself in the tight places. I learned to handle the ice ax with confidence and to manage my strength. I'd saved someone who was falling, and felt the assuring tautness on the rope when I slid myself. What I hadn't felt until one day on Mount Moran in the Tetons was the pleasure of a day going right in the mountains from beginning to end.

Mount Moran is a massive black hulk with a skillet-shaped glacier filling one of its amphitheaters. I climbed that day with my friend from Idaho and with a professional guide, Herb Swedlund. By then I'd lost fifty pounds, realizing that 205 pounds might not be the most wholesome displacement for a five-foot seven-inch man. Swedlund was a mountaineering comedian, a skilled cragsman but a cutup who made jokes about hanging by toenails over five thousand feet of air. But on this day Herb was upstaged by the mountains themselves. Everything about this particular mountain and the quality of the day was benign. We shared a relaxed camaraderie that removed all temptations to grimness. The sun flowed through the clusters of pine and cedar thousands of feet up on the rock slopes, warming the stone as we approached. When we got to the rock we found it steep but prodigal with holds and pebbled pitches that gave perfect friction to our soles, and we flew up the face. Swedlund told his jokes to an appreciative audience. We yodeled and sang on the summit.

The idea of a death wish made me smile. Being on the summit on that day didn't mean outdueling some ogre that I'd invented and invited into my life. We sat on the broad summit and gabbed and sucked in the sun. And on that day, climbing ceased being an ordeal to be outlasted. In the years that followed I went with my friends, Rod Wilson and Doug Kelley, or Monte Later or John Peterson, to mountains increasingly higher or more difficult—Pharchamo in the Himalayas, Devils Tower in Wyoming, Huascarán in the Andes, and others. With a Swiss guide I climbed the Mittelleggi Ridge of the Eiger in Switzerland. If I were to claim that the ego drive had disappeared from those climbs, testing those old warhorses of will and fitness, you are entitled to bring the polygraph. But by now the climbing idea had expanded and softened for me. I found human qualities in it that made mountain climbing something better than a game of chicken with ids. It meant sharing a day with people who themselves had probably scrubbed out the breakneck fervors in climbing and now felt good about taking time for the companionship of the climb, going to the mountain with a lighter tread—and probably a few extra pitons.

The Matterhorn has always symbolized that passage for me. The mountain was there on the wall of my third grade class, as it must have been for millions of other schoolkids. It looked monolithic and invincible, its summit adrift in the sky. When children hear about mountains and imagine them, the Matterhorn is the mountain they imagine. Seen from the valley of Zermatt in Switzerland, it leaps into the heavens in an almost perfect symmetry, its white summit crown imperious in the sky, seemingly one great thrust of stone miles above the forests and rivers beneath it.

It is not one great thrust of stone. The Matterhorn is a magnificent wreck, its faces and ridges broken by ages of exposure to wind, ice, frost, and water. But it is a mountain of glamour and notoriety because of its striking architecture and its history, which is sinister and ghoulish. Its allure popularized alpine climbing for the first time a hundred and fifty years ago. It resisted the first attempts and was finally overcome in an ascent that made its reputation. Four of the climbers died coming down. And, because it is the Matterhorn, thousands have gone to its not particularly difficult ridges, and eight hundred have died, most of them because they were ignorant or foolhardy. Some were just unlucky.

It became, I have to say, my mountain. I'd read the lore and conjured the phantoms from the cemetery below its slopes. I knew the names of its first victims and read the biographies of the leader of its first ascent, the driven and mostly irascible Edward Whymper. I climbed it for the first time when I was thirty, when I was not very proficient but so imbued with the Matterhorn in all its imagery that I climbed it well with a Swiss guide, Gottlieb Perren.

After climbing had mellowed for me and I could approach a mountain feeling competent in the climbing craft, the Matterhorn became something more believable for me than when I first climbed on it. Then, it was something to "do" if you went to the mountains, a hash mark on the sleeve.

Gottlieb was one of those stolid, Teutonic Swiss alpine guides, a man with striking blond hair and big shoulders that gave him the look of a film star when he walked around the streets of Zermatt in sunglasses. On the mountain he was terse and uncommunicative. Although he would eventually operate three sports shops in the valley, mountain guiding then was his work and constituted his persona. The Perren family was among the gentry of Zermatt. It was there when the tourist explosion came in the 1800s, one of the few families of Zermatt given a permanent voice in the village's councils. When Zermatt commercialized, the Perrens went into hotels—and stayed, of course, in mountain guiding.

Ultimately I climbed the Matterhorn seven times with Gottlieb or another Swiss guide and once with Rod Wilson in the 1980s, when we alternated leading the rope. So is there any credible excuse for climbing one mountain eight times, spread out over thirty-four years?

Sure there is. If a walk around Lake Calhoun agrees with you or refreshes you, you'll probably do it again. Eventually that walk creates a relationship, you and the lake, something familiar and good, ongoing. After a while, it produces a kind of intimacy, something that seems to go beyond restoring yourself. The mountain, the lake, or the woods becomes a renewable part of your life's experience, too good to consign to memory banks and slide shows. So you go back again. I think the recycling of my earlier times on the Matterhorn goes back to my second climb with Gottlieb, after we'd cleared the one technical rock pitch on the mountain and sat for a few minutes' rest in the emergency hut near the mountain's Swiss Shoulder. He was wearing one of those dazzling wool ski sweaters and actually smiling. He carved off a slice of sausage and took a long drag from his canteen. In it was a mixture of tea, honey, and some splashes of wine—without doubt the true nectar of the Alps. He offered the canteen to me. I sipped from it as a courtesy. It might be the nectar of the Alps, I thought, but for me the water bottle was safer. "Today," he said, "sehr schon." Very beautiful. I nodded. Despite the accelerating popularity of the Matterhorn climb, days with mobs roaming the ridge, we were practically alone.

We'd started at 2:30 A.M., nearly half an hour ahead of the others in the Hornli hut. I'd heard the clumping of Gottlieb's boots approaching my room on the second floor, a prelude to the climb that always got me stirred up. I rolled over on my sleeping mat on the wood floor and was grinning into his flashlight when he opened the door. "Guten morgen, bergführer," I said. Gottlieb grunted and went downstairs. We had dark bread and coffee, roped up in the hut, crossed the snowfield separating the lodge from the Matterhorn's cliffs, and started up, headlamps spearing the dark stone and competing with a flood of stars.

I tilted my head as far back as I could on the top of my pack. I'd been there before, but the ridge was a colossus. The night magnifies mountains. It invests them with mystery and a domineering power often not present in sunlight, when the green sweep of the timbered slopes beneath them softens the austerity of the heights. In the lower going, though, the Matterhorn's Hornli or Swiss route is practically a trail. At eleven thousand feet it steepens to require legitimate rock climbing. But it is luxuriant with good handholds and footholds. If you are fit and moving well, you can advance over a thousand feet an hour. I was fit. At forty-five I climbed with as much dexterity and stamina as I ever would. Often in the mountains, speed can mean safety. A climb of the Matterhorn is one of those times, assuming speed is coupled with good sense. The climbers come in packs later in the morning, rope after rope. And after noon, the frost begins melting in the cracks between loose rocks, launching frequent rock slides.

"So we get to the top quick?" Gottlieb said. Technically, that was a question. Actually, it was a declaration. *Schnell.* Let's hurry but let's be careful. The rule among most Swiss guides is that if the client doesn't ask for a breather, he doesn't want or need one. In a couple of hours we reached the emergency hut, where there is a more or less mandatory pause. Dawn was coming. The summit head of the Matterhorn lifted massively above us in the snags of clouds and the half light. The snowfields of the polar landscape around us emerged silently from the night and the first rose light colored the higher slopes. I walked to the edge of the hut's outside planking and felt the chill and the hostility generated by the Matterhorn's North Face.

What a moment, I thought. Belonging. I had figured out some of the mysteries of the mountains and how to manage myself in the face of their moods. Here, as in the Tetons a few years ago, I had begun to feel that seductive sense of ownership, if just for this moment. Then I'd written: "Each time I walk through the corridor of pines of the Signal Mountain road and look out on the Grand Tetons by starlight, I'm fired by a sensation of proprietorship. The Grand, Teewinot, Symmetry, Nez Perce, Moran—they are mine. Ours. I want to embrace the mountains, the faces and the voices they evoke. And I tingle and ache to be on one of the ridges now, waiting for the exploding sun."

But I was seven thousand miles from the Tetons, looking not at the Grand and Teewinot but at the emerging snowfields above the Matterhorn hut. We strapped on our crampons. Sparks flashed when their metal teeth crunched into stone in the places where a pitch of perpendicular rock interrupted the snowfields. Below the Matterhorn's summit is a series of thick fixed ropes, meant for security in an exposed part of the climb where the route swings from the ridge to the approaches of the North Face. The technique is to pull up with one arm and use the other for handholds. It goes faster that way and it's less tiring than going up arm over arm. No climbers were above. The two of us were alone, approaching the summit of the Matterhorn at sunrise. Gottlieb looked back down the protective rope with a nod of approval. He was sick of battling crowds on the summit. He appreciated being allowed to move fast, which was his form of being at ease in his mountains. His pause gave me a moment for thanksgiving.

Reaching a summit, as we were about to, is a reward of its own but a transitory one. The more lasting prints and echoes of the hours of the climb don't necessarily come from the summit. A climb puts you in an alien high world, where you try to understand its caprices and where you are excited by its power. But you remember the sections where the two of you moved together in harmony, coiling the rope, enchanted by the sudden warmth of the sun on your face when you come out of the shadow. On this day we were stepping through ice and snow and facing the rising wind, passing through a time imbued with shifting sensations and yet understanding that the final, elusive reward of the good climb is the freedom that it grants.

I think the professional guide saw that as well as the middle-aged wanderer from America's Midwest. Climbing was the guide's work. It kept him in quality schnitzel and wine. But he was born in the Zermatt valley and the mountains ran in his blood. So the temperamental differences between us peeled away. We were alone on one of the most glorious mountains on earth, going to the top, two men, hardly friends, but bound together by the magnetic synergy of a moment like this. It was not only the rope that linked us. It was also that quality that welds the mountain traveler to a remote and wild world where for a few hours his blood and spirit can race with the wind and reach for the sun.

We walked together to the summit at 14,770 feet. It was 6:30 in the morning. The air was clear and the north wind raked our faces. A few hundred feet away, the wind tossed miniature snow flurries around the big iron cross on the Italian side of the summit, giving it an embattled look. The wind subsided, and the cross stood as solemn and timeless as ever. Gottlieb pointed his ice ax to the east, and here was the exploding sun. It poured rivers of gold through the snow canyons separating the Rimpfischhorn and the Strahlhorn. The sun, rising impatiently to escape the barriers of granite and ice, frolicked over the snowfields and then broke above the mountains in full power, a huge orange globe hanging over the peaks.

Gottlieb blinked, the Teutonic guide, a man who had stood on the Matterhorn's summit hundreds of times.

"I've never seen it like this," he said.

We didn't stay long. I inhaled from the gusts of cold wind and stared into the immensity of the white world and into the sun. The energy and vastness of it seemed a benediction. But it was not a place to linger. We got down, shared a cognac, said good-bye—and climbed again three years later. It wasn't quite the same, but would you want that? The Matterhorn became a reunion for me as I grew older, a fixed milepost of my journeys, a version of the place to which the child returns to store and rediscover his secret things. It meant reuniting with the feel of the rock and the snow and the wind, with the hands of those I climbed with, and, I suppose, with the ghosts of those who'd climbed on this uncanny mountain in the beginning. I suppose I also came back to find out whether I was still up to it.

In 1992, at the age of sixty-four, I climbed the Matterhorn one more time, maybe the last time. The crowds were a nuisance and the French-speaking guide pretty much an unfeeling brute, and my crampon strap broke just below the fixed ropes. But I reached the top and gulped the west wind and ate my salami and looked out at the Monte Rosa on another part of the Swiss-Italian border miles to the east. Still there, summits luminous, its lower slopes subdued in the huge shadow cast by the ridges around them. Soon the miniature houses and tiny meadows in the Zermatt valley nine thousand feet below began to sparkle in the sunlight. Still the same picture, after thirty-four years. The world is racing helter-skelter toward a new millennium, but some of the things closest to our emotions don't change at all. Why would anybody want to say "this is the last"?

The corner I'd turned years before, I think, may have had something to do with separating my needs in wild nature from my appetites as I got older, replacing the thrill chaser with the pilgrim. When you climb on the Eiger or camp alone in the northern Minnesota winter, risk never vanishes. But the glandular part of a mountain climb or a long solo bike ride by now has pretty much given way to something more durable and congenial. I tried to express that one day in a letter I wrote to a twelve-year-old boy who seemed disappointed that some of the great mountains had been climbed. He wanted to know what would be left for him.

I offered consolation. I said there would be mountains galore down the road for him when he grew up. But I said he should not try to measure his achievement by the size of the mountain:

> You can learn to love the earth, Gerald. And while you are doing it, you
> will find certain moments when you and the earth are united, when you
> feel you are part of the wind and rock and you share their strength and
> beauty. And it will not be a moment for feeling awed or inconspicuous
> but for understanding that however we, or you, define God, there is a
> divinity in this moment. You don't have to be alone to experience it, but
> perhaps you will be. There's a path in the Grand Teton Mountains called
> the Cascade Canyon Trail. It lifts you out of the valley of Jackson's Hole
> and into the heart of the spires and waterfalls. For three miles it carries
> you beside the jade stream, which sometimes swishes thoughtfully and
> sometimes roils and charges. Later the trail rises through the glacial
> canyons and avalanche chutes, past a tiny lake called Solitude and scales
> the steep slope of granite and scree to a flat tundra. It is a barren place
> of glacial gravel, dwarf pine and struggling alpine flowers. It's called
> Paintbrush Divide. It's the kind of goal we can manage today on one
> last hike of the fall. On another day we can climb the mountains, when
> we have equipment and time. But you don't have to reach a summit to
> deserve the special grace of this place. So we can hike it alone, a walk in

the mountains through the Douglas fir and the swishing stream. We don't need conquests or gravity-defying deeds today. This will be our small requiem of the season, walking on a quiet mountain trail.

The boy wrote to thank me, saying he thought this was good advice. I don't suppose I'll ever know if he found his mountain, or whether that mattered, or whether he hikes that trail to Solitude with his family, with no summit hungers to placate. I found my own pretty well under control, and the hikes to Solitude and into the northern Minnesota woods brought a nearness to something benevolent that seemed to elude me until one day I walked the trail to Eagle Mountain in northern Minnesota. It's hardly a mountain—more like a woodsy hill with a charming overlook into the lakes.

If God is peace, I thought, why should it be so hard to understand what it is that stirs us with gentleness and thanksgiving on a trail in the woods? Theologians spend their lives trying to define God, and fallible worshippers grope through a hundred sermons and meditations trying to do the same. The woods that day seemed incorruptible. It was the kind of hour when we feel kinship with and comfort in nature, and when we feel cleansed. We may be alone, but we don't feel alone. Someone, something may be walking with us. If that is true, why do we struggle so hard to understand what has happened to us?

The lift of the spirit the outdoors gave me broadened with the years. I don't mean I was seized by urges to conduct lakeside services. I did pause to give thanks. I tried to open my senses in ways I hadn't before. There was a time when I would bang or claw on a mountain but carry nothing much away except the summit photo and a strong appreciation for the nylon rope. Climbing later meant enough time for introspection, if that seemed right. It also meant looking beyond rappel ropes and ice screws. I'd never been conscious of the smell of the mountain rock after a rain. Now I found it pleasant and distinctive. The aroma would linger long after the climb was completed, in the same way the smell of the campfire will linger for the camper long after the songs have ended. The smell of that rain-freshened rock became the incense of the mountain.

This reformation didn't mean the finish of inching around the thin edges. As I learned more about the high country or the cold country and felt equipped and at ease exploring it, my horizons widened. With friends, or sometimes alone, I went to the Himalayas, the Andes, Alaska, and northern Minnesota in winter. Some of this was in search of a true wilderness experience at a time when, in America at least, there is not much true wilderness left. My own definition of it led me back to northern Minnesota. The waters and woods up there are thick with visitors in summer, which is good and wonderful. In the middle of winter, once removed from the snowmobile trail, the silences and aloneness that Sig Olson struggled so hard to preserve are still there. The last wilderness in Minnesota, then, may be winter in the deep north woods. Reflecting on that, I realized that I'd never spent a solitary day on earth when I had not heard another voice or seen another person. That was hardly original. Human beings aren't natural hermits. But I packed my tent and sleeping bag and small camp cooker, bought some freeze-dried food, and skied into the Boundary Waters beyond the Echo Trail and Angleworm Lake. There was no other human, and there were no other voices.

Two woodpeckers hammered on the upright corpse of a jack pine. A Canada jay would glide down now and then to inspect the intruder. Painted rocks, the art of the Indians, materialized when the sun's rays loosened the snow and sent it flowing down the cliffs. I skied through thick forests of Norway pine, through marshes, and past the prints of moose. What a day. It was eerie and free, stepping through a time primeval. I sang and talked to the woodpeckers, but at about four o'clock the sunlight began to vanish and I put up my tent on the frozen shore of Home Lake. There was enough water from a nearby stream to save me the time-consuming business of melting snow on my cooker. I ate freeze-dried beef stroganoff as a celebration of the new year, because this happened to be New Year's Eve. After stowing my gear in the tent, I lit a small reading candle and hung it overhead in its protective case. Next I got comfy in my sleeping bag and opened the pages of Erica Jong's raunchy *Fear of Flying.*

Somewhere into the second chapter I was laughing up a storm. In the middle of this I heard a sound outside the tent. I poked my head out and saw a large and amiable moon but nothing else. In the morning, the snow outside my tent was spread with moose tracks. My visitor during the night was large and antlered. The moose must have heard the laughter and figured the occupant for one of those tourist nuts who couldn't tell the time of year. He also might have had a lament: "Can't we get through one winter without hearing the sound of a human voice?"

Nature is not always so kind. If you impart human qualities to it, an exercise that sometimes can deteriorate into the absurd, you have to recognize that some days it can be cruel. It was that in January of 1970 in the Beartooth Mountains of Wyoming and Montana. Nothing in my life left me so demoralized. We'd been snowmobiling in the Beartooth for several years. There was an obvious trip there, over Beartooth Pass, nearly eleven thousand feet high along the route of the summer highway, from Red Lodge, Montana, to Silver City, Montana. The local snowmobilers had been making it for several years. Under normal conditions, it's a ride that can be negotiated in five or six hours. Weather had turned us back two or three times in earlier years. In 1970 I called Monte in Idaho and suggested we might put together another group for that year. It grew to sixteen before we started, too many for close organization.

That didn't seem critical, though, because the weather forecasts were promising and we had the keys to a summer souvenir store, Top of the World, as an overnight shelter. Because that was going to be our lodging for the night, we had no need for tents or sleeping bags. I second-guessed myself about that later. But if you have done what you think is prudent preparation, then no amount of second-guessing will be of much value, or bring back a man who died. Still, it was years before I ended the hindsight. Jim Marshall and Paul Dickson of the Vikings were two of the travelers. Jim brought a couple of photographers, thinking this might make some dramatic footage for his growing audiences. I invited some friends. Monte brought others. When I broached the idea to the *Star*'s executive editor, Robert W. Smith, he suggested that Hugh Galusha might enjoy it. Smith was a highly civilized and nervy editor with highly civilized friends, including Hugh, who was the president of the Ninth Federal Reserve District. He was also a native of Montana and a longtime activist in the affairs of Yellowstone Park.

Hugh brought with him Wally Dayton of the department store family, a conservationist and wilderness enthusiast. Most of these people were experienced snowmobilers. Galusha wasn't, but the machine wasn't hard to operate even on the mountain road. Hugh was a droll, easily amused traveler in addition to having a penetrating mind on a hundred issues and a lifelong devotion to the high country. But in midafternoon we ran into a ground blizzard. The winds must have reached close to eighty miles an hour as we approached the summit of

Beartooth Pass. They choked the machines, which were then relatively primitive. In a few hours we were benighted.

Because some of the machines were able to keep going after the others died, we were spread over two or three miles of the mountains in small groups. Wally Dayton and I and three others spent the night a few feet below the summit, sharing our body warmth by hugging each other through the night. Marshall and Dickson and three others walked for hours until they reached the shelter of a lakeside forest, where they built a fire. Hugh and two others dug a shallow trench to protect themselves against the wind. They had a plastic tarp to cover them, but the wind blew it over the mountainside and the trench gave more the illusion of safety than genuine protection. The other two spent the night trying to improve the trench, but Hugh seemed exhausted. He made no complaint. He said he would be all right, but his voice was growing fainter. They tended him as best they could, trying to keep him awake, talking to him and trying to warm him with their bodies. Half an hour before the five of us walked down to join them at 6:00 A.M., Hugh died from the effects of exposure and fatigue.

The horror for me was the death of a worthy man in what was intended as a frolic in the snow. We were grown children romping around the mountain landscapes, laughing and gabbing among the great peaks two miles in the sky. No rationalizing language could erase that that frivolous purpose. There was one pale consolation. Hugh's last day on earth in so many ways had been an abundant one. That, though, was no consolation at all to those who loved him.

The Himalayas are the kind of place where you have the time and the atmosphere to sort through those vulnerabilities of being human, the human's aspirations and follies. And I try to. So, I think, do those who travel there with me. These are no longer mountain climbs. They are treks into the heart of the Sherpa country, the Solo Khumbu of Mount Everest, or the route of the Kali Gandaki, where Marco Polo once walked beneath the great peaks of Annapurna and Dhaulagiri. The Himalayas are the highest and mightiest, but they offer the traveler something more, an authentic odyssey onto another plane of the spirit, because this is the vortex of the Eastern religions that have shaped the times of the Orientals, and the world.

When you come to the Himalayas, you do it both as a pilgrim and as a child. It is a land for the spirit and for restless feet, where you will find a nature unmatched on earth in its immensity and its power to numb the eyes of the beholder. Mountains of snow and ice rise into the stratosphere. Cascades nourished by their glaciers thunder beneath the creaking suspension bridges. The trail will take you through forests of rhododendrons with blossoms as big as balloons. It will introduce you to a teenage girl with coffee-colored eyes that seem to say "Someday I hope I can see your land." You travel with Sherpas, mountain people who crossed the passes from Tibet six hundred years ago. You can't walk with them without feeling that here is a humanity that comes closer to what their higher power and ours intended. What you like most about them is their seldom-disguised joy in walking through their mountains, breathing the thin air, singing their heads off in camp and their outbursts of intuitive fun.

The famous place of fiction in the Himalayas is Shangri-la, which does not exist. Everybody would like to think it does, me included. There's an irresistible romance in the idea of searching for transfiguring peace and wisdom. And there are many times on a trek when you do find something strangely soothing and mellow. But it is always something a little beyond. If there are no red-nosed reindeer, we also have to admit that there's no place where the enigmas of creation and the blows of daily living can be explained in one sunburst of revelation. When you remove the illusion, though, what you find may not be transfiguring but it *is* amazing. You are on a voyage that brings you to a vast architecture of nature and those expressive faces in the villages. The faces of Nepal somehow summarize the faces of humanity, picturing its struggles and its whimsies and hope. You see it in the small children peering into your tent, in the old Tibetan merchant bantering with us on the trail, and in that girl who hopes someday to travel to our land. She places her hands together beneath her lips and says "namaste." I salute the God who dwells within you.

It is better than Shangri-la.

I can testify as mortal truth that I've found no Shangri-las while I was riding on the seat of a bicycle. I certainly have encountered inexplicable and amazing things. In some ways, the cross-country bike ride may be the most fulfilling of all for those who are drawn to the open road and who, let's admit it, are looking for Shangri-la. Setting aside bicycling's racing culture and the superhuman creatures who can go three hundred miles in a day, cross-country bicycling can be a memorable and charming way to meet lands and folks away from the metropolitan bedlam. It gives you the country unguarded and real, with all of its aromas and farm dirt and rippling leaves and a barking dog. It is something you cannot capture from the front seat of an automobile. The whirling spokes somehow make you part of the elements, and you can blend with the grain fields and the birches. In some ways it's better than a walk in the country, because the bicycle gives you movement—not speed, but just enough movement to impart a feeling of easy passage, something close to a travelogue film in slow motion. But the bike ride yields far more: breezes in the face, the sight of lady's slippers by the roadside, an aging red barn in the setting sun. It is the country in all of its integrity.

I started riding seriously in the mid-1970s. I rode long distances alone and put my readers in the picture, figuring they might be interested in the trials and discoveries of a man riding eleven hundred miles around Lake Superior in one week. What I remember most acutely from that ride wasn't so much the striking seascape and the fatigue, although both were engraved in my brain and my seat for a long time. Someplace near Nipigon, Canada, I was trying to make mileage before breakfast. My timetable required one hundred and fifty miles a day. I'd ride for thirty miles in the early morning, telephone my story to the office from a restaurant, have breakfast, and ride some more. Near Nipigon a highway patrol car passed me going in the other direction. A few moments later the patrol car pulled up behind me. I asked the officer if I'd done something wrong.

"No, just like to ask a few questions."

None of them had anything to do with traffic laws. The guy just wanted to talk. He was patrolling long expanses of empty highway early in the morning. What it came to was that the guy was lonely. We talked for thirty minutes, totally busting up my timetable.

So I shortened my breakfast, changed my gear settings, rode a little faster the rest of the day, and life around Lake Superior went on. In time people began to write to me, asking to come along. I couldn't think of a reason why they shouldn't. With the newspaper, I organized an annual bike ride, which became a kind of community on wheels. Over the years it took us to hundreds of towns and introduced us to thousands of faces we'd never seen. Yet as gratifying as that's been, I don't know of any biking experience that's brought more into my life, and quite as much bewilderment on the road, than my journeys with Amy, my older daughter. She drew up the agenda for the first one, from

New Haven, Connecticut, where she was attending college, to Minneapolis. It ended abruptly near Flint, Michigan, when my front wheel hit a trough in the road, dumping me on the pavement.

My fall was passably graceful except that it ended with a loud crack, the sound of my cheekbone fracturing. They operated the next day, mending my bones but terminating the ride. In the week we spent on the road, my daughter and I decided that traveling together cross-country put some unexpected spice into our relationship and into the miles, so a few years later we biked from Minneapolis to the Tetons, a distance of more than a thousand miles. About nine thousand feet of it was uphill, and most of it was squarely into the west wind.

"Did we ever consider," the young scholar asked someplace near Casper, Wyoming, "doing this from west to east?"

The answer was no. The Tetons represented a culmination, a logical destination aesthetically and geographically, I said. She thought Lake Calhoun and the IDS Tower would have made a reasonable substitute, but she didn't press the point because the trip had been too full of events and random hilarity to argue. It had also been a pretty precious time in the reunion of a father with his now undeniably adult daughter. I'm not sure whether it had been as momentous for her as for me, although I think it had. She was a young woman, finishing college, preparing for law school, full of ideas and insights I'd never heard from her. I don't want to omit streaks of temper. We never left each other's side for more than an hour or so, although it might have better served the cause of harmony if we had. This meant we quarreled some days. All right, a few times every day. We argued and badgered each other, but it was never done with any teeth, and we rode side by side for miles on the prairie, laughing in the wind and grumbling, learning a little more about each other with each mile. It was fascinating tracking her mind. It sprayed out notions and schemes like a rain shower. It made judgments and played games. It flashed back to her childhood, and a few minutes later it would be looking into the intramural brawls in the Democratic Party or laying out a strategy to bring some fairness to the distribution of money and opportunity in America. She talked about the law profession she would be entering in a few years and the kind of marriage she hoped one day to achieve. Some evenings, when she looked tired or out of sorts from battling a cold that developed near the Missouri River, I put my hand on her shoulder and told her I couldn't imagine having a better or less predictable traveling companion. Those flattering thoughts didn't save me the next day, when she barked at me for doing a lousy job drafting into the wind.

I'd look back near the top of some hideous grade outside of Dubois, Wyoming, thinking she might have pulled over to rest. But she was always on the road, moving uphill, her helmet bobbing, sweat glistening under her nose.

We were friends. We loved each other as young woman and father, but we knew each other so much better now. And while she would pretend to be appalled by my riding habits or my restlessness to get going, I'd find her sometimes looking at me tenderly when I was trying to explain one of my stupidities from our household of the past, before her mother and I divorced.

I know of no other journey I've taken that meant as much to me then, or means as much today. I will remember looking down the mountain road behind me, seeing a young woman enjoying the open road, the breeze tossing her hair—and even the abominable sounds coming out of her transistor radio.

7/ Newspapers Fumble for a Soul

In American pop history and in the early movies, the death of a newspaper was crowded with scenes of mixed tragedy and bitterness. Tears flowed in the city room amid the general damnation of fate and the newspaper's owners for letting it happen. Moody drinking parties usually followed when the last edition went to the printer.

Gradually, the American reading public was conditioned to newspaper mergers. They were a fact of life in American journalism of the twentieth century. Emotional appeals from loyal readers and last-ditch attempts by management and sacrifices volunteered by the employees got to be familiar. The end of another newspaper didn't seem quite that tragic anymore.

In April of 1982, the *Minneapolis Star* breathed its last, ending almost uninterrupted publication that reached back into the 1800s, if you discounted strikes and tracked its genealogy diligently. It had been around for years under other nameplates, in competition with a platoon of daily newspapers in Minneapolis. Eventually it merged with another afternoon newspaper called the *Journal*. Their names were combined and hyphenated. When the *Journal* half of the title lost its usefulness and disappeared, it didn't matter to thousands of old guard readers in Minneapolis that their newspaper was now called the *Star*. For decades afterward, when it was no longer the *Star-Journal,* they called it the *Star-Journal*. It's the way of readers' habits and allegiance. And it was one reason for the public's somber response to the doomsday of the *Star* in 1982, when it was folded into the surviving partner of the Cowles's Minneapolis newspaper dominion, the morning *Tribune*. But on the day when it happened, someone clearly forgot to inform the last graveyard shift of the *Minneapolis Star* that the death of a newspaper in America was a routine symptom of the times. No one had the nerve to tell the stricken reporters and editors and photographers that the death of a newspaper was no longer an occasion for sepulchral mourning.

The city room of the *Star* on that day was crowded with scenes of mixed tragedy and bitterness. Tears flowed amid the general damnation of fate and the newspaper's owners for letting it happen. Moody drinking parties followed when the last edition went to the printer.

Scores of people on the newspaper's staff received notice the day before. They either could not be absorbed into the consolidated staff of the new paper, the *Star Tribune,* or would be placed in other jobs. The carnage was not limited to staff members of the *Star.* In all legal respects, employees of the *Star* and the *Tribune* were considered members of the same staff. They were grouped in the same management-union contract, under the same work rules, and lined up at the same payroll window. When it came time to assemble a single staff from the separate newspapers, lists were made. It was the ugliest of times. There weren't enough jobs to go around. Choices were made from the lists. The criteria: what's better for the newspaper, for the readers, for the stockholders. An even uglier time. There was a certain amount of leaning over to be fair to employees of the setting *Star,* a hardheaded decision recognizing that tens of thousands of *Star* subscribers were losing their newspaper and might not be panting to buy the new one unless it preserved some of the flavor and the personalities of the old one. A substantial number of people forced into unfamiliar jobs were men and women with seniority from both newspapers, people of distinguished service and union protection. Their problem was what a pro ball club's personnel office would call "the numbers crunch." They were invited to remain with the combined newspaper, but doing work that might give them no professional satisfaction. For them it was an exile, and most of them did what the newspaper's unhappy management expected: took early retirement. For these people, it was no consolation to read that afternoon newspapers were going under throughout the country, that what was happening to the *Star* was happening everywhere, and that corporate mergers in America were commonplace.

Does this chronology sound familiar? It should. It's the story of the American workplace in the last four decades of the twentieth century, from textiles to telephone companies. There's no reason to believe that the loss and disruption of lives at the *Star Tribune* in the early 1980s was any more wrenching than it was in the layoffs when Pillsbury was sold to an English conglomerate or in the rest of the downsizing butcheries of the 1980s and 1990s.

But the *Star* was my workplace. It was ours. The heartbreak and accusations of betrayal were being voiced by people I'd worked with for years or for an entire career. And while I had few intimate friends at the newspaper and never got much involved in the gossip and beer busts, I was depressed reading the list of the new combined staff, the men and women who had made the cut. It was painful because it summoned the invisible faces of those whose names weren't there. It just seemed a savage way, Darwinian, to arrive at a solution, moving and sorting bodies, although if I ran the newspaper I would have had to ask the same question: Is there any better way to do it? The casualties included young people whose lack of tenure made them expendable, but also veteran employees who either chose early retirement to avoid being moved into jobs that were an affront to their years of service or accepted those jobs under protest. It gave me no special elation to see my name with those of Larry Batson and Barbara Flanagan as the general columnists who would write for the new *Star Tribune*.

Tim McGuire, then managing editor of the *Star,* asked me to write a column for page one reflecting on the years of the *Star* I remembered, its daffier moments and its more touching ones. I told of the moral union that a good newspaper builds with its readers, and for all of the inevitable thrashings of the last years, the *Star* had been a good newspaper in trying to cover its town and the people in it. I couldn't avoid seeing something operatic about its passing, in the passions and melancholy at the newspaper and all of the subplots that went into it. I shared a snatch of irony when I settled at my desk on the last morning. A few feet away I could hear Paul McEnroe running through his early-morning checklist, the newspaper's milk run, telephoning the agencies and offices for overnight news—the fire and police and sheriff's departments, and one more.

The last call McEnroe made on his checklist on the last day of the *Star* was to the coroner's office.

When I scan more than forty years in the business, and the monumental changes that overtook the business in those years, the *Star Tribune* merger rises larger each year as a landmark of daily journalism's new age. Technology was going to erupt in a few years and change forever the way newspapers put themselves together. It was already a significant presence. In the late 1970s, I wrote the first *Star* piece to be processed on a computer keyboard. They gave us a three-hour course in how to run the computer, which was linked directly to the mainframe system and did not require the uncanny virtuosity you see in the hands of the nation's millions of computer jockeys today. What I knew was how to log on, how to run the keyboard, and the telephone number of the mainframe gurus to call when something went wrong. They had a Pavlovian response to almost every anguished telephone call from the newsroom: "Store often."

To store on these computers, what you had to do was hit one button at any point in the composition. I can't remember whether the button said "save" or "store." It was something complicated like that. Two weeks after I pioneered computer writing in the newsroom, I launched into a long piece on a ski trip through the middle of Yellowstone. It was full of skiing through geyser mists and accidental encounters with bison and flopping into open water where it should have been frozen. The piece was going to run to at least six sheets of what we then called typewriter pages and was scheduled for the cover of the Variety section the next day, deadline around 8:00 A.M. or so. I wrote it in the late afternoon and early evening the previous day because I was speaking in Hudson, Wisconsin, that night and had worked out a timetable under which I'd leave the office no later than 6:45 P.M. At 6:45 I was two paragraphs from the finish. I'd packed most of what was necessary into the piece and had room for a marginal sunset scene and felt good about the project—until the screen went blank.

Crash.

Nearly two thousand words vanished, never to reappear.

I drove to Hudson miserably. They tend to have long cocktail hours in Wisconsin, so I didn't speak until 9:00. The question and answer period took us to 10:00. I got home a little before midnight and was up again at 2:00 because (1) I had to write my daily column, (2) I had to do nearly two thousand words on Yellowstone, and (3) I wanted an early-morning conversation with the mainframe guru for therapy and counsel. I wanted some assurance that it wouldn't happen again. He was polite but unapologetic. "Yeah," he said, "I can give it to you in two simple words.

"Store often."

He was still saying it on my last day at the plant.

More than technology was entering and leaving the city room and mahogany offices of the *Star Tribune* executive parlors in 1982, set off by the prolonged recession of the early 1980s. Newspapers are invariably victims of any extended hard times. This was no Depression, but unemployment was severely up. American industry was in the midst of a historic change from the smokestack to services and electronics. Foreign competition compounded it before the flood of foreign-made products forced corporate America to abandon its smugness and its arrogance toward the customer. But this was a major league convulsion, and newspaper advertising sank. Directors looked alarmed. At the *Star Tribune,* Donald Dwight was forced out as publisher—too late, in the judgment of most of the stockholders. Chuck Bailey, in every way the leader and the conscience of the *Tribune*'s old newsroom, resigned emotionally in disgust over the disarray in the company's corporate leadership and in sympathy with the victims the merger had created on his staff. From Buffalo, New York, hardly the Red Cross of American journalism, the team of Roger Parkinson as publisher and Joel Kramer as editor was imported to control the damage and to chart a course to brave new horizons. In the midst of this, the board of directors met and divested themselves of John Cowles Jr., the newspaper's chief decision maker and de facto chief executive. This was an authentic, familial bloodletting in the best traditions of the medieval palaces. The Cowles family controlled the newspaper's majority stock, and still does, which meant that some of the relatives came in and unhorsed John Jr., presumably for the good of the newspaper and the good of the readers, but mostly for the good of the stockholders. The deposing was done under the thin umbrella of chivalry, but it was done nonetheless. While there were a half dozen explanations for it, practically all of them came down to money. The newspaper was losing it—meaning it was making substantially less than it had been—and had been in disarray in its leadership, which was muddling through the times, infatuated with stadium building and gilding itself with new offices in the midst of the muddle. Cowles Jr., while he was unlucky to be in charge at a time of national trauma in newspaper economics, clearly was responsible for much of the mess.

As a publisher, John was fundamentally a promoter, reserved in style but temperamentally a kind of urbane bulldog. His works as a civic hustler were high-magnitude stuff. Years before, he'd engineered the construction and promoted the concept of the Guthrie repertory thea-

ter, firmly implanting Minneapolis as one of the centers of world theater and eventually energizing drama throughout Minnesota. Cowles
raised the money by running down the list of the heavy hitters of
Minneapolis business. In the late 1970s and early 1980s, when the
Minneapolis campaign for a downtown domed stadium hit the wall,
Cowles got the newspaper involved corporately in ways that aroused
forty-five members of his newspaper staff into an act of retaliatory
anger. They paid for an ad with dozens of signatures decrying what
they saw as a direct conflict of interest: the newspaper financially sup-
porting a project that it ought to be free to cover objectively. Cowles
maintained that in no way should the staff feel intimidated, because
he was exerting no pressure. He probably wasn't. What the news people were talking about was that principle dearly beloved by the management of newspapers when it lectures its employees about staying at
arm's length in dealing with potential news sources. There didn't have
to be a direct and overt conflict, the employees said. The appearance
of conflict was bad enough.

But John Jr. was no shrinking dilettante. He had stamina and he
had the clout of his newspaper when he lobbied the custodians of
downtown Minneapolis money. Theirs was a loose confederation of
Renaissance-type corporate dukes who usually found a way to tie in a
high civic purpose with the balance statements of their businesses. The
scholars call this principle enlightened self-interest. The Minneapolis
business leaders in those years saw themselves as a high-minded,
practical-minded collegium of good fellows who could get things
done.

But in his periodic rampages against the architects of a domed stadium in downtown Minneapolis, sports columnist Patrick Reusse, then
with the St. Paul newspapers, skewered this coalition of money and
power in downtown Minneapolis. He called it The Brotherhood. It
was a catchy image flowing with Patrick's distinctive acid. It conveyed
something sinister, and it almost always gave Patrick one of his more
pungent columns. The picture of a downtown Minneapolis syndicate
wasn't totally inaccurate. Its self-interest was clear but its achievements—underwriting the Guthrie Theater and promoting the Nicollet
Mall, for example—brought indisputable and lasting value into the
community.

The syndicate as originally constructed, of course, is now dead.
Downtown money and self-interest have abetted the juggernaut cam-

paign that began in 1996 to build a new stadium for the Twins, but it wasn't the same old chummy roundtable of downtown hierarchs. It was closer to a strong-arming conscription of everybody who stood to make money if the new stadium went in. If you need proof of the disappearance of the more fraternal old gang, consider the futile hours jock-promoter Harvey Mackay spent struggling to round up corporate support to buck up pro basketball at the Target Center. Harvey was trying to wangle a million or so from the very people who would benefit most from the downtown jock events. The campaign dwindled off into the usual fog and self-serving statements to the press, and the public, predictably, was forced to bail out the millionaires. The downtown syndicate is dead because the corporate leadership that sustained it no longer exists. The Daytons no longer run Dayton's. The Pillsburys are admiring the lake, which they certainly deserve to. Some of the city's most powerful bankers and merchants now have no special attachment to the city, sentimental or otherwise, beyond the base of prosperity it gives their business.

But it was different in the early 1980s, and when John Cowles Jr. approached Governor Al Quie to promote the downtown stadium, he did it as a corporate spokesman. And when he and his accomplices lobbied the legislature, they had the audience usually accorded to corporate heavyweights. One of the alleged lobbyists for the downtown dome happened to be Mike Lynn, the Vikings general manager. But Lynn's was strictly a Trojan horse operation. Privately, he wanted to kill the downtown dome, but Max Winter, his boss at the time, was going to be pivotal in the decision. Lynn was cagey. His plan was to fly to Hawaii to persuade Max that the downtown dome was not the way to go. He was shot down in that plot before he ever got to Hawaii.

Cowles flew there first.

Lynn has never been shy about acknowledging his ingenuity as a high-level sandbagger. "That's right," he said. "On the record and in every statement I made to politicians, I was on the side of the domed stadium in Minneapolis. What I really wanted was a new open-air stadium in Bloomington. Max wasn't yet all out for the Minneapolis dome and I knew I had to get to him before John did. I didn't. Max bought the dome idea." Lynn thus joined the Metrodome advocates, who now had pretty much worn down the legislature in the dome version of the Thirty Years' War. Practically nobody in the legislature or in Minnesota loved the dome, but no one in St. Paul or Bloomington gave the legislature any sensible option. The Metrodome came in. Teeth gnashed around the state with the sound of a chorus of unhappy chipmunks. But the Twins won two World Series because of it, and nobody ever thought to put the patrician and enigmatic figure of John Cowles Jr. in the middle of the celebration.

To Cowles's credit, he never asked for any piece of the spotlight. Nor did he get any from the newspaper public after 1982. He'd made some questionable decisions investing company resources during his tenure. The Cowles's purchase of a newspaper in Buffalo, New York, might have been pushed by John's corporate pal, Otto Silha, but Cowles was part of it and was held responsible. The economics of newspapering were sour at the time. At annual company meetings, John Jr. would address the stockholders in a sonorous baritone that suggested a man in comfortable control. To the company board, however, the picture seemed less cozy as time went on. There was no room to feel comfortable in the early 1980s if you ran the *Star* and *Tribune*. The *Star* was disappearing as one of the cash cows. In the late 1970s John Jr. brought in Donald Dwight from Massachusetts to become the publisher of both newspapers. Dwight's performance alienated the directors as the company's money troubles expanded.

It wasn't hard after a few years to assume that Dwight's stewardship was somehow connected with the money problems. He was suspected of mishandling a brief strike by newsroom employees late in 1980 and mishandling the demise of the *Star*. At least those were some of the grumblings. The politics of the boardroom got thicker. Cowles stuck with Dwight in a show of loyalty that was pretty much Cowles's managerial style. But by the end of 1982 the company's profits had shrunk some $10 million over a two-year span, deepening the board's disenchantment with the company's leadership. The villains in the drama cluttered the stage: the death of the *Star,* the residue of the 1980 strike, the Reagan recession, an awkward attempt by some in the Cowles empire to merge the Des Moines and Minneapolis newspapers, the Buffalo newspaper deal, Dwight, Cowles's use of several million dollars in corporate assets to lubricate the stadium deal, the transfer of company corporate offices to ritzy quarters in the IDS Tower, the use of company resources that seemed cavalier to the board, and the growing evidence that John Jr. was not especially good at managing the business his father created—and on and on.

The list was unlovely. The board members, some of them members of the Cowles family, of course, removed John Jr. as president and publisher, a vote unhappily tabulated by the board chairman and a longtime friend of John Jr.'s, Otto Silha.

Now John Cowles Jr. was free to explore new worlds of teaching physical fitness and acting, a venue that ultimately presented the former publisher and board chairman of the *Star Tribune* nude on the stage. This might strike some of the old newshounds as a peculiar metamorphosis for a man of John Jr.'s corporate pedigree, but it was not so peculiar to John's friends, familiar with his closet urges to emote. I regretted John's departure because I liked him and his family and I thought I understood his promotional drives. I remember reading the bulletin board announcement of his removal. I was standing next to Frank Wright, then the newsroom chief of the merged newspaper. It was a Saturday morning and the hallway was empty. The other upheavals in the newsroom were still fresh. "Isn't somebody going to stop the bloodshed?" Frank asked.

It stopped eventually, with the infusion of Kramer and Parkinson and with changes in some of the editorships, but mostly because the country's economy got hot again. If you're a monopoly newspaper, you shouldn't have all that much trouble making a profit.

The feeling was pretty general among the newspaper's working stiffs that a John Cowles Sr. in command could have found a way to avoid most of the consternation. John Cowles Sr. was one of those newspaper publishers whose corporate wisdom and causes left prints on the nation, certainly on the part of the nation where he published. He turned the *Star* and the *Tribune* first into money makers and then into vehicles for social and political reform. He was an internationalist who helped dig Minnesota out of its heritage of Midwest isolation. He put racism under scrutiny in Minneapolis and in America, and he got his newspapers into social issues like birth control and more equitable housing. He also helped get Ike Eisenhower into the White House by bringing him to Minnesota to demonstrate his popularity among the voters. Cowles Sr. was familiar in his newsoom, which he would visit frequently to stay in touch with his reporters, editors, and photographers, and especially to make the new staff members feel welcome. He was a fountain of questions. Although he was deferring in his manner, they weren't courtesy questions. They needed some thought to answer. He'd walk in from his office and noodle around. He had an amiable round face and wore glasses that gave him the appearance of a neighborhood banker visiting with his customers in an open house.

For reasons I never learned, he and his wife, Elizabeth, developed an interest in some of my early work for the newspaper, and ultimately I was invited to spend a weekend at the company's game farm, Glendalough, near Battle Lake in western Minnesota. It was the scene of frequent company gatherings to which executives and staff workers were invited. The agendas included talk, a game dinner, talk, some recreation, and more talk, spilling over into the next day. My invitation contained an impish aside from the hosts. Suspecting my closet sympathies for Republican causes, they said, they would try to place me overnight in the Eisenhower Cottage, the one in which Ike slept when he was a guest there in the spring of 1952. I had to apologize for not being able to get there before 7:30 P.M. because of a prior commitment. As a courtesy to the other guests and the hosts, I asked them to go ahead with their normal dinner schedule and I'd blend in when I got there.

I arrived around 7:30 and found John and Elizabeth Cowles sitting in lounge chairs outside the dining room. They said the door to the Eisenhower Cottage was open and dinner would be ready when I'd cleaned up. I rejoined them in fifteen minutes and looked around for the other guests.

None appeared. I was the weekend guest of John Sr. and Elizabeth Cowles—solo, the designated pigeon for the inquisition. Elizabeth—Betty—Cowles had a husky alto voice that was spellbinding but also worrisome because it spoke of thousands of cigarettes inhaled. She may have had emphysema even then. They pumped me with questions during the salad and through the pheasant and after the chocolate pie, about my life, my views, and the quality of Slovenian cooking. Mrs. Cowles retired soon afterward but the conversation—the relentless interrogation by John Socrates Sr.—repaired to the fireplace room. It was never threatening or testing. The guy simply was inquisitive. He had reporters and columnists on his staff, and he wanted to know their feelings and how they read the part of the world they knew. He wanted to know something of their personal histories and he wanted to know what they thought about Vietnam. What was their impression of the condition of the family farm in Minnesota, of the current image of the American abroad, of the future of the two-party system in America? It went that way for two hours. It was fascinating and suspenseful, and it left me with the same feeling I had near the end of my first competitive mile run in high school. At that stage I wasn't interested in scoring points. My one overpowering thought was finishing.

John Socrates Sr. wore me out, but it was a satisfying fatigue and mercifully the interrogation ended there. Instead of talking world politics the next morning, they handed me a mallet. The Sunday recreation at Glendalough was a game called crokey, played under the general auspices of the rules of croquet, except the mallets were bigger. The mallet head, in fact, could easily have been mistaken for a small beer barrel. My partner was Elizabeth. She was also my mentor. She explained the subtleties of the backswing and the need for an aggressive mentality. I was shy on backswing subtlety but managed the rest of it, and we lucked out at the finish, edging John Sr. and the family friend who was his partner.

I saw Betty Cowles again only once. She was dying and thought the best way to die was to bring back into her life, for an hour's visit, people who were close to her, relatives, friends of the family, a comparative stranger she remembered from an important episode in her life, or this person or that who wrote in a way Betty found agreeable.

We visited for an hour in front of the fireplace at the family home in Minneapolis. I've never seen another person leaving the world as gracefully and as indomitably as this lady.

By the mid-1980s the newspaper had righted itself and was gearing up for the new age. I confess to not being on the inside of most of the new technological marvels. Although each year I found myself moving a little deeper into the ranks of the venerable crocks, I tried wherever I could to avoid the old lion's skepticism of what was happening on this dazzling new frontier. What's happened basically is that the newspaper had to tie in to the new age dazzlements to survive.

I can speak with authority only about the newspaper on which I worked. The newest of the new waves were the on-line nets and electronic highways that transformed the metropolitan newspaper from its ancient role as town crier into an informational gusher. Before the waves struck, the *Star Tribune* had reshaped itself and was making large money again. Roger Parkinson's chief charge from the boardroom was to avoid any big showdown with unions that were already weakened by the antiunion politics and industrial facelifting of the 1980s and 1990s. He negotiated a long-term contract at little pain to the *Star Tribune,* and he left by common consent afterward.

Joel Kramer was a cool and cerebral guy with a sure hand on the economics of newspapering in the Twin Cities and the practical possibilities and limits of Twin Cities journalism. I say this mostly by inference. I worked under Kramer's stewardship for twelve years and scarcely knew him. He strode the corridors of the newsroom with one hand jingling coins in his pants pocket, surely nothing Freudian there, and his mind seemingly on the first or next Pulitzer Prize or the novelties of the overhead lighting system. The two of us almost never managed eye contact, which on second thought might speak well for the editor's taste. This was one of his peculiarities of which I'm sure he was aware. It's not easy to be remote in a hallway six feet wide with nobody else coming or going, but Joel was gifted in this kind of scene, and he achieved it. We had a meaningful conversation every two or three years. He was considerably more sociable and comfortable in the happy daily patter of the newsroom when he was in the midst of his age peers, a generation younger than me. I had no complaint with him and no feeling of surprise when he became the newspaper's publisher. Without question he was a guiding force in restoring the newspaper's stability after the disorders of the early 1980s, and he was just as unquestionably a sound newsman. The newspaper's Pulitzer Prize for its reportage of the arson-tinged irregularities in the St. Paul fire department reflected great credit on the two reporters, Chris Ison and Lou Kilzer, but Kramer supervised the editing and did it with high craft.

The fellow who actually ran the newsroom for most of my last ten years with the newspaper, Tim McGuire, was a man with whom I connected in a more personal way despite lapses of months when we had no need for contact. When he reached Minneapolis and the fading *Star* in the late 1970s—and his late twenties—McGuire was an unlikely prospect for stardom in the business. At the time, the search was on for a managing editor to replace Dave Nimmer, who left the *Star* for television in 1978. Nimmer left because he was unsure whether he was temperamentally suited to act as a working disciple of the uncrowned messiah of Twin Cities journalism, Steve Isaacs, the *Star*'s editor. Steve's agents had learned about a smart and energetic young editor in Florida, with instincts for brashness but showing promising symptoms as a new wonder child of newspapering. Isaacs flew to Florida, was impressed, and offered McGuire the job. In the *Star* newsroom, of course, he was an instant curiosity.

McGuire was perceived as Isaacs's protégé, which suggested the captain of the *Titanic* bringing in a new man to examine the ship's blueprints after the first iceberg showed up off the starboard bow. McGuire arrived from Florida revealing no immediate evidence of knowing much if anything about Minnesota. Because of a physical disorder, he was short and squat and charged around the halls with some difficulty. This did not foster the dominating presence to which most editors aspire.

But it did earn him a slowly growing respect for his tenacity. From the first day, he disclosed a total lack of timidity in the face of his new surroundings. McGuire eventually dominated the newsroom. He was an Irishman with a round red face that sometimes gave off sparks of combat and sometimes peals of giggles and guffaws. The intramural nonsense in the newsroom turned him on and made him feel he was part of the lodge as well as the lodgekeeper. His mind was nimble, ambitious, and resourceful. He was also a chance-taker. In view of that quality, it might not have been a coincidence that he turned out to be the newspaper's chief cheerleader on the cultural benefits of gambling in Minnesota. He looked like a bustling gnome when he moved around the newsroom. But as he moved higher in the decision-making councils of the newspaper, his zeals and chutzpah pushed him into new portfolios of expertise in microchip journalism and in the business of the newspaper. He also got tougher. He devoured the newest advances in the industry's technology and the latest theorems coming out of the groupthink tanks of the industry consultants. Early on he impressed Kramer so much that he was advanced to the job of managing editor of the combined *Star Tribune* over one or two more obvious choices. McGuire splattered the future with ideas and solutions. He also aroused animosity among staffers who thought him noisy and unfair in how he dealt with some of their friends.

I never pretended to be in the loop about most of that. Office politics usually soured me. McGuire and I would talk two or three times a year, about projects or personal matters. The talks usually lasted five minutes. He was a verbal guy, and I didn't have much time for vows of silence myself. But we understood each other pretty well and didn't tax each other with language that was unnecessary. We clashed here and there. But we both tried to separate the professional side of our meetings from any personal innuendo. He was casually vulgar at times and liked throwing himself into red-faced furies as an act of intimidation when he was arguing. But of all of the editors I worked with, I found him to be the most warmly tuned to the human side of the newsroom, capable of tears in the presence of a colleague in pain.

What I remember best about him were the few times when we joined in the fugitive scenes of mischief we both tried to orchestrate on the job whenever there seemed to be an excuse. Newspapering's moldy old garments as "a game" never went out of style for me, and evidently not for McGuire. He pulled only two columns I wrote in our nineteen-year association at the newspaper. Both involved some puckish fun I was having that day with the newspaper's longtime sports columnist–*cum*–radio star–*cum*–close personal friend to millions. McGuire and Kramer had vowed to protect this personality from all attempts at puckish fun.

"You know I have to take this column out," McGuire said on a visit to my office late in the afternoon.

"I don't know that you have to," I said. "But I know that you're going to. I thought I was safe. I thought you were in L.A. attending another conference on how to better American journalism by encouraging daring and original writing."

McGuire said he was sorry I wouldn't be able to appear in the newspaper the next morning because obviously I was ready to leave for the day. This was rank gamesmanship. McGuire was saying there were still forty-five minutes in which to produce a substitute column and wondering whether I would or could. McGuire knew I would and I sent him a memo the next day thanking him because I thought the subject matter of my substitute column was an improvement on the original.

Later, in my last year with the *Star Tribune,* we sat at the same conference table a couple of hours before the verdict in the O. J. Simpson criminal trial was announced. The newspaper's editors by then scheduled staff conferences incessantly—strategy conferences, state of the art conferences, team meetings, and self-improvement seances. By then the business of newspapers had undergone a redefinition. The business of newspapers had been to publish the news. Now they have two businesses: publishing the news and holding team meetings. The agendas have become interminable. I've never been a scofflaw temperamentally, but one of the priorities on my personal agenda was escaping staff conferences. My role as a columnist essentially made me a freelancer inside the walls. In addition to that, I had considerable time in grade. If I didn't attend the meeting, I was probably not going to get a notice from the team leader warning of my imminent deportation.

But the conference in advance of the Simpson verdict was one I needed and wanted to attend because it undoubtedly was going to affect my work that day. McGuire sat in as an observer to be in the picture. One of the senior editors outlined our plans for coverage. Since I was writing for the next day, it was assumed that the Simpson verdict would be my column. The senior editor then discussed deadlines. He noted that depending on when the Simpson verdict came in—which turned out to be sometime around noon—we might want to put out a special edition. An Extra. Newspapers today publish extras with the approximate frequency of sleigh rides in Kuwait. But McGuire had spasms when he was revved up by putting on those moldy old garments of the newspaper past. So did I.

Putting out special editions was practically a costume party. It might have been kids playing doctor, except that an extra cost money and had no impact on the average reader. To begin with, the readers had already heard the big news. The extra edition went out on the streets, not into the homes. The press run amounted to a few thousand copies, and might have had some passing value as pure show biz: "Migawd, I just heard about it and here it's in the newspaper already." But mostly it was grown people playing at stop-the-presses newspapering, and I clutched at the chance to do it.

McGuire winked at me during the senior editor's presentation but said little. What he was doing was conspiring. The wink said, "Can you do a column in time to be part of the extra?" Well, yes. You could if you wrote the column before the verdict came in but tried to impart some of the voltage of the day of decision. All you needed for that was the scene in front of you on television. I wrote mostly about the television carnival and the judge's foolishness in creating the carnival. I wrote also about the deepening racial polarization in America that resulted from the telecasting. Those were worthwhile issues, I thought, and could be discussed without regard to the verdict. I finished two minutes before the verdict came in, inserted a paragraph of comment when it did, and sent my column to the city desk. There was nothing essential that had to be changed in it the rest of the day, and I later thanked McGuire for his economy of language at the staff conference.

I remember with no warmth, though, the chronology that led to the departure from the *Star Tribune* of Larry Batson, one of the most versatile and literate journalists I've worked with. He'd been columnist, editor, sports editor, sports columnist, and roving investigating writer. He was a shambling, bulging guy whose slow and jowly speech did nothing to disguise his Ozark upbringings. When he wrote his periodic vignettes remembering the Ozarks, he brought his readers around the campfire, listening to a drawling old troubadour from the hills spinning out the improbable pratfalls or wry little revenges of the odd but earnest folk who lived there.

For one memorable week when Batson wrote for the *Tribune* and I wrote for the *Star,* we competed in covering Evel Knievel's failed attempt to fly the Snake River in Idaho in a homebuilt rocket. We talked often at lunch or on drives to and from the flight's promotion headquarters. Let me correct that. I talked often on drives or at lunch. Some of my soliloquies were wily attempts to ambush Batson into conversation. What I got were monosyllables and grunts to pass the butter. I concluded finally that the guy was an instinctive Sphinx despite his surpassing gifts as a writer and his shrewdness as a reporter. Enticing him to talk sociably was beyond mortal powers. And yet at last, driving back to our hotel one afternoon, I heard the unthinkable—unsolicited talk from Batson. "By the way," he said, "I pretty well figured out how you use your hands and arms as punctuation marks and dependent clauses when you talk. I wonder if you couldn't do us both a favor, though, and try not to use your hands and arms that way when you're supposed to be driving."

I desisted, although I have to say it blighted the quality of our conversation. We had a good professional relationship based on mutual regard for each other's experience in the business. Batson spent months doing research on a subject that was unlikely to inflame the readers with its urgency and magnetism: the growing water shortage in America. He talked endlessly to experts and farmers and hundreds of other people from coast to coast. When he put it together his premise *was* urgent and convincing. It was so good that it went down to the wire in the balloting for American journalism's most prestigious prizes. He spent more months putting together material on racism in the Twin Cities, overt and hidden. He'd begun to write, but the newspaper shifted some gears and policies and decided that here was a series that demanded a team and had to be broadened. Batson found himself working with new and more editors and finally winding up in a no-man's-land of newspaper politics, eventually with nothing to do. In the head-to-head sessions with his supervisors, he was not his own best advocate. He was a mule-headed Ozarkian whose presentations to McGuire and Kramer didn't score. He brooded and then quit to take early retirement.

For the newspaper, I thought, it was a shabby waste of an uncommon resource. I expressed that thought in a column, with which the newspaper didn't interfere. In fact, I don't remember more than a handful of times when the newspaper's editors or executives made any show of being aggrieved over a piece I wrote attacking one of the newspaper's policies or its sacred yaks. Its acceptance of millions of dollars in tobacco advertising was something neither I nor thousands of its readers could square with the newspaper's history of advocacy in public health. I didn't campaign for any legalized ban on cigarette advertising in the newspapers. Just drop the advertising, I said. Do it voluntarily as newspapers in Canada have. I'd ask Parkinson to justify the newspaper's double standard of constantly identifying tobacco as a killer and then taking its advertising. Roger would usually cite some First Amendment issues. The newspaper didn't have to like the product to provide advertising space for it, he would say. And then Roger would add, "Well, it's a line of business. We make revenue on it. When are you gonna get off this? I hate to keep taking your calls."

But he didn't say don't call again. So I never felt any real intimidation factor when I wrote opinion in my column. McGuire didn't like my guerrilla war against gambling, but he didn't intervene. In the earlier years, only an ostrich could fail to notice an anti-Catholic bent in the newspaper's editorial pages and sometimes in its news columns. While I no longer worshipped in this church, I wrote a piece in the *Star* in the 1970s inviting a reader to drop his subscription to the newspaper if he was offended by that bias. Steve Isaacs ran the *Star* in those years. He read the column in the first edition and nearly choked. He didn't say, "Don't do it again." He did say, "Give us a look in advance if you're going in that direction again." You might have called that prior restraint, but why bother? I had no interest in going in that direction again. The point about bias, or what I saw as bias, had been made.

None of this implies any particular bravery on the part of the columnist. You have no business writing opinion columns unless you're ready to handle the buckshot that follows, fair or otherwise. It does mean that the Cowles newspapers' supervisors pretty much followed the creed of John Sr. and let the opinionists offer their opinions and take the consequences without being subjected to winds of disapproving ice from the bookkeepers or editors.

When I left at the end of 1995, the newspaper was fully locked in the arms of the corporate office manias of the time. It had launched itself into the wonderland of cybernetics and all of the potential for new profits claimed for it. Special departments were set up to handle on-line services to business and individual subscribers. Big money was budgeted to develop these resources and the venture was undertaken eagerly. The newspaper's staff was kept informed almost daily of the newest bonbons and was invited into the action. In all of this, the *Star Tribune* had small choice if it intended to stay even with or ahead of its competitors in the information explosion, which introduced jungle law into the competition: Nobody's turf is protected anymore. The phone companies will be doing what the television companies once did exclusively. Newspapers are peddling on the Internet. All of the old rules of engagement are dead. The electronic highway is wide open, and no speed laws are enforced.

The newspaper in Minneapolis also did what most metropolitan newspapers have done—invested tons of money consulting with the think tank wizards who enunciate gospel in restructuring the news operations of today's newspapers. Restructuring got to be a crusade led by the jingoists from the consulting firms. It was all about building teams in the newsroom, empowering the staff, reshaping the decision-making process, dispersing authority. Story ideas used to be pursued by reporters and editors. Now they were surrounded by teams and newsroom SWAT squads. A new language was invented. When Pamela Fine was brought in to become the de facto managing editor of the newspaper, she learned that she was not the managing editor. She was the news leader. Managing editor sounded like the vestige of a tyrannical figure out of newspapering's archaic past. Definitely not the image you want to preserve in today's collegial newsroom. The person in charge of matching reporters and editors in appropriate niches became director of player personnel. That is not made up. It was an actual title. McGuire and Kramer carried the message of this new Camelot of journalism exuberantly. If people are going to laugh at those cartoonesque titles, they said, let's have some fun.

But somewhere and somehow—may good sense be praised—the managing-editor-in-fact was recycled as the managing-editor-in-name.

The temptation among the older newsroom dwellers to mock all of this alien apparatus was impossible to resist. But most of that restructuring has now become part of the newsroom landscape in Los Angeles and Chicago and New York as well as in the Twin Cities, and much of it will undoubtedly stay until the next generation of restructuring wizards. Bank employees and pants salesmen could tell stories just as harrowing; the Dilbert principles live in the American workplace today, and they're not going to be blasted out overnight—if at all. The only valid test of the reinvention of the American newsroom is what it means to the readers (apart from the stockholders). The question in Minneapolis and hundreds of other cities then becomes: Is the newspaper serving the needs of its readers better than it used to?

I worked for what was essentially one newspaper for more than thirty-five years, and I still call it my primary source of news. In the 1960s it filled the traditional role of the metropolitan newspaper and did that adequately. It distributed news and advertising. It told who was at war, who won the ball game, who died, and how to plant tulip beds. It provided a few smiles and often ignited thinking in its editorial pages. The writing was competent or better and reporters usually stayed with their beats for twenty or twenty-five years, a practice not always in the best interests of the reader.

The newspaper, in short, largely did what it was supposed to do.

Comparing the newspaper of thirty-five years ago with today's newspaper is like comparing a neighborhood flyer with an encyclopedia. The newspaper of today gives news, it gives somebody's opinion on practically every page, it tells you how to have better sex and what clinic to check out if you don't. It gossips about stars and nobodies. Its photos—no, make that images—are more vivid and compelling today and often are given the right of way over words in telling the story. Those images have a higher priority than they used to because of television and the public's absorption with living pictures. They also have another use—making a statement about the social diversity of our times. A photo of holiday sunbathing at the beach used to routinely show white sunbathers. Today's photographer is going to be more observant. Today there are lots of colors at the beach.

What you notice first when you look at the cover pages of today's newspaper is how busy they are. Not chaotic busyness, you'd hope. What you see is a reflection of television and the quick-read principles of *USA Today*. You want movement on those cover pages, eye-catchers and grabby graphics—charts, punchy type, the works. Today's newspaper concentrates some of its punchiest writing and vignettes in side columns called rails, featuring blurbs and patches of news and human follies, smallish takes that often actively compete with the traditional news columns. It glories in capsulizing the news in one-paragraph digests in an inside section of the newspaper to accommodate readers who don't have time to take the newspaper seriously. It assembles huge staff resources from time to time to do blockbuster, carpet-bombing pieces that will take a subject like transportation of the future and spread it over eight pages, interrupted only by the Audio King ad on page eleven. The piece will wring every imaginable syllable from transportation of the future without necessarily answering the question of why we let the concrete layers get us into this mess in the first place.

I make these observations mostly with goodwill and no malice. You couldn't start in this business more than forty-three years ago without being startled by some of its appearances today. To the primary question of whether the newspaper better serves the interest of the reader today than it did then, my answer is probably yes. It's vastly more entertaining. The content is uniformly more literary. The fare tends to be more provocative. The newspaper spends a lot of energy trying to convince the reader it has its fingers on the pulse of all fads and is standing on the cutting edge of all known trends. It makes sure it satisfies every Internet wonk in town, and it will tell you all you need to know about the latest threat to health in a cup of coffee, as opposed to yesterday's threat, which was entirely different. Today's newspaper, mine and most of the others, is mortified at the thought of being behind the pack in understanding some new lingo or twist in teenage behavior, which may be obsolete tomorrow. So it assigns reporters in packs to interview the teenagers, taking their gobbledygook seriously, as though it were the discovery of a new planet.

All of that is faintly bewildering and may camouflage more important stuff. I look at my newspaper today and I see a substantially improved main news section, evidence that the newspaper has worked hard on it and spent money on it. I look at the newspaper and I see good staff coverage from Washington, instead of some of the token coverage of years past. I see a local globe-trotter like Frank Wright running from Saudi Arabia to Nicaragua and giving the newspaper's readers a personal yet professional scan of what's going on, and I like that. I see highly talented sports columnists dressing down a coach for unlimited failures and crimes against honesty and the public when the coach's primary problem may be that some teams in the league are better. But I read them because they invariably write well and at high level of entertainment, and because I know they are almost always better when they remember that you can be funny or deadly and provocative and still cut your victim some slack and show a little generosity.

I see this newspaper, like every metropolitan newspaper, struggling with and experimenting with its most important mission of all, covering the town right. Sometimes it succeeds powerfully, and the bite of that story clings to you for days. Sometimes it simply falls on its can, like the rest.

The newspaper is better today because it has to be. Otherwise it would get killed by television. Yet there seem to me to be some troublesome traps in what we're getting in today's metropolitan journalism. Today we will take a local issue and engulf it with herds of reporters and photographers and editors. We will hold a strategy session and organize the de rigueur focus groups. Minute dissection of optional directions will take place. Potential hazards to the story's credibility and the reader's tedium quotient will come up. The story may or may not be critically important, but a strategy session is almost mandatory; without it, the principle of empowerment in the newsroom will be compromised and the benefits of groupthink will be lost.

I'm not saying there aren't some virtues in this cast-of-thousands approach to identifying and pursuing the news. The idea of teamwork is important in almost any event involving human beings, and in a newsroom the satisfaction of a group of people moving on a story in concert and bringing it off successfully can produce an emotionally powerful wallop. I've shared some of those moments. But the groupthink idea in the newsroom has developed its own life and can be reduced to silliness. Consulting experienced and expert reporters and editors about where and how to go with a story is one thing. Wasting time by making a show of bringing people into the decision process, some of them unseasoned and out of place, is another. Senior editors still make most of the big decisions about what appears in the newspaper and how it appears day to day. They should. They are well paid and usually well enough endowed with self-esteem to deal with wrathful readers aiming flamethrowers at their tails. They are editors because they are willing to run the risk and take the responsibility and the occasional spurts of glory.

We can have newsroom meetings every day, we can have good and responsive newspapers, but we can probably have better and more responsive newspapers with fewer newsroom meetings. I think what we have in local news today is a lot of bright and motivated people sitting around and discussing story lines and spending an inexcusable amount of time on Process, the current godhead of corporate America. Because of Process, a lot of them may not be doing enough that is productive, both for the newspapers and for themselves. Some of those bright people aren't being exposed to enough of the guts and faces of local news to become authoritative in writing it. There are also new orthodoxies that govern some of the groupthink. Because we are now thoroughly sensitized to minorities, to gays, lesbians, pro-lifers and pro-choicers, to the problems of farmers and urbanites, atheists and vegetarians, we have editors and reporters who are scared stiff that they have missed one of them someplace in the story. And when that mentality takes over, the caricatures about political correctness become a reality in some of the newsroom decisions. Sometimes the result is reporters writing for editors rather than for readers.

The good newspaper understands that reporting on diversity is tricky. It will get complaints from white majorities that "this stuff is going too far; it's too much." It will also get complaints from minorities and special interest groups that the new coverage they're getting is still tokenism, that the paper still hasn't got the proportions right. You know now why senior editors are paid well. But some of them simply work harder at trying to resolve those dilemmas. A good start, of course, is to put diversity into your newsroom. The *Star Tribune*, the only newspaper I know very well, has done that better than most. One of the best things the newspaper has done in years has been to give a prominent commentary role to an African-American writer, Syl Jones, who has the writing skills and art and experience to be able to look at white-black relations in his town and to look at hypocrisies on both sides. It is not going to shock his readers to learn that he finds more hypocrisies among the white mainstreamers, who, he sighs, don't know a fig about African-American culture. But he looks at racial relations in America as both prosecutor and poet and sometimes as a gagster, so you're probably going to get something worthwhile when Jones writes on race, whether it's spiky, condescending, or funny.

The newspaper's biggest challenge today, in terms of being relevant to the lives of its readers, is the original one: bringing to its readers what's actually happening in town. I don't mean the ball games and the metal concerts and the fires. They belong, and they are always going to be there. What I'm talking about is making government news, downtown news, neighborhood news, people news incisive and compelling; finding out what's important to the lives of the readers in the news from the government catacombs; getting past the surface glitz in the suburbs and beyond the surface violence in the ghettos, putting them into some kind of texture, exploring for reasons and looking for developing currents, comparing today in race relations with what used to be, why it's changed, and what the faces of change are.

Every newspaper knows this. In its fashion, every newspaper devotes energy and resources to reaching beneath the surface. What separates the good newspaper from the mediocre newspaper is the difference in the intelligence and nerve with which that mission is pursued. That and the level of leadership in the newsroom, which is where the nerve and intelligence have to begin. Genuine charisma in a newsroom leader is not always available to add to those other endowments. When it is, the newspaper can be great and the whole community benefits.

The newspapers I most enjoy reading are the ones that make a special cause of digging out people whose lives have something to say to the readers about the times, about pursuing life in ways that can be brave or kicky, lives that have something to say about novelty or hope. This does not have to be Pollyanna stuff. Towns are made up of human beings, who still happen to be the most interesting thing you're going to find in tomorrow's newspaper. You will see a good deal of this in the metropolitan newspapers of the Twin Cities. You should see it more aggressively and more creatively done.

One thing I don't immediately grasp about today's slick daily newspaper-magazine is its bashfulness about getting close to the people it serves. There are some papers in this country that are regarded with genuine affection by their readers. I think that relationship can be attained by the newspaper without sacrificing any of its professional integrity, any of its aggressiveness in pursuing the news. I don't think that relationship is necessarily achieved by filling the newspaper with homey feature or personality stories, although God knows if you had to go in just one direction in building a better feeling and higher trust among the readers, that would be a way to go. I'm talking about the tone a newspaper strikes in approaching its readers. I think it should be saying, "Here, we want to give you the news as honestly and as accurately as we can, and sometimes you're going to get mad at us, because you don't want to read that news that day. But we're printing it because we think it belongs and we think in the long run, knowing that, you'll trust us. We're a lot of things as a newspaper. We print news and try to keep the public's books. We're entertainers and figure freaks in our sports pages. We'd like to be one more thing."

The newspaper can be a friend.

It can be part of the community in ways that stick to the skin of the reader, not just by sponsoring glamorous sports events and getting into physical fitness. In how it projects its stories, how it writes and displays them, it can be saying, "We know a lot of you are in pain. We feel it. We want to understand it."

A newspaper is capable of projecting that humanity in its own town, while it is also projecting tough news. I know that because I'm a child of the American newsroom, and I've never lost my fondness for it nor my respect for the essential devotion to a calling that you will see in most good newspaper people and newspapers, and the ones I've worked for have been good ones. Nothing has ever fascinated me as much about the newsroom as the extraordinary meld of personalities and talents that fill it. In the typical daily newspaper you're going to read a range of stories taking the reader into the television studio, the power dens of politics, and the locker room. The stories will be in-depth accounts of this entertainer or that, or a puff piece about a jock—the usual fare. Celebrities make news. The irony often is that the man or woman writing that particular piece is a far more interesting character, largely unknown to the public except by byline, and most of the readers don't remember bylines. Columnists are substantially more visible to newspaper readers and usually have no trouble creating an identity. They can help to give the newspaper a personality. Its true personality, though, is the sum of what it brings to its public every day, and if I published a daily newspaper in America today, I'd invest money in what television has been doing for years—personalizing itself to the audience.

Except for columnists, and particularly sports columnists, newspapers historically have been bashful about telling their part of the world: We're proud of the way these people report or shoot pictures or organize coverage. We think we have arts critics and business writers who do it better than anybody around, and we want you to know them better.

You can do that with advertising or personal appearances or promotions and in a half dozen other ways. I have thoughts like that after watching a two-minute promotional piece for a local television station advertising the wonders its news team performs. Well, they may perform very well in their special venue. But the morning after the ten o'clock news, I'll pick up the newspaper and read a dozen strong local news stories untouched by television, and I'll ask, Who delivers the real news, after all? For all of the flaws in its daily work, a newspaper when it is aroused and when it has strong staff and leadership working in harmony can produce some breathtakingly good work. The Minneapolis newspaper has done that in its Olympics coverage. It has done that, and so has every other good newspaper, when it charges into a breaking story with all resources available and reaches the doorstep the next morning with both the chronicle of that story, in detail that clamps on the reader from start to finish, and its impact on lives. And in case you're likely to miss any of it, you'll be told on the front page that you can't afford to, because here is more on pages seven, eight, and nine, and continued on page twelve.

On the other hand, the Minneapolis newspaper's coverage of the early weeks of the scheme by the Twins and Governor Arne Carlson to build a new baseball stadium was a large plate of pap that flatly served the interests of the promoters.

Daily newspapering. So much in it is sloppy and some of it is misguided and sometimes when you were looking for something comforting in a column you get something snide. But much of it is good and strong reporting, giving you a portrait of the day you can't get anywhere else. Maybe I have those thoughts because each day as I left the newsroom I had the feeling that I'd just spent a day at the soap opera. It was a menagerie of creatures who fizzed or growled, bitched at management or conspired to sell a marginal feature to a gullible editor. Most of them I found infinitely more entertaining, and usually more gifted, than the economist I had just interviewed for an hour. I'd like to see on television now and then a takeout on a Dick Youngblood—who for sure ought to be taken out from time to time—or a Kim Ode or a Peter Vaughan of the place where I worked, or their St. Paul versions across the river. I'd like to see a piece on a Steve Ronald, an editor you very likely don't know but who for me embodied not only the skills and good sense I appreciated in the newsroom but also that quality of honor that can still find a place in the newspaper turmoil.

Finally, the question I'm asked about the newspaper today more than any other, and certainly with a riper flavor of accusation, is this: When are newspapers going to clear all those liberals out of the building and give us some honest news?

The newspapers of America periodically do the mea culpa story. Critic's premise: most newspaper reporters are liberals. The premise is usually delivered with a judgmental wrath borrowed from the Inquisition. The newspaper's mea culpa story's response is this: That's right. We have them. We shelter them. We don't know what to do about it.

An explanation usually follows to account for this embarrassment of liberals on the staff. It has variations, but the core explanation is that most newspaper reporters come from liberal arts educations and are inclined to look with sympathy on the predicament of the needy. Or because their jobs require it, they come to experience firsthand the chasms between rich and poor in America; and when they see corporate greed, they see it bulging with dollar signs into the millions.

That is usually part of the explanation. And then I look at myself. I would probably plead no contest to the accusation of being liberal politically. I am liberal because of my upbringing in the mining country and because of my liberal arts education and because I saw firsthand the disparity between rich and poor in America. Liberal doesn't mean being naive. It doesn't mean you cry at shopping-center openings. There is room in the definition for demanding that people take responsibility for their acts, which a lot of the self-proclaimed individualists never do. Did being liberal shape my outlook as a columnist? Of course it did. Did it affect my reportage at, say, the Democratic and Republican conventions in Florida in 1972? I doubt it. The Republicans were almost as hilarious as the Democrats. I suppose I should have reported that after the Republicans' final night, I spent three hours in the suite of the Lunds and all of rest of the Minnesota Republican hierarchies, most of whom would have been called liberal at the time. I tried zealously not to be corrupted by the Republicans, to be on guard against this after-hours grazing influencing my reportage. I think I succeeded. I don't think I was corrupted by the Republicans. And the Democrats on the final night were beyond corrupting anybody; most of them couldn't stand up straight.

Incidentally, corporately, I happen to be an unblushing capitalist, a free enterpriser without shackles or nose rings. For years I've received part of my revenue through the operation of a travel club, authorship of books, and public speaking. This income is duly reported to the government. In reading the business pages one year, I learned that my little company had paid more in corporate income taxes than General Dynamics, which paid nothing. I was glad to be able to step into the breach.

Most of those mea culpa stories admitting a preponderance of liberal thinkers among the newspaper's reporters will end up with a serious attempt at analysis. Does a liberal bias among reporters affect political news coverage?

The answer usually is this: It's hard to say. That answer will not send readers soaring into a paroxysm of discovery, but as a matter of fact, it is an essentially honest one. There's one crucial safeguard for the readers. Newspapers of today are so conditioned and battered by the charge of newsroom liberalism that they are going to comb every line of a political story to protect truth and the readers from proliberal mischief. That does not always protect the reader from a political bias in the reporter's selection of material, but any clear spinning of the story to make villains out of the conservatives or lambs out of the DFLers is going to reveal itself, and the consequences of that could be hard for the writer in the job reviews.

Those protections aren't fables. Newspapers of today search their souls and probe for any vagrant symptoms of liberal thinking in their news stories. The vigilante mentality has gone that far. Beyond this, a newspaper's ombudsman, a person paid to make judgments about the newspaper's iniquities, is one more protection for the reader. At the *Star Tribune,* I felt that this job—not the most comfortable one for anybody worried about security—was done conscientiously. But I'm not sure what you can do as a practical matter to stampede those liberal reporters out the door. Decapitation of one in five has been suggested. The newspaper could require a sort of political Rorschach test before it hires. That is not a facetious thought. It may come. But way beyond this is a more germane question: What is the potential impact of the liberal-flavored newsroom at the polling place?

Newspaper stories today elect precious few politicians, even if the stories were skewed for political purposes, and it would be hard to get that kind of story through today's jittery copy desks. Far more politi-

cians are elected or defeated by the radio talk shows, whose custodians are almost uniformly noisy headhunters who keep screaming
about liberal bias in the media. Where they're elected mainly, though,
is on television, with money and with shrewd or truth-warping sound
bites. There is also this thought to comfort Americans who are worried about political ideologues in journalism affecting elections: In the
1930s, 95 percent of American newspapers supported the Republican
candidate against FDR. Many of the newspapers, including the *Chicago Tribune,* ruthlessly used their news pages to campaign against
Roosevelt.

Roosevelt won in a landslide. In hindsight, I don't know about that
decapitation formula to get rid of news people with a liberal twist.
Change that formula from one in five to one in six. My old crony
Doug Grow was still writing columns in the *Star Tribune* at last observation. Taking his head off is a sloppy way to change his attitude.

8/ Minnesota: Lotusland in Icicles

A man honking his car horn was arrested in a western Minneapolis suburb shortly after midnight early in the fall of 1991 after a citizen's complaint. The incident made the front page of newspapers outside of Minnesota, and when the readers learned why, they howled.

Inside the newspapers of America on that day the sports pages were jammed with the story of the Minnesota Twins' tenth-inning victory over Atlanta in the final game of the World Series in the Metrodome.

The two stories were connected, of course. You had to be a lifelong inhabitant of Minnesota to understand that. You might actually have predicted it. The boisterous motorist nailed by the gendarmes was celebrating the Twins' World Series victory. He went out of his head and beeped his car horn. Red lights in the mirror followed that rash act. Consider. In other cities of America, the acts of jubilation after a World Series victory often include mass overturning of cars, street riots, creative acts of arson, and other miscellaneous destruction. In Minnesota, a man honked his horn in a residential street and got arrested for disturbing the peace.

And although in downtown Minneapolis that night, thousands of Twins fans behaved with Minnesota's version of wanton conduct—smiling at strangers and doing high-fives—no other police action was reported.

I recall this episode in an open confession of awe. Despite a lifetime in residence here, I've never stopped underestimating Minnesota citizens' obsession with the sanctity of moderation in all things. I know that this is a generalization that can be challenged. Life can get pretty tempestuous in Minnesota when the largemouth bass season opens. I'm also aware that the past twenty or thirty years have eroded some of the conceptions about Minnesota behavior, and some of them are now obsolete.

But not many. Which spurs a question: How much have we, has Minnesota, changed?

That stereotype about the Minnesota passion for orderliness, incidentally, had clearly reached most of the American public by the World Series of 1991. One of the headlines on that car-honking story read "Lawlessness Strikes in Minnesota."

I *will* make one generalization fearlessly. No public psychoanalyzes its behavior as ardently as Minnesota's public, or reads or listens to the psychoanalysis of visiting shrinks and scholars as relentlessly as Minnesota's public. I don't believe the same zeal is present in Mississippi. I know it isn't in North Dakota. I'm not sure why this is, although there are road signs. Somewhere in the 1960s, several odd symptoms of life in Minnesota began attracting the scrutiny of sociologists and professors. Local cartoonists (Dick Guindon) and commentators (Garrison Keillor) made a living on them. Local newspaper columnists grazed the same pastures. I was absolutely impressed in my early years with the *Star,* for example, by the theories of one of the homebred scholars, Professor David LaBerge of the University of Minnesota. The winter was particularly severe. I'd grown up a few miles from Canada and had long ago made my philosophical peace with Minnesota winter. It was going to be long and cold, but eventually it would end. It could actually bring some joy to your life, if you had (a) long skis, (b) three sets of jumper cables, and (c) an insulated fish house.

Professor LaBerge, who wanted to bring good news to Minnesotans in this particular winter, offered the theory that certain kinds of constructive activity outdoors can stimulate people erotically. In other words, snow shoveling—done in moderation, of course—can enhance your sex life. I shared this electrifying news with the newspaper's readers. It was met by a substantial amount of mail, most of it from the male in the family. The men were mad because the professor had no idea of the size of the family driveway. The men of Minnesota now were expected to deliver some action at the end of the long hard day, both in the driveway and in the bedroom. They claimed to have been ambushed, and I was the instigator. The professor, who was also president of the Bach Society, was mildly shaken by the repercussions. I offered him a consoling thought. Inasmuch as Johann Sebastian Bach had twenty-two children, I said, he certainly had to qualify as one of the outstanding snow shovelers of his time.

If I needed any more evidence of the cult of weather in Minnesota, this just about closed out the testimony. It also reinforced an impression I've had about Minnesota most of my life, and I have to acknowledge that when I look at Minnesota in all of its bafflements and joys, I look at it primarily as a citizen and not as a newspaper columnist. One reason Minnesota is so fascinated by itself is the citizens' uncommon view that their state, a place in which more than 4 million people live, is a community. There's an intriguing test you can apply to this idea. If you happen to be traveling through London and meet an American and you trade small talk, one of the first questions is going to be Where are you from? If the traveler is from Atlanta, he or she is very probably going to say Atlanta. If the traveler is from Los Angeles, the answer is probably going to be Los Angeles. If the traveler is from Minneapolis or St. Paul, the answer is very probably going to be Minnesota.

You can wrestle with the psychology of this, but that is the response you're likely to get. It can lead to more provocative questions, all of them based on an assumption that I think holds up: over a period of time in this century, the large majority of people who live in Minnesota decided this is a place they like, a place where they can feel comfortable and productive. They have held to this belief through several decades of powerful changes in how Minnesotans make their money, how and why they elect their politicians, and what the state looks like ethnically. That belief has also held in the urban Twin Cities, although with less conviction, because this is a part of Minnesota where change has produced unprecedented violence.

Some sticky questions emerge as Minnesota approaches a new millennium: How fundamental are the changes over the past fifty years and how valid are some of those old conceptions about Minnesota's personality and values? In the next century is this still going to be a place where you can spend a useful lifetime?

In 1973 *Time* magazine published a cover story that approached the breathlessness of the announcement of an archaeological discovery. The discovery was Minnesota and its novelty. What made the state novel, *Time* found, was its strong and unhurried quality of living, its in-house achievements, its role as a citadel of world-class medicine, theater, and music in the middle of the prairie, and the services it was exporting to all continents.

Here was a place in America, *Time* said, that worked. The State of Minnesota. It was led by a young Swedish-American governor, Wendell Anderson, a hockey hero at the University of Minnesota in his college days, the portrait of the clean-living, clean-talking, ambitious but level-headed young politician out of the happy foundry of DFL politicians that gave the world Hubert Humphrey, Gene McCarthy, and Walter Mondale. He appeared on the magazine's cover, holding a large dead fish. He was smiling, his collar was open, and he was the personification of the place that works. This was a young politician said to be so wholesome and so credible that he could campaign on a platform of raising taxes hundreds of millions of dollars—to shift the burden of financing the public school system from property taxes to income taxes—and still get elected. The implication: where else but in Minnesota?

The piece drew a picture of a place in America where government was orderly and practically without sin, where giant businesses and any-sized businesses genuinely believed in the idea of corporate good citizenship, cooperating with the government when that made sense and allowing for the public interest in some of their corporate decisions. It was a place of natural beauty where families could picnic in their backyard and enjoy visits from woodchucks and mallards within sight of the rising glass towers of downtown Minneapolis. It was a place almost free of strife, its social attitudes dominated by the sturdy principles and the devotion to work brought to the cornfields by the early waves of immigration from Scandinavia, Germany, and Ireland. Later its culture was flavored by Jews, Slavs, other southern Europeans, African-Americans, and the homestanding Native Americans who, the magazine acknowledged, were mostly broke. It was a place of prosperity and diversity, where the arts flourished and the banner of education was held high, and where you hardly ever heard a disparaging word.

If you looked closely at this portrait, you could almost see a yellow brick road running through the place from Winona to Warroad.

Was this picture of Minnesota in the early 1970s extravagantly naive?

No, it wasn't.

Now take that picture of Minnesota as a land of prosperity, of social conscience and relative stability, graced by a nature prodigal in its gifts for both recreationalist and viewer-of-sunsets. Does the picture still have relevance in the late 1990s?

In crucial ways, yes—possibly more than skeptical minds are willing to admit.

There's a quote in the *Time* article that now strikes a hard gong of irony, though. Minneapolis underwent racial street riots in the mid-1960s, reflecting a national racial unrest, reflecting the rebellion of youth and minorities in the 1960s. The city reacted by trying to bring the problems out into the open and bringing the advocates together, forming the Urban Coalition. One of the coalition's leaders said this of Minneapolis then, in 1973: "For a black, Minneapolis is one of the truly outstanding cities in the U.S. to live in. The problems here—housing, education, discrimination, unemployment—are manageable. There just isn't the real, deep-seated hatred here that blacks often encounter in other cities."

This is not the kind of talk you're likely to hear from black leaders in Minneapolis in the 1990s, at a time when racial frictions stoked up by police incidents—the black gang–hatched murder of a white cop, the shooting of a black teenager by a white cop—have created a bunker mentality in the black settlements of north and south Minneapolis from time to time. It is not the kind of conciliatory talk you're likely to hear from city residents, white and otherwise, whose fears deepened dramatically in the mid-1990s with record outbreaks of murder in the Twin Cities.

That is one of the jolts of reality that has intruded on the near make-believe that smitten biographers of Minnesota from outside the state saw in Minnesota in 1973.

It doesn't mean that the black leader was chasing an illusion in 1973. It doesn't mean that the problem solvers of all colors have receded from the goal of finding answers and bringing the races closer together in the Twin Cities and in Minnesota. The upward movement of blacks into the middle class in the city and the suburbs is not as dramatic as the tensions in the city, but it is nonetheless a telling part of the racial equation and racial change in the Twin Cities.

What it does mean is that Minnesota offered a refuge to the poor and the voiceless and the broken families. They came, and some of them brought their problems. Those problems increasingly get to be resented by those who were here first. Stereotypes come in the door when willingness to understand goes out the window. The big majority of the poor and voiceless who obey the law and live worthwhile lives come to resent the stereotypes. And when all of that happens, the utopia of 1973 looks comically distorted and easy to ridicule. Finally it means that if poverty and drugs and violence afflict the inner cities of New York and Los Angeles, they now do the same in Minneapolis and St. Paul.

That is America and the world in the 1990s. But it's only a piece of the world, and it doesn't mean Minnesota has gone to hell and all of the claims made for it are hot air and hypocrisy. What holds Minnesota together as a community, if that's a fair term, may be a lot stronger than the forces of change and trend-chasing that might fragment it.

The traveler in London who identifies Minnesota instead of Minneapolis or Coon Rapids as the place where he lives might be moved by a half dozen reasons he never bothers to define. The thought tantalizes me because his impulsive statement of "home" ties in with the way I look at a lifetime here in the windchill and the waters and the abundance of this place. I think about that because it has been the medicine of Minnesota that saved my life and the nature of Minnesota that has enlarged that life with scenes that are forever part of my coloring book. It was the foresight of Minnesota's pioneers in chemical dependency that may have saved my self-respect. I'll admit you can get soggy about all that. I've never looked on the place as anything close to utopia. How could you when you spend an hour at lunch at the Lincoln Del listening to a couple argue over the exhibits to avoid at the Minnesota State Fair?

But let's say Minnesota has come to be a community more than the state of New York is a community or Florida is a community. If so, why? And if a cardinal characteristic of a community is shared experience, what is Minnesota's? When you search for that, you inevitably have to sift out the forces and events that have acted to bond this particular province of America. You have to start with the state's university, for more than a century the centerpiece of Minnesota's absorption with education and with arts and culture. It was an institution proudly owned and essentially revered. It was everyone's college, the people's university. Its tuition was inexpensive, its faculty sound, and its national reputation strong. Over the decades, it schooled millions, directly or indirectly. It extended the fruits of its research and its medicine into the lives of every one of the state's citizens. More than any other institution in Minnesota, it brought the state's residents together in a solidarity of proprietorship and benefit because, beyond all of its roles, it served. For a dozen reasons, many of them outside the school's control, the University of Minnesota today is less in its reach and its impact. That does not minimize the residual effects of its imprint on the lives of millions.

The bonding in Minnesota came from the beginning in the bedrock of the Scandinavian immigration of the middle and late 1800s. The history the Scandinavians brought to Minnesota was noticeably shy of social storms and political hatreds. They brought to Minnesota a certain durability demanded by the ruggedness of their life in Norway and Sweden. They brought a fondness for order, a willingness to experiment politically, and a stoical faith that this, too, will pass, whatever the aggravation of the moment. That particular trait may have been the most valuable in the 1800s, because one of the first things the Scandinavians met in Minnesota was twenty-below-zero weather. And finally what they brought was more Scandinavians, so that eventually that shared experience so critical in the building of kinship spread from border to border in Minnesota. It was augmented, of course, by Germans and Irish and Belgians and Jews and African-Americans and Slavs and Greeks and—

How are you going to name them all? May their tribes increase.

But despite the later arrivals, Minnesota became a community for better or for worse primarily because it was homogenous for so many years, a land of white Europeans, mostly white northern Europeans who shared traits and ideas and, when it came to that, recipes. Lovers of diversity cheered the immigrations that came afterward, through the Hispanics and the Orientals in the 1980s. If you have any belief at all in the strength and goodness of democracy, you joined the cheer because those later immigrations changed the face of Minnesota by multiplying the faces of Minnesota and spicing the flavor of the community broth.

If you're honest, you know that not everybody cheered.

And yet that stubborn notion of Minnesota as one big, loose neighborhood in a land of harvests, lakes, and eight thousand potholes in spring hangs on, for some very good and hardy reasons. They manage to link the people of Hallock in the beet and wheat country and the people of Wabasha in the southeastern bluff country, although the two lie hundreds of miles apart. One of the strongest links is the Twin

Cities themselves. Minneapolis and St. Paul. The metropolis. The metropolis essentially is made up of people who migrated from Hallock and Wabasha and four hundred towns like them. Instead of the traditional city versus country clash, a visit to the metropolis became a family reunion. One of the institutions that made it a family reunion and buying binge in years past was Dayton's department store. If the university was the people's school in Minnesota, Dayton's was everybody's store. A reason for that was Dayton's early insistence that the customer mattered and the customer should be treated with dignity and courtesy. There was more to the creed. If a disagreement over a returned purchase ever developed, there was a strong chance that the customer was right and a sentiment that, moreover, customers tended to be honest.

Some of these ideas were considered revolutionary and subversive in retail selling until then.

Adhering to them, Dayton's made a ton. What you did when you went to Minneapolis in the fall was to watch the Gophers play football, visit the relatives, look at the lights on Hennepin Avenue, and shop at Dayton's.

This sequence is not likely to occur today. The point is that in the building of Minnesota's habits and attitudes, the existence of a Dayton's was a contributor of high magnitude. And beyond this relationship with customers, the philosophies of the Dayton's founders were crucial in advancing the idea of corporate generosity; the business volunteered 5 percent of its profits to the public good. Scores of Minnesota businesses adopted that principle, which contributed immensely to building a momentum of giving in Minnesota: corporate giving, outpourings from foundations, and private giving. It would definitely include little old ladies in tennis shoes, without whom the Salvation Army couldn't exist. Today, Minnesotans—far more than the people of most states—give millions of dollars each day above taxes for schooling, for health care, for the disabled, and for other services.

That is an act of community.

Although the dollar is being squeezed and political climates are changing, private giving remains a characteristic of life in Minnesota. Dayton's has undergone vast changes and—apart from the national titan of Target—no longer can claim the sentimental place it held among Minnesota shoppers (or share of the market). But the concepts of its founders still linger in the ethic of much of Minnesota business.

Similarly, WCCO-AM does not hog the public airways as it once did. But because of the reach of its clear signal, and because of its personalities, the Twin Cities radio station became a daily presence, an unmistakable bonding force, in the lives of hundreds of thousands of Minnesotans. The voices of Cedric Adams, Clellan Card, Bob De-Haven, Halsey Hall, and later Howard Viken, Charlie Boone, and Roger Erickson were as familiar to listeners in Two Harbors and Worthington as they were to Twin Cities listeners. Because it was a state-wide station, it dealt in statewide news and statewide (does it need to be said?) weather.

In fact, there was a period in the 1960s and 1970s when WCCO-AM became an absolute, howling autocrat on the subject of weather. It became the King Lear of weather. It was going to save you from blizzards and tornadoes. It was going to spare you falling bricks in your basement and red dust from the Dakotas. It came with special sound effects ranging from high pitched-beepers to ooga horns. The ooga horns were so loud and penetrating that one night they woke me from a sound sleep on the couch in the shank of the evening after I'd drifted off in the middle of a ball game. It happened that a week before, I'd seen a movie on submarine warfare. WCCO's ooga horns came blasting out of the night, disorienting me. For an awful moment I imagined myself on the deck of a submarine off a Pacific atoll, the captain ordering a crash dive with his ooga horns.

In my column the next day, I expressed mild discomfort with this system of terrorizing the public. I suggested that the station deserved homage for alerting the public to the hazards out there. I also suggested that one of the real hazards to the public was the threat of death by heart attack caused by the sudden assault of those unseen ooga horns.

The station responded fiercely. It put on the mild and lovable Joe Strub of the U.S. Weather Service to tell us how indispensable WCCO-AM is to life as we know it in our time. It denounced me for being irresponsible in suggesting that there might be a calmer way to do this, and in offering the theory that it is possible to survive lousy weather in Minnesota without hearing about it first on WCCO.

The station also quarantined me. In the past I'd been invited onto its airwaves to make my annual appeal for contributions to this charity or that. I'd also been invited to talk about my books. Now the gate clanged shut. No books. No charity appeals. As a potential guest, I was consigned to the station's black hole. In six years, however, the management changed and I was pardoned, cleansed. That happened even after I'd cautioned Roger Erickson to bring in a fresh atomizer because it was only three months away from the school closing season and he sounded terribly raspy and just not ready for the panic.

Television and the aggressive marketing of FM radio reduced WCCO's voice and influence over the years, but it was unarguably an important and entertaining voice in building that border-to-border neighborhood. So, in fact, was the Minneapolis newspaper, particularly the Sunday *Tribune* with its huge reach of thirty and forty years ago, now lessened by the economics of production and delivery. But for years the Sunday Peach section—swamping the reader with ten stories on the University of Minnesota football game and twenty-five photos, including the ones from Russ Bull's Machine Gun Camera—was a fixture in scores of thousands of homes in Minnesota in the fall.

The geography of Minnesota and its outdoors tended to work a natural solidarity. We're a little remote. Modern technology has dissolved the isolation, but well into the twentieth century Minnesota's uncivilized winters and its distance from American mainstreams produced a state-of-siege fellowship among the dwellers that still survives today when the windchill gets abnormally ugly. And a continuing link in the lives of practically all Minnesotans today is their admiration for the natural treasure of the state's outdoors, the waters where they canoe and fish and swim, the forests where they can walk or hunt or ride, and the parks where they can take their families.

Lastly but critically, there is this: the politics of Minnesota has reinforced and built some of the more constructive sides of Minnesota as a large but still definable neighborhood. Sometime in the middle of the twentieth century a consensus emerged in Minnesota about what could be done in its society. It was an attitude that paid no particular allegiance to either political party.

For three or four decades in the middle of the century, the partisan politics of Minnesota coalesced into a general understanding that was never voiced in any joint communiqué from the Republicans and Democrats but seemed to exist nonetheless. The state had uncommon resources. It had a public with a history of strong commitment to and support for education. It had a stable society and diversified industry usually willing to cooperate with government in capital development and in meeting societal needs. That being true, the politics of Minnesota ought to be shaped by progressive action by its government, using Minnesota's resources in innovative ways to better lives and to protect its natural riches.

That is not from some DFL platform of the 1950s. It fundamentally defines the direction that Minnesota politics took from the late 1930s through most of the rest of the century, at least until the parties began to fragment and the state's political leadership waned into mediocrity. Some of the strongest reform legislation of the century, in fact, occurred with Republicans Harold Stassen and Luther Youngdahl in the governor's office. One of their ideological successors was Elmer Andersen, a Republican businessman and former legislator who governed in the early 1960s and brought to his office the same appreciation of a sensible government role in molding a stronger and more equitable society. When the DFL came into power in the middle 1950s, of course, the process took on speed. So did the innovative legislation. Some of it, in the fields of health protection and education trailblazing, in meeting the problems of the disabled and the poor, and in governmental planning, became a national model. Some of it wasted money, and the inevitable corrections occurred on Election Tuesday.

But the net effect was to create in Minnesota a public consciousness about political power, that it could be wielded inventively and still responsibly, and that it could be done openly. And for a few productive decades in Minnesota, both political parties more or less agreed with that premise, when Democrats quite candidly called themselves liberals and Republicans quite willingly called themselves moderate, or progressive, or liberal. That consensus of goodwill, of the constructive works available through strong political action, has taken obvious hits in recent years with the deterioration of political parties and the fighting over dwindling funds. But for much of the century it gave Minnesota—as a community—a political vitality that brought politicians and researchers here in regiments to try to duplicate it.

Some of the forces around which Minnesota built this rough solidarity have gone south. Others have modified, but one that hasn't changed and won't is the Minnesotan's fixation on the weather. Talking about lousy weather in Minnesota will survive ethnic diversity and brawls over yet another stadium. It will outlast the Republicans and the DFL. It will be here when the ozone layer goes to hell, and it will be here when the environmentalists and the motorboaters in northern

Minnesota finally agree. Talking about lousy weather may be the one, the irremovable condition of life in communal Minnesota.

One of its virtues is that it spans the decades. It is *the* common denominator of life in Minnesota, making everybody equal and uniformly surly until the county snowplows go back into the garage.

But what about the rest? What about those bridges of commonality that tended to bring people together in Minnesota, and the gee-whiz picture of the Minnesota society discovered by the *Time* piece and perpetuated by Gopherphiles?

Is there any serious resemblance between the Minnesota of twenty-five and forty years ago and the Minnesota of today?

I think there is. Before you examine that case, you have to identify the pieces that no longer fit in that picture, another way of saying that the picture is now discolored. It would be a miracle if it weren't. How badly discolored it is depends on your view of reality and may depend on the level of your forgiveness. But what's different about Minnesota doesn't mean that all change necessarily has been in the direction of loss.

Most of what's different and most of what's worse is probably a closer reflection of the world around us than any special delinquency or sins in Minnesota, although there are enough of those to occupy squads of moralists. Minnesota's political parties used to be among the nation's leaders in sprouting productive ideas and attractive candidates. Minnesota's political parties today are essentially cartoons. They don't speak for the broad centers of their constituencies and don't speak with much civility or sense under any conditions. Their caucuses and conventions have become a battering ram for single-issue hawkers and pleaders, and their endorsed candidates are often paste-ups of the delegates' twisted view of political reality and of the needs and wishes of the voters. As a result, no politician in Minnesota takes the party endorsement seriously as an open door to election. What the party endorsement usually earns you in Minnesota today is defeat in the September primary. The parties inflicted this destruction on themselves with the best public relations intentions, to "open up the process" to the people. The people turned out to be the special grinders who took command of the process.

But this phenomenon is not peculiar to Minnesota. Slick or brutal television campaigning, not the political party, is now the open door to election in America. This reduces the influence of political parties.

In some state elections, it disarms them totally. One of the side results is distraction and often a general mess in the state legislatures, Minnesota's among them. Another result is the steady disappearance of high-quality public servants at all levels of government, and most of the good, well-adjusted characters who used to be considered party professionals or den fathers—Republican Wheelock Whitney, my kind of millionaire, or Democrat George Farr and others of that stripe. These are people for whom politics was not only a business but a potluck party to be enjoyed, people for whom it was never in bad taste to say something generous about the enemy. And the electables somehow no longer include people like Wendell Anderson, who emerge from the broad currents of their parties and their publics. Anderson came to grief in the 1978 election because of a voter backlash over his self-indulgence in getting himself appointed to the U.S. Senate, and because of his odd attendance record during the time he was there. But the qualities that put him in as governor, and would have guaranteed him years in the Senate if he'd been patient, were ones you don't see much anymore in the higher precincts of Minnesota politics. He was a generalist with some original conceptions of what was possible in government. He was accessible and bright, willing to strike a compromise and yet bold enough to campaign on a tax hike to equalize the school financing burden. Similarly, the gentle-mannered Al Quie could advance in Republican politics. What you're more likely to see in Minnesota elections today are mavericks, both rich mavericks and underdog mavericks, or lightweights who press the right one-issue buttons, or opportunists who switch their principles like rock singers switch costumes—which means it's a Rod Grams and a Paul Wellstone and an Arne Carlson who've been making it at the ballot box in the 1990s.

While the nosedive of party politics is a national trend, what's different about the decline of the political party in Minnesota is the ferocity with which the one-issue screamers have pushed their causes. It makes their particular lopsidedness more lopsided than the national average of lopsidedness.

All of which means that the art of politics in Minnesota has deteriorated. One of its large casualties is the art of excellence in government; there aren't enough good and balanced public servants around anymore to keep good government creative and responsive. There also isn't enough money. That is a universal condition in government today, and one that may also explain a more wrenching decline in

Minnesota over the past twenty-five years, the decline of the state's university.

It's a critical change in Minnesota in any serious measurement of the quality of life in the state. What's happened at the University of Minnesota runs parallel to the experience at other major state universities, but not at all of them. None of them is immune to the trauma of the money crunch and to shifts in focus dictated by technology and the speed of the times. The country is educating millions more students than it used to. State colleges and vocational schools have expanded. The role of the state university in all of the complexity of today's education has been examined to death by waves of reformers and visionaries. It's happened with a vengeance in Minnesota. There's no way to deny the reality of what they and the citizens are seeing at Minnesota's big school—the loss of some of its excellence and a lot of its faculty and leadership, partly because it lost its chummy relationship with the legislature, partly because it has gone through a succession of less-than-magnificent university presidents.

But an even larger reason was the provincialism of the legislature. Sometime twenty or thirty years ago an idea emerged that attracted the instant enthusiasm of town boosters and their politicians: practically every town ought to have a college. There was even a formula floated around: no college-age youngster in Minnesota ought to be any farther than twenty-five miles from the nearest college.

Nobody ever bothered to explain why this theory would suddenly bring intellectual brilliance and cost savings to a state that was already one of the best educated in America. Well, yes, more colleges were needed to make higher learning available to kids unable to attend the university. The state had to expand its satellite and specialty colleges.

"But it didn't have to do it on the scale it did," David Lebedoff tells us. Lebedoff is one of the likable political geeks in Minnesota, an author, observer of political phenomena, and a good head. He also calls himself a university watcher, which means he has his head on a swivel. A new cosmic event might come from any direction on campus.

"A big thing that happened is that the legislators fell in love with the idea of a college in their backyard," says Lebedoff. "So money started to go into the country to build schools. What started out as a reasonable expansion of educational opportunity in Minnesota turned into a frenzy of building. And eventually they overbuilt. They wasted millions of dollars on buildings that weren't needed or that eventually were closed. Money for brick and mortar. The loser was the university, because there's only a limited amount of money available for higher education, and the university got squeezed."

The university also took hits from other directions, from the loose spending of a gadfly who attached himself to the school's athletic department, from the prosecution of some of its athletes for assault and worse, to the infinitely more damaging disorder in its medical school, one of the most prestigious in the world, that culminated in charges against the renowned transplant surgeon John Najarian, largely the result of a series of investigative stories in the *Star Tribune* developed by reporter Joe Rigert. Najarian was accused of mishandling university money and ignoring the law and rules in promoting the drug ALG, which was used to prevent the body's rejection of organ transplants.

Najarian was cleared in federal court. I'm not sure about the strength of the government's case. I knew Najarian through my newspaper and radio work. I also knew scores of his patients' parents, to whom I'd talked as part of my work. They told first of the unlimited time he made available to them to talk about what lay ahead for their children, what the prospects were, what his judgments were. They talked first of his thoughtfulness before his skills as a surgeon. I also knew about his headlong administrative style and some of his dodging of protocol. I don't know what else he dodged. I did know, as a resident of this place, about the thousands of lives he'd saved directly or through his research and his aggressiveness. I agreed in my column that this performance could by no imaginable stretch of logic put him beyond the reach of the law. Respecting his achievements didn't mean he should be exempt from going into the dock.

It did mean some of us applauded his acquittal.

And finally the University of Minnesota hospital, one of the finest teaching hospitals in the world, could no longer compete with the private hospitals in an environment of health care managed by giant insurance conglomerates and had to merge itself into the Fairview system. Dozens of college hospitals will follow suit, for the same reasons.

It follows that you can't blame the legislature or the arrogance of medical school stars or the mistakes of the school's administration for all of the university's distress. But it wasn't all fate, either. The university and its overseers in the Minnesota Legislature took turns blundering on important decisions for years, and the result is a university that no longer receives the unconditional trust and affection of a public that once viewed it with so much pride. Its medical school, although it remains strong, has lost prestige. The university is still critical in Minnesota. It's just not as good, and that is a very important loss from twenty-five years ago, and painful damage.

So was the systematic undermining of what once was called "the Minnesota miracle," the scheme of Wendell Anderson and his legislative pals to democratize the financing of Minnesota's public school system. Paying for public schooling in Minnesota, regarded then as now as one of the better systems in the country, had been getting bogged down in the rising public clamor to reduce property taxes, which were among the highest in the country. They had to be to underwrite the kind of schooling on which the citizens were insisting. The Minnesota miracle put the burden on income tax, which allowed a sizable cut in property tax. The explanation: It was a fairer way to do it. It would assure equal education in the school districts, regardless of their wealth. The Minnesota miracle was applauded at home and around the country, for a while. It wasn't applauded with much enthusiasm by Republican insiders, who always doubted the luminosity of the miracle. They argued that a disproportionate piece of the new income tax money went into teacher salaries. That may have been true, although it's also pretty axiomatic that attracting and holding high-quality teachers usually has something to do with high-quality education.

In any case, the miracle gradually eroded when the formulas began changing. The biggest erosion occurred when Governor Rudy Perpich and the corporate giants of Minnesota, the Minnesota Business Partnership, discovered common ground. The met several times to find routes to a goal they shared. State income taxes, the partnership's leaders lamented, were awful. Minnesotans paid the third-highest state income tax in the country. It was stifling possible business expansion and giving the state a bad name among businesses that might migrate here. It was tempting those already here to move. It was the same litany Perpich had been hearing for years, and the state kept prospering. The level of personal income taxes, the partners said, was making it hard for Minnesota businesses to attract promising middle managers from around the country.

Somebody said, "Well, why not make up the difference with higher salary offers, which will then be passed on to the customers?" The response was, "We're doing that." They were, and they didn't like it,

.

but they kept prospering and outpointing their competitors despite all of the corporate and political wails that taxes were killing Minnesota business. Yet this time Perpich was getting tense himself over the bad-business-climate oratory. All right, he said, we ought to get that state income tax number down from third-highest in the country. Never mind, of course, that Minnesota annually ranked third or better in the country by most educational and quality-of-life tests. Rudy wanted Minnesota to disappear from all of the top-ten tax lists. Not a whole lot of thought was given by the Business Partnership to the services Minnesota was going to lose by lowering taxes. It was cordially assumed that the resulting increased business activity would put more money into state vaults.

When the issue got to the legislature, most of the politicians, not surprisingly, could see no harm in lowering Minnesota on the pits lists of states with the highest income taxes.

The deed was eventually done. The tax was reduced by close to 16 percent. Minnesota happily slid down the lists and scrubbed the Minnesota miracle. Eventually the heaviest school financing burden returned to a rising property tax, and that portrait of Minnesota as a social Garden of Eden of America lost a little more of its color. And yet some fairness is demanded for the business combine's role in changing the school financing formula. The Business Partnership at the time was a good deal more progressive than it became, more thoughtful about how it looked at the broader scope of what was good for both Minnesota and business. It was one of the pioneers, in fact, in proposing the open enrollment plan that gave high school students a choice in where they went to class, an idea in which Minnesota once more led the nation.

But a smudge in that Garden of Eden far more grisly than school financing began to spread in the 1980s: the mounting number of violent deaths in the Twin Cities and increasing fright among the citizens. Social critics, remembering the lotusland images, talked and wrote sardonically about the hypocrisy of claiming that life is better and calmer in Minnesota and then stacking up the bodies like any other city in America where violence had become part of city's daily time sheet. It was and is hard to present a credible argument the other way. Because theirs was essentially a prosperous and quiet white society fifteen and twenty years ago, Minnesota and the Twin Cities were hardly cauldrons of social confrontation then. Drugs, the migration into the Twin

Cities of people who were troubled and broke, and the easy availabil-
ity of guns changed that.

More and more palms and apple trees vanished from that mythical
garden.

The garden had already begun to lose its lushness when the Minnesota Legislature in the early 1980s opened the floodgates to the gambling epidemic that now engulfs the state. Until then, advocates of
horse racing would come into the legislature every two years with a
bill to legalize pari-mutuel betting. Mostly they represented the interests of the breeding industry and the horsey personalities of the western Twin Cities suburbs who wanted to see their colors paraded on a
Minnesota track. It was an understandable ambition, although the
legislature didn't listen to it seriously until the national recession of
the early 1980s, triggered by the passionately promoted supply-side
economics of the Reagan years. Traditional (that is, Democratic) sources
of cash for the states from the federal troughs in Washington began to
shrink, worrying the public servants in St. Paul and every other state
capital. Legalized gambling, until then vigorously shunned by the
states for good and defensible reasons, now looked more appealing.
We'll bring in taxes, the horsey personalities told the Minnesota Legislature. The bill passed, although there was no mass public pressure
for it and the tax monies it brought in were trivial. In time other
gambling-is-good thumpers began arriving at the state capitol. A few
minor league delinquencies in church bingo operations had turned up.
Why, somebody asked, are these people allowed to run gambling operations and other law-abiding, honorable Minnesotans can't? Most
of the arguments weren't planted by the law-abiding, honorable citizens but by the distributors of pull tab gambling equipment who stood
to profit.

So-called charitable gambling was expanded in Minnesota with a
speed and permissiveness that outstripped all other states. Fundamentally, it ran out of control for years and still does in a lot of towns.
One reason for that was the cover of charitable gambling. A good deal
of the proceeds went into causes that were met with sympathy or enthusiasm in the benefiting towns. In addition, most of the charitable
gambling operations were run by politically powerful or prestigious
organizations in town—the military service clubs, other service clubs,
and associations to aid the disabled. All have clout in the legislature
and in the city councils. When bookkeeping discrepancies were found

by the examiners, a tap on the wrist was usually the penalty of choice. The bookkeeping got sloppier. The number of people personally profiting from the operations increased. The regulators were intimidated by the political pressures—and still are.

Mainly, charitable gambling in Minnesota is still a mess. One of its offshoots was to encourage the state of Minnesota itself to get into the gambling business. The passage of the lottery bill in Minnesota meant more than the disreputable sight of a state government going into the pockets of its citizens, spending the public's money to advertise, fooling thousands of suckers into believing they could get rich. It meant also that Minnesota was now saying, "Hey, never mind that we liked the way we ran government around here and we liked the way people managed their lives and we liked what makes Minnesota different. Now we want to be like everybody else. We want to make money by taking it from the dummies."

Money was made, all right. Neither the enlarged charitable gambling nor the state lottery resulted from any mass public pressure. They came in because the gambling industry was persuasive and because Minnesota wanted to be like everybody else. The spread of gambling in Minnesota was seen as inevitable in view of the times and the glamorization of gambling via television and print advertising. It *wasn't* inevitable. And it didn't spread nearly as virulently in other states as it did in Minnesota. And when it did it was over the private mumbling and grumbling of a large number of citizens who thought that it was wrong and that it made society more corrupt and loopy. And, of course, they were right. But there was no organized resistance.

And finally, when the Indian reservations said, "Why can't we promote the same stuff that's going on off the reservation?" there was no way to deny them ethically or legally. Congress produced predictably sloppy and ambiguous legislation allowing reservations to operate gambling if that specific kind of gambling was already legal elsewhere in the states. It took the reservation and gambling industry lawyers no time to discover that games like blackjack, although not technically legal in Minnesota, were permitted to operate on "gambling nights" and other ad hoc promotions by some of the service and private clubs. Since practically no arrests had ever been made, the games must be legal. The sloppy national legislation bred sloppy state legislation. Compacts were negotiated with the reservations by state politicians ignorant of the compact's implications, or in some cases with a political interest in what was going on. Those compacts were uniformly one-sided in favor of the reservations. Las Vegas–style casino palaces went up. The gambling industry's profits soared. On one reservation, hundreds of thousands of dollars went annually to people who could prove they were residents of the reservation. For friends of the Indians, there was something deliciously ironic about this. Here were Indian folks who were systematically swindled years ago, their land taken and their poverty ignored. These same folks were now making (or somebody was making) millions of dollars from the white descendants of the swindlers who stole from the Indians.

Now a new argument surfaced. To balance the casino's advantages, why not more gambling? "Minnesotans like to gamble more than other people do," the gambling hustlers claimed. They don't. There's no psychological evidence that Minnesotans have more itchy gambling glands than anybody else. What they do have more of than other people today are places to gamble—the lottery, thousands of pull tab vendors, more casinos per square foot than anywhere in America except Las Vegas and Atlantic City. It got so bad that the race track, the pathfinder of the gambling industry in Minnesota, went broke, swallowed by competing gambling operations. It was later downsized and resurrected.

Allow me a personal aside. I think gambling in Minnesota is a travesty. But I do like that picture of history avenged. If the suckers are going to blow the family grocery money on numbers, let it be in an Indian casino, where the gods of history can smile. The trouble is in the hasty legislation that opened the doors not only to Indian profits but also to gross mismanagement and tribal feuds. It failed to look seriously at the issues of "tribal sovereignty," a concept that is part fact and part romantic myth. Tribal sovereignty became a shield to deflect nosy prosecutors and human rights protectors. For a while it kept federal investigators away from the cooking of casino and tribal books. That is being remedied, but the huge sums being spent on gambling in Minnesota must be appalling to the ghost of Luther Youngdahl, who thought he got rid of it in the 1940s with acts that had to please all good and sturdy Scandinavian Lutherans, to say nothing of the other good and sturdies in Minnesota.

The damage gambling has caused cannot be measured on a calculator. The calculator might be able to quantify the millions of dollars that have flown from homes that can't afford the losses. It might even be able to give rough numbers on the thousands of new cases of gambling addiction in Minnesota. What it can't show is another and even more costly kind of dependence generated by the gambling flood, the growing dependence on gambling money of state and local government agencies, of private institutions, of youth groups and even schools.

What this means is that once gambling revenue gets large enough, it will be almost impossible to root it out of government financing. The lottery brings in a certain amount of money to the state. It's still trifling alongside the major tax revenue, but the lottery is, after all, a disguised kind of tax and there may be no political will down the road to get rid of it, even when the public interest would be better served by dumping it. In the towns, charitable gambling gifts often go to public bodies like the police department. That being true, a logical question in some of those towns is this: Just how zealously are the beneficiaries of those gifts enforcing the law governing pull tab gambling?

Several years ago I was asked to speak at a luncheon of the ministerial association of a large Minneapolis suburb. My talk dealt primarily with some of those hidden cancers of gambling in Minnesota. The applause at the end of my talk was about normal, but I admitted privately to the luncheon chairman that I was surprised by the meagerness of the questions afterward.

"I should probably tell you," he said, "that half of the ministerial association's budgeting comes from charitable gambling."

Is there an answer? Sure. It will lose steam after it gets so bad that the citizens themselves demand action to remove the multi-billion-dollar monstrosity they allowed to happen. That is pretty much the cycle of gambling in history, which tends to have a long memory.

There are more smudges in this expanding canvas of the new age Minnesota. But as a citizen who was born a year before the stock market crash in 1929 and spent his boyhood in the Depression, lived practically all his life in Minnesota, and as part of his work has chronicled life in Minnesota, let me make a brief reevaluation of the place where I live.

I never saw it as a paradise in the cornfields. It gave me my education and tended my health and made me aware of both the glory and the frailty of wild nature and the possibilities in human nature. I would never claim those things would have not happened in another place. I do know they happened in Minnesota, and I may be better for that than if I had been in another place. I was never sure about a specific "Minnesota mentality," about Minnesotans being nicer than people in, let's say, Alabama. I don't believe that. Human nature is pretty much the same around the world. People are as generous and nice in Sri Lanka as they are in Minnesota, when it's possible for them to be generous and nice. What's different about Minnesota is the environment for a good and constructive life, for good and constructive works, created both by the settlers and those who came after and by the generosity of the land. From the beginning, Minnesota served the needs of its people by serving millions around the world, first through its vast stores of iron and wood and the richness of its farmland, and then with its medical research and healing that saved the lives of multitudes.

I don't think this is a romanticized view of Minnesota past or present. Whatever the depth of the smudges, the vitality of the place where I live is not diminished. Because it valued education so highly, and invested in it, and because its workforce was strong and its industry resourceful, Minnesota is prosperous today. It has absorbed the corporate gyrations of the 1990s—the downsizing, restructuring, and merging—better than most, because its business is diverse and resourceful. Its most sophisticated and some of its most critical industries of today, high technology and medicine, are businesses and services in which Minnesota leads. And it leads because there was a climate here for intellectual and corporate exploration and a willingness of government and industry to reach common solutions. That may have become closer to a one-way street in recent years with public bailouts of Dayton's and Northwest Airlines and growing concessions to the sports promoters. But in the end those political decisions have been based on a rough consensus of what business the public is willing to help and how valuable it is to their lives or to Minnesota's. The stadiums have been built for those ball clubs the public thought were worth having—sporting clubs that in themselves strengthened that feeling of community. In California, they labeled a baseball team the California Angels for marketing purposes. But they didn't really mean it. It still belongs in Anaheim or Los Angeles. In Minnesota, the football team and the baseball team are truly Minnesota's, and no marketer or advertiser is going to ignore that.

It's still attractive and viable, Minnesota, with most of its popular kinks and ardors still in place. Thousands of people still throng the scarcely adequate highways for the weekend up north. It doesn't matter if at least forty or fifty cases of neurosis develop every year because the traffic drives the motorists batty in their relentless search for serenity in the pines. The place up north still summons the settlers, maybe more magnetically than ever. If you don't believe that, you might try buying a cabin up there.

No, Minnesota has not solved all of its problems. It may be that the state has not accurately identified those problems. Art Rolnick, a respected researcher for the Ninth Federal Reserve District, believes Minnesota's prosperity and stability, for all the reasons we love to talk about, are likely to continue over the long haul. But he also believes that neither the metropolitan leaders nor the state have shown the political will to attack the greatest threat to stability and quality of life in the Twin Cities. "Putting stadiums in the middle of downtown doesn't do it," he says. "I don't know that putting a Target in the middle of downtown Minneapolis would do it. Those things attract a lot of talk but I don't know that they contribute substantially to strengthening the city. People come in and watch the ball game and go back to their bedrooms and lawn chairs in Minnetonka without spending much money in the little shops around the stadium or basketball arena. By the way, where are all those shops and stores that were going in around the Metrodome? What they are is parking lots.

"What has to be done to strengthen the city is lift up the poorest and the voiceless to levels where they cease being problems and become contributors. That may take money, but more than that it takes an attitude. It means we have to truly see this as a critical problem, both to the security of the cities and to their prosperity. You just can't ignore it. Downsizing isn't hurting America as much as that is. If a middle management guy loses out in downsizing, he'll get another job that may pay less. How big is the difference between $125,000 a year and $90,000? That is not life or death for the guy. What is life or death in America is putting some of those other people, the ones who can't boost themselves, on the ladder most of the rest of us have been climbing all our lives."

It can be done, and Minnesota is a place where it may happen sooner than elsewhere. I took that tack in a talk a few years ago, and afterwards a man asked me why I kept having these expectations about Minnesota. I said I never spend much time chasing illusions, but I do have eyes to see and a minimal amount of brainpower. I said this place is not going to be confused with the Land of Oz, because the natives are right, there are only two seasons, winter and road repair. And until the World Series got us aroused, the biggest passion around here was going to see the ice melt on Lake Harriet. But I like the fact that we don't have a whole lot of crooks in the meeting halls of Minnesota, that people have been willing to go into their pockets for good schools and clinics, and that we have created a Minnesota medicine, beginning with the Mayo Clinic and the university and extending now to the private hospitals, that has made the difference in millions of lives around the world, and made our own health stronger than most. I like the fact that for all of the howling about a miserable business climate in Minnesota, some of the country's biggest corporations continue to prosper here with record profits, and that a disproportionate number of the five hundred biggest corporations in the country operate in Minnesota.

I like the fact that this is still a decent place to raise a family, and that when experts try to figure out how a state can better manage its affairs, or how a company can build stronger bridges with the community and therefore become a better company, they usually come to Minnesota.

That still is Minnesota, by and large. This is a place where the public has set aside, for itself and for those who come after, hundreds of parks and preserves and waterways that can nourish people for a weekend or a lifetime. It is a place where high technologists flourish and reach global markets, but you can drive into the bogs of northwestern Minnesota and find an isolation that reaches back into the centuries. It is a place where, just two hundred miles from the great glass towers of the Twin Cities, with their humming electronics and their bustling brokers, you can ski through the woods and hear the baying of a wolf.

It is not a bad place in which to have spent a lifetime.

9/ The Mirror Is Not Always Kind

Three days after a quadruple bypass operation, I received a call in my room at Abbott Northwestern Hospital from one of my readers, extending his best wishes for a speedy recovery and offering to share the hospital story of one of his relatives.

"I thought you'd be interested in knowing he had the very same operation six months ago," the man said. My interest in hearing this story was limited. The steel wiring in my breastbone was causing throbs. My left calf was swollen to the size of a vacuum cleaner bag where a vein had been removed to create new channels to my heart. To aid urination during the convalescence period, they had inserted a catheter in a place where catheters were never intended to be inserted. In this condition, I fumbled for the language of courtesy to accommodate the helpful reader. I settled on a white lie. "Sure," I said, "I'd like to hear about it. How's he doing?"

"The operation went very well," the man said. "But he had a reaction to the blood thinner afterwards and they had to amputate one of his legs."

After thanking the caller for his medical report, I felt a tingling in the toes beneath the swollen calf and began worrying about the imminent departure of my left leg. I tightened the thigh-high white hosiery I was wearing to reduce the swelling and thought this would be a good time for my daily talk with Ms. Silver Linings, the happiness nurse on the floor. I hit the button and Silver Linings arrived with sunbursts of predictions of my imminent discharge from the hospital and of a robust future life that would easily carry my age into three figures.

I said this was encouraging but I would be content if she pulled the instrument of torture from the place not built for catheters. I pleaded pain, inconvenience, and the probable onset of internal poisoning. She said if I was going to live to be 100 I'd probably have to adjust to all three. The catheter stayed.

The white stocking stayed and so did the postoperative fog that settles on the mind and body after its critical parts have been disassembled and rewired. The hundred daily irritations shift in and out of the procession of healers and blood siphoners. The ache and disorientation mix with the fugitive moments of exhilaration when the mind realizes that life has been restored, and then with the prayers of thanksgiving. At the end of that day, my thanksgiving included the caller with the relative who would have had a sensational operation except for the loss of a leg. The human mind's ingenuity in trying to comfort the sick with the unlikeliest potions of consolation has always astounded me. When I told the story to Verne Gagne and Jerry Gruggan a few hours later, Gagne laughed so violently he shook my bed and threatened the fresh wiring in my sternum. But what? The caller deserved to be remembered. His intentions were good. In realizing this, my thoughts might have taken me into premonition. Months ahead, voices like his would make the difference between renewed life and personal destruction for me.

Life deals grief and pain indiscriminately. Some of the grief is deserved and some of it is practically invited. Usually it comes in intervals. For me it came in a volley of sledgehammer hits packed into the six months between December of 1992 and the following May. I came within a few days of a massive heart attack and needed the quick mind of a woman internist and the hands of an accomplished surgeon at the eleventh hour to save my heart from strangling. A few months later I was diagnosed with cancer of the prostate gland.

A few months before that, my second marriage ended.

Four days before my surgery for prostate cancer, I was arrested for drunk driving on a Saturday night in Maple Plain, Minnesota.

All of those episodes involved my own complicity in one form or other. Because I try to practice a faith, somebody brought up the subject of God's will. It's worth considering. But sometimes the penitent in me collides with the journalist skeptic. I'm not sure I know God's will when I see it. I've seen football coaches and politicians explaining victory in terms of God's will, but I doubt that God is a superreferee or the head judge of the electoral college. So I could hardly write off that tidal wave of grief in my life as any particular act of God, although if one of the events qualified it would probably be the red lights of the

Maple Plain policeman in my rearview mirror that night in May. After all of the years in which the newspaperman in me tried to isolate truth and variously tried to track it down, the arrest for drunk driving brought a particular and savage truth into my life, about the price of drinking, the price of self-deceit, and the damage I'd caused to people who mattered to me.

Personal disclosures by public personalities risk being awkward and messy. If they're going to be made, they should be done with merciful attention to the audience's limited endurance. Further, they ought to perform a service. It's something I tried to do in the newspaper in the aftermath of the drunk driving arrest, and I tried to look at cancer and heart surgery with a thought for people who were indifferent to their risks or were terrified about learning the truth.

The other reason I brought readers into some of that personal angst and the rearrangement of organs had something to do with the way I construed my column. It was personal on some days. This didn't mean I had to spill all, which I didn't. In sorting through that massed trauma of five years ago, I don't know why I should have been surprised to learn that all of it bore some sort of internal connection that tied arterial blockage to cancer to the humiliation of arrest and to divorce.

There were two links. One was alcoholism. The other was my belief—held in the face of impressive evidence to the contrary—that a life of professional satisfaction and mile-a-minute shifts in energy could pretty much go on into a boundless future. The first clue that this theory was full of cheese came on a tennis court late in 1992 when I felt mild chest pain and hard breathing after a few retrieves off the backhand of George Farr, my longtime tennis partner. Farr was a few years older and not especially famous for hitting unreachable backhands. Puzzled, I stopped to breathe. While I was gathering myself, I remembered the sharp bite I'd felt in my chest biking a few months before, a sensation that felt like swallowing cold wind in the morning. In fact, in either my naïveté or my denial, I'd attributed the pain to exactly that. But in my office late on a Friday afternoon, I felt a recurrence of that dull ache I'd experienced on the court. Only now I was sitting and not running down a ground stroke. It felt as though a soft, invisible fist was squeezing the muscles in my chest.

I telephoned a friend on the staff of Abbott Northwestern and asked if she could recommend an internist. She asked if I had a family doctor. Feeling silly, I said no. She made a nondescript sound of mock sympathy. It might have said, "OK, Hercules, maybe we should try medicine instead of immortality." She gave me the name of Dr. Parin Winter, an East Indian woman born in Tanzania and a member of a clinic specializing in disorders of women. "She also knows a little about the disorders of men," my pal at Abbott said. A half hour before I was going to leave for the weekend, Parin Winter called. I described my symptoms. Because it was more or less demanded by membership in the jock lodge, I tried to minimize the pain while trying to be reasonably accurate. I also gave her some history. "I can't imagine being able to climb the Matterhorn a few months ago and having any serious heart trouble," I said.

Parin Winter was silent for a moment, possibly scanning her medical books for evidence that climbing a mountain was proof of a perfectly functioning cardiovascular system. She apparently found no such citations. "Have you been getting full annual physicals?" No. "When was the last time you took a stress test?"

Silence.

"I think you should be at emergency at Abbott in an hour," she said. "I'll make an appointment for you. There may be nothing wrong with your heart or arteries. But there probably is. You need to be looked at." The lady spoke these words with that lovely lilt that characterizes English-speaking East Indians. But she was decisive and serious. I found no trace of judgment in her voice for my delinquencies in health care. What I did find in eighteen hours was pure prophesy. Two hours after I entered the hospital I expressed my disappointment over the decision of Parin Winter's associate to keep me overnight for tests. The external tests in the afternoon gave me full clearance. My pulse was low and my heartbeat was firm. My blood pressure was good and I was Hercules reconstituted. Plus I had to do a book signing at B. Dalton in the afternoon, a radio appeal for the mentally retarded in the morning, and a speech to book lovers later in the day.

"Well," the doctor said, "you might have an interest in what the angiogram and the stress test have to say."

I did. I said yes, bring in the treadmill. I welcomed it. This, I thought, is what I do. I walk and run. My legs are strong. They were, but after six minutes on the treadmill there was a jackhammer loose in my chest and the angiogram revealed arterial blockages of 90 percent, 75 percent, 95 percent, and 100 percent. My heart hadn't been damaged, but my arteries were a ticking bomb. They gave me three options:

medication, an angioplasty, or a quadruple bypass. Listening to the methodical analysis of the cardiologist, Dr. Jim Daniel, I got the impression that there was no choice at all for a man with the numbers the angiogram turned up. His wasn't a flat recommendation for an immediate bypass. The doctor was aware of the popularity of lawsuits in today's society. What he did was guide the conversation. I voted for the bypass. One of his aides then slipped me a card with percentages on it. With hospitals and HMOs increasingly scared about litigation, that card represented a medical version of the Miranda warnings. With a bypass, the little card said, my chances of dying on the operating table were 3 percent. The chance of heart muscle damage was 15 percent, the chance of a stroke 1 to 2 percent. I regarded these numbers with reasonable gravity. I then asked what were the chances of loss of wisdom teeth.

"None," he said. "But outside of your coronary arteries, you're in good shape. You can shave the odds of all of those things to practically nil."

Practically.

"Yes. Practically."

That was a comfort. Later in the day I asked the cardiologist what had happened—how could I have drawn on all of that energy for so many years, made my body slimmer and durable, while my heart arteries were systematically choking?

"A lot of things can make you vulnerable to heart trouble, and you have no control over some of them. There's family history, for one. But you say there's no history of heart trouble in your family." None.

Overweight is another suspect, he said. But my weight had been normal for more than twenty-five years. My blood pressure was low. I was active. I'd never had diabetes. I stopped smoking thirty years ago. I stopped eating cheese puffs.

"But you're sixty-four," the doctor said. "If you're going to have heart trouble you're about at the magic age. You're male. That's another contributor. The bigger ones probably are your cholesterol count, which is higher than it should be, and stress."

Everybody has stress, I said. Even Buddhist monks have stress.

"They may. But with that schedule of yours you may have been going for the gold medal."

I met the surgeon, Dr. Bob Emery, the morning before the operation. He walked into the patient lounge briskly and confidently, which is the way you'd like your surgeon to be walking the day before surgery. He'd performed more than a thousand of these, but he seemed stimulated by the prospect of getting back to the operating table. Every one new, in other words. Life or death all over again. I almost cheered. You don't want a heart surgeon coming to work looking bored about punching in. He was trim and athletic, a smallish man with a slip of mustache, rather like a surgical Alan Ladd. He introduced himself and spoke economically. He said that it looked like a bypass four ways, that he had good people on his team, that I was in good condition apart from the arteries, and finally: "It's going to work. You look ready."

On Operation Monday they rescheduled me from the afternoon to the morning. The patient who was down for Monday morning apparently suffered a minor setback. "The guy is an attorney," Emery said later with a crack of a smile. "We take newspapermen ahead of lawyers. It's the law of natural selection." I wanted to ask Jim Daniel's assistant, with his Miranda warnings card, what the percentages of having a stroke on Monday morning as opposed to Monday afternoon were, but medical folks were in my room with shavers and a sedative. There was a small clutch of people waiting in the corridor when they started rolling me toward surgery. Mark Hanson, my pastor, was there. Amy held my hand while we wheeled toward the operating room. The sedative had made me drowsy but I could feel her confidence. "See you after the operation," she said. "Don't get into an argument with the doctors."

My daughter. Way to protect the family image.

I remember the overhead lights seeming to dim as they rolled me into position, people in green gowns, surgical masks, something reassuring from a nurse. Nothing more. The rest was a wipeout. I'd come in with an idea of what they were going to do, and if there was a miracle in the operation today, it was that the marvel of this medicine is now routine and no longer exotic. The patient is laid open and the breastbone pried apart. Retractors bend the sternum in opposite directions to give the doctors and nurses ten inches of working space. Emery removed the saphenous vein from my left leg. From the left side of my chest he took the internal mammary artery and diverted it to provide more new channels. While this was happening, the heart was stopped, its life-giving functions performed during the operation by a heart-lung machine while the grafts were made. The blockages were outflanked. To protect my body they chilled it to seventy degrees and then cooled my heart even further by packing the cavities with a solution of ice slush.

Hours later, Emery confided, "You looked like a large frozen daiquiri."

He couldn't have spent much time dreaming up metaphors. The crux of the operation finished, he reunited my heart with its blood supply. With my heart now pumping again, revving up to its pace of one hundred thousand times a day, I could be safely weaned off the robot heart, the machine. It was shut off, and the sternum halves were folded back together and spliced with stainless steel wire, now locked into my body for the rest of my life. In six days I was released from the hospital.

Skilled people, an athletic surgeon, Minnesota's pioneering medicine, and a woman from Tanzania, diagnosing over the phone, had saved my life. I blinked as the attendants wheeled me to the elevator and then to a waiting car. I'm not sure I deserved all that. I did talk briefly to Emery before I left and expressed my thanks.

"I'm curious how you look at your work," I said. "You save lives. But you do up to three of these a day. Do you feel the same professional challenge for each of them?"

The doctor shrugged pensively, a gesture that seemed to say, "If I were the patient, I'd certainly hope so." What he said was, "Yes. A person's life depends on it. And you always want to do things as perfectly as you can. You can compare it with Olympic judging. You want to do a 10 every time."

I said that was impressive and in my case, at least, I wanted to thank God they didn't let the Bulgarian judge in.

When I went into my rehabilitation at home and had time to look back through all of the turbulence of the weeks before, two questions I hadn't asked in my short seminar with Jim Daniel stuck in my head: Did drinking have any connection with the blockage of those arteries? Did it aggravate the stress that certainly had a connection with the heart trouble? No answer was available to me. I doubt that the doctor could have answered. How much drinking? Over what length of time?

If there was ambiguity about that, there shouldn't have been about the connection of drinking with the breakup of my two marriages. I don't know that I could have acknowledged it in the days after my heart surgery. But I could six months later and I do now, although there were other causes: the usual frictions, selfishness (mostly mine), and the complacencies (mostly mine) that erode a relationship.

Rose Heuberger and I were married for twenty-two years. We met on a blind date in Minneapolis, arranged by one of my cousins. She was a grade school teacher who'd walked a picket line in the early 1950s, at a time when walking a school picket line was still a pioneering act. She'd been class valedictorian at Milwaukee State, played the cello, and sang in a respected Minneapolis women's choral group, the Cecilian Singers. These notable feats may have been equaled in my mind by the fact that she was the daughter of Swiss immigrants living in Milwaukee. My introduction to Rose included generous slices of zither concerts at the Swiss Club in Milwaukee and wall paintings at the high-gabled family house depicting scenes from the Bernese Oberland and cows grazing in the high meadows. Nobody in the house seemed to have any strenuous objections to my practicing my yodels, learned on the weekend passes of my army days. Above all this, Rose was venturesome. She was a whiz in the kitchen and relaxed and inventive as a housemate. She was also altogether sappy about loons and butterflies, her favorite teaching aids in school.

We were married in 1954 in the sacristy of the church at Marquette University in Milwaukee, an act that spared me hellfire for the moment. Rose agreed that the children would be raised in the Catholic Church, although I didn't insist and they weren't. I didn't attend church regularly at the time and eventually moved to the Lutheran Church, although I suppose I've never left the Catholic Church sentimentally and still find myself aggressively defending it when that seems right or when Notre Dame plays on Saturday. The wedding reception was held in the Heubergers' gingerbread home. My parents and aunts and in-laws living in Milwaukee came, along with some of the Heuberger clan. The wedding and reception, as I remember, cost eighty dollars. Nearly forty years later, on the eve of my daughter's wedding to John Bessler in Minneapolis and the subsequent reception for three hundred and fifty at the Humphrey Institute, I reminded Amy Klobuchar of that remarkable fact of economics in Milwaukee. I did this as the proud father of the bride and the chief patsy of her wedding book-keeping. She was unimpressed.

"What was the price of a cup of coffee in those years?" she asked. I said about fifteen cents.

"There's your answer," she said. The lady is both a lawyer and a politician. She produces answers like that. I'm not sure what it resolved, but I readily agreed that it was an answer.

Rose and I lived for almost all of our twenty-two years together in a home we built in Plymouth that resembled the interior of a small chalet. We had two children, Amy, born in 1960, and Beth, born in 1963, and lived normally. On vacations we hiked together as a family in the Teton mountains of Wyoming and the Black Hills of South Dakota, and one year in the Swiss Alps, where we sponged gloriously on the Swiss relatives. The disruptions began in the early 1970s. I came home in sorry condition one Christmas Eve after drinks at a friend's house, in no shape to put together the kids' presents. Rose handled it. I'd get home late for dinner, and the kids must have talked about it. Rose conducted no harangues. This wasn't continuous, but it happened often enough to raise warning flags. I told her one night I was embarrassed by it and I apologized for the unfairness and said I was attending AA meetings. I was, but I'd done none of the groundwork and made none of the admissions. Our marriage drifted, through no fault of hers.

While that was happening, Beth began experimenting with alcohol and drugs, for which I might have been the role model. Increasingly she isolated herself, and she dropped out of high school at sixteen despite an IQ at least equal to that of her sister, who became class valedictorian and went on to the Ivy League. Beth and I warred silently. It was impossible for us to communicate beyond the weather without beginning to suspect each other's motives. It was futile and the estrangement deepened whenever we tried.

Years later, after struggling with chemicals and her lack of education through her entire adolescence and young adulthood, Beth—now Meagan—enrolled in a college in Iowa. She recreated her life and became an academic star after all those years of alienation. She'd found in herself a person she never knew, one who could explore and write and argue philosophy. What she found first was the motivation to risk walking into a new world. She found that motivation not in her father or mother or sister, but in Meagan. And after all those years of mute avoidance and stonewalling, we began to rediscover each other and to talk about Kant and Adler, which may truly be an act of God. The rediscovery wasn't that hard. Temperamentally, Meagan and I were a closer match than her sister and I were. "Talking to you," I told her over the phone, "is looking into a mirror."

But in my last years in the house the sisters quarreled incessantly while their father was filling up most of the day and part of the night working at the newspaper, running a talk show, giving speeches, writing books, and generally being an absentee.

I initiated the divorce in 1975. There was no provocation for it. What would you call it, just another middle-aged man with wanderlust, serving himself, ripping up the lives of three people to give himself new air and space?

What else is there to call it?

On the day of our divorce, I wrote my column about our marriage. I thanked Rose for the times she forgave my follies and for the times when she didn't. I remembered the times we had supported each other and I asked her to join me in believing that the court decree did not pronounce a failure. We had times of beauty in the outdoors and in watching the children grow, in doing nutty things around the house and in knowing each other so well. "We're leaving," I said, "without really knowing the times we helped each other with a small act never reported, or the times we wept for each other."

We're still great friends and confidants, and we're still in and out of each other's storage rooms. She borrows my tent for her campouts on the North Shore, and when we come together for a family Christmas I still hang around the kitchen long enough to go home with a load of spritz cookies.

I'm not big on soap operas, but I imagine most of us have some of those scenarios in our lives, and I suppose I ought to ask Lois Berkland Lura what kind of character I played in her particular soap opera. We met in the 1970s, at the most grievous hour in her life. Her husband, Dick, was a member of the high school faculty in Edina and a part-time deputy sheriff in Carver County. They lived on a hobby farm outside Chaska with their three small children. It was almost inevitable that they would. They were both farm kids from Iowa who met in their college years. She attended nursing school in Minneapolis and became a registered nurse. Dick was a visual aids expert at school, a cop, a commuting student studying for his master's degree at Mankato State, and a member of the Chaska school board, a highly popular young man who attracted the instant affection of the kids at school.

On a late fall night, he and his partner were rushing to the scene of a traffic accident when their patrol car crashed into a freight train at a poorly marked intersection. Both were killed. Three or four friends of his called me at different times the weekend after his death. They thought Dick Lura's energies and the impact he'd made on scores of young lives could be the subject of a newspaper column. I thought about it and called his home, apologizing to the young woman who answered for intruding on her grief. I asked if she objected to my visiting to talk about her husband. She thought it was all right, and I drove to the farmhouse, where her father was helping her with her chores through the funeral and its aftermath. We visited for forty-five minutes. She and her family lived in a turn-of-the-century frame home with a huge round oak table in the middle of the kitchen-dining room and an ancient pedal organ dominating the living room. She told of their courtship, and about her husband's exuberance in whatever he undertook and the ten years of a strong and fruitful marriage. She was a small, brown-haired woman of thirty-one with an obvious energy that was subdued in her grief. She seemed crushed and yet brave, trying to accommodate the visitor. I left with a packet of letters her husband had written to her before their marriage. They were spontaneous and newsy and filled with affection and a touch of happy-ever-aftering. I quoted from some of them in a column I wrote the next day, giving the reader a glimpse into what seemed to me to be a pretty precious love story—now destroyed, and the children left fatherless without warning. I returned the letters with a note of sympathy.

She was a person the newspaperman will meet in his travels and his work, but not one he will meet every day.

Our paths came together again considerably later at a football game at Metropolitan Stadium. She was wearing an all-weather jacket imprinted with one of those familiar pocket patches bearing the neighborly advice of rural Minnesota: Please don't eat the yellow snow. I congratulated her on her contribution to hygiene in Minnesota and we talked about her family and exchanged some dutiful evaluations of Minnesota weather in November (ghastly as usual) and the condition of the Vikings offense (about normal). Several weeks later we talked on the phone, and a couple of weeks after that went cross-country skiing in Carver State Park.

Three years later, on our return from a trek in the Himalayas, we were married in a church in Chaska. The auspices for the marriage weren't especially glowing even then. Lois had reservations about it two or three weeks before the wedding. Some thirteen years later, after we'd divorced, I conceded to her that her instincts in this were spectacularly better than mine. The difference in our ages, thirteen years, wasn't vital. But our wills collided often. When we traveled together we were impulsive and close, frolicking through the woods and making the mountain country our private dominion, the way it is in the coloring books. She was inquisitive and irrepressible and nourished some obsessions that floored me. She was, for one thing, an absolute manic, compulsive newspaper reader. I wrote for one and kept reasonably abreast of what was in it. But Lois consumed it, from the front page through the ads and obituaries and classifieds and all the way to the stock markets and finally the weather in Albuquerque on the back page.

For months we'd planned a trip to the Teton mountains, her first. Mountain country excites her, and I was primed in my role as the itinerant guide. We left Old Faithful in Yellowstone for the drive down the stunning Lewis River Canyon, then into Grand Teton National Park, Jackson Lake, Jenny Lake, the great pinnacles and all that. We pulled into the Wagon Wheel Motel in Jackson around supper time.

"Welcome to the mountains," I said.

Lois looked up from the newspaper she'd been reading. She saw the marquee of the motel. "What did you do to the Tetons and where are they?" she laughed, building her defenses.

"A half day behind us," I said. She hadn't looked up from her newspaper for three hours.

This might have been one of the all-time most unflinching endorsements of the American newspaper, but I also found it an inviting part of her personality, her stubborn pursuit of all that happened on this day in the life of the world, whether she found in it the newspaper, on television, or in the company cafeteria. Mountains in the sky offered scant competition when she was in the throes of this search.

From her training in nursing but more through her intuition, she often insisted on taking charge. When we traveled and met a genuine emergency, an injury or sickness or some other medical crisis, I've rarely seen a person react with quite the same swift competence. This was beautiful unless there was somebody else on the scene who also intended to react with swift competence, maybe a doctor or another nurse, in which case all hell erupted. She was a nurse and a dabbler in civic events, but ahead of all the rest she was a mother and a nurturer. The death of her husband left her with two sons under six, David and Jamie, and a daughter, Ann, slightly older. After the accident, she tended them alone, stimulated them to get involved in school, and guided and instructed David in how to deal with his diabetes. She gave him a regimen, and no compromises. She drove them around to this game and that meeting, worked at a hospital, cooked at home, and read her newspapers maniacally as usual. All of her children grew up to be popular students in high school, all graduated from college with honors, and all married successfully.

What forestalled us from winding up in the lost luggage of divorce long before we did was that we genuinely cared for each other. She had a hundred appealing notions and quirks, one of which was a fixit mentality that sooner or later put her prints into the scene whenever Lois thought Lois's intervention could bring sudden light and direction. I say this in gratitude because her inspired meddling in a hospital—while we in the midst of our divorce—probably saved me from death by cancer.

For more than ten years, we'd split, we'd grieve, and then we'd look for excuses to get back together, dumbfounding our friends. Finally the sheer weight of that struggling drained our energies to reconcile, and when Lois filed for divorce the second time in the summer of 1992, I didn't argue. There had to be a resolution one way or another, and this was the way. We reached a settlement that seemed harmful to neither.

We remain friends. One thing missing when we talk today is argument over alcohol. It didn't disappear easily, nor did some bad cells the doctors discovered almost as an afterthought in the spring of 1993, a few months after the bypass operation. They might not have found them at all except for Lois's intrusion when she visited my hospital room a few days after the bypass, in the midst of the divorce. I've never been able to decide whether in a previous life she was a detective, a swami, or a process server. It's enough that in her present life she is an observant and protective occupational nurse. In the hallway that day she told a doctor she'd been concerned for years that I might have prostate trouble. She had reached this conclusion in the way wives reach such conclusions, usually because of the proximity of the bedroom to the bathroom. She said she'd urged me to see a doctor about it and that I, of course, had disregarded her advice.

This is more, I'll have to note regretfully, than could be said about our struggles to keep our marriage upright. Of our thirteen years of

legal union, we achieved a balanced distribution of time and energy—
we were together half of the time and separated half of the time. We
took turns initiating the reconciliations. Friends trying to support one
or the other competed with friends on the other side. What encour-
aged some of them, appalled others, and mystified most of them was
that we kept trying to get back together. There were days, weeks, and
months (but not quite years) when we not only declared love but quite
obviously meant it. When issues between us seemed resolved, our
marriage was romping good fun. Putting it prudently, though, our
relationship was volatile. My intervals of drinking were the largest
wedge in this eruptive pie. I minimized them, of course, and Lois kept
giving me evidence to show how destructive is the power of denial and
how critical is in-house treatment. There were years in our relationship, including one span of five years, when I was completely sober.

It didn't mean, I know now, that I'd come to grips with dependency.

I'm not sure that alcohol—while it certainly was an element—was
at the core of all our disputes. We shared qualities—intensity, abrupt
judgments, willfulness—that tended to get us into verbal scrums. We
shared other qualities, of course, that brought us closer together: curiosity, impulsiveness, a yearning to walk the faraway places, social
concerns. But most of the squabbles, whatever induced them, ended
when I raised a wall of silence. It was my response to contention and,
I suppose, to unsightly truth. Lois's short list of my defects was probably accurate: I was afraid of intimacy, tried to control by withdraw-
ing, and refused to reveal my feelings. The list tended to lengthen as
our haggling went on.

"I think he should be given a PSA test," she told the doctor. The
PSA is now well entrenched in urology clinics as a marker for the possible existence of prostate cancer. It has its critics, but millions of men
have taken it and, in the biopsies that followed because of it, cancer
has often been detected. All of which meant that one of the last of the
cavalcade of medical sleuths who visited after the heart surgery was
Dr. Rodger Lundblad, a urologist with whose country doc style and
long piercing instruments I was to become well acquainted in the
months ahead. He explained the PSA and its role in cancer detection.

"Just consider it one more piece of routine before they let you out
of here," he said. "I wouldn't worry about it." A day before I left he
brought in a reading of six. "A little high," he said, "but it's in no way

definitive. I've had that reading myself. Go home and get strong and we'll do another test in two or three months. Don't worry about it."

I didn't. Getting my lungs and heart back and worrying about those odd spasms of the muscles under my wired breastbone didn't leave much time for fencing with demons that might not exist. I went back to work, got stronger, and celebrated with a bungy jump off a bridge in New Zealand. When I got back I called on Rodger, whose practiced fingers told him—and definitely told me—that I had an enlarged prostate gland. It is a condition as common to older men as falling hair. Rodger and I were now on a first-name basis. There's nothing quite like the awkward intimacy that develops between the patient and his urologist, from whom there are no secrets. He recommended a biopsy.

In about a week, Rodger came with his devices, thin probing lances that looked at least a yard long. The results came back in a few days. No cancerous cells were found. I breathed again. He said there was always a chance that a more thorough test would produce another result. He had found enough evidence of blockage to warrant the standard TURP—transurethral resection of the prostate—procedure. This was done under local anesthetic in a relatively minor operation that required a few days of hospitalization. Thirty minutes before I was discharged from the hospital, one of Rodger's young associates entered my room carrying a report. He said an additional, wider biopsy had been done during the TURP. I listened quietly. He said the new tests had produced a result different from the first. He tried to be considerate, but there really aren't many ways you can say it. He used the word *malignant* to describe thirty-six out of fifty-five tissue samples they'd taken during the procedure to break up the prostate blockage. The doctor was saying I had prostate cancer.

My face must have colored, because I felt a rush of prickly heat. I stood there not sure whether I ought to tell the young doctor thanks for letting me know. I don't think he was sure whether he ought to offer me his arm or to maintain his professional look of hopeful solemnity. I excused myself briefly and went into the bathroom to towel the moisture from my face. The urologist left, and I was alone. I tried to tell myself this was no pronouncement of death. This wasn't the Big C of the neighborhood's whisperings back in the mining town of my boyhood, the words that meant death, cloistered words that in some households even imputed a kind of shame. That was fifty years ago. This was the 1990s.

It was still the Big C.

It was the Big C, but now there was a chance. I tried to shake those sighs of dread I remembered from older folks in my hometown when they heard the diagnosis pronounced on their loved ones. Most forms of cancer can be treated today. They can be slowed or stopped if they're found early enough. But it's still cancer, highly lethal. A nurse walked into my room, savvy and aware. I'll never stop being grateful for her simple act. She knew what was up. "You're supposed to sign some papers for your discharge from the hospital," she said. "Let me handle it. Why don't you leave now and go home and think what you want to do. It's better there than here." She looked squarely into my face. "You're going to have better days. You're going to be all right."

I walked numbly through the corridor and took the elevator to the main-floor exit of Abbott Northwestern. My car was at home and I didn't feel up to calling the friend who'd brought me to the hospital a few days before. I looked around for a taxi, holding my overnight bag and trying to organize my mind. No cab was in sight. It was a gorgeous April day, reflecting the sun's warmth off the concrete walkway where I stood, trying to clear myself of this semiparalysis in the brain. Call a cab. I started for the doorway and heard a voice behind me.

"You look a little lost."

Wendy Anderson, once governor and senator, now a lawyer and university regent, now my Wednesday-afternoon tennis partner. We had a deeper history than that. I liked his politics and his personality when he was the governor. I'd been startled and annoyed by his decision to have himself appointed to the U.S. Senate in the double switch he worked with Rudy Perpich in the 1970s: Popular young governor resigns. Inflammable lieutenant governor succeeds him. Newly installed inflammable governor appoints popular ex-governor to fill a vacancy in the Senate. I'd expressed surprise at Anderson's decision in my column, but I didn't trash it. I thought he'd ride out any negative reaction from the public and sit in the Senate for years to come.

In the summer of 1978, though, facing a challenge from Republican Rudy Boschwitz, Anderson politicked on the Iron Range on the issue of expanding the motorboat routes in the Boundary Waters Canoe Area. The mechanizers were the loudest lobby in northeastern Minnesota and claimed to speak for the vast majority of the northeastern Minnesota voters. They didn't, but they did exert powerful political clout and were in a position to embarrass any Democratic candidate who opposed them. Anderson backed them for months while the language of a Boundary Waters bill, initially authored in the House by Representative Don Fraser of Minneapolis worked its way through Congress. I blistered Wendy a half dozen times in my column. In the congressional protocol and in the leveraging of power, his position on the bill as a senator from Minnesota was crucial. Eventually, after the bill was modified with compromise language supported by the Boundary Waters advocates but opposed by the mechanizers, Anderson spoke in favor of the bill and voted for it. It passed and became law. His decision alienated a lot of his supporters in northeastern Minnesota and may have contributed to the general malaise of his campaign. He was beaten decisively.

I doubt that my columns had any serious impact on the election. But I know they hurt him, and I regretted that because he'd been a constructive public servant for years. We met a year later and talked guardedly although cordially enough. He never mentioned the columns. A few years later we began playing tennis, but practically never talked politics. In fact, we talked only briefly on most subjects except hockey and traveling in Scandinavia. Yet we both enjoyed the time we spent together.

In the early 1990s the *Star Tribune* published a piece about Anderson's finances, with a how-far-the-mighty-have-fallen tone. I thought it was fair enough to look at an important political figure then and now, but the positioning of the story on the front page and the depth of it seemed to suggest that his life after politics had been an embarrassment both to Anderson and to his associates. I thought that part of it was unwarranted, and I said so in my column a few days later.

The only mention he ever made of it was between sets during one of our matches, six weeks later. "My mother wanted you to know that she appreciated that piece," he said. I had to fight off a smile walking back to the baseline. The guy had principles. I'm not sure whether he or his mother was saying thanks, but he didn't bellyache when I took him apart on a political issue years before, and he wasn't going to spread a lot of cream of gratitude for a supportive story. I liked that then, and I appreciated the concern in his face when he saw me outside the hospital, clearly troubled. He was waiting for his car after visiting a friend and asked if I'd been doing the same. I told him about the doctor's report.

"I'll drive you home," he said. We rode through the residential streets of south Minneapolis and then into the suburbs. It was such a divine spring day, trees leafing out, the sun splashing the windshield, that no special gloom intruded in our talk about cancer. But we did talk about cancer. We talked about how today's medicine had restored normal lives to hundreds of thousands of people who would have been condemned just ten and fifteen years ago. "I think you're going to be one of those," Wendy said. "I'll plan on it."

I wasn't sure I was going to be one of those. How far had it spread? All of the statistics of successful treatment for prostate cancer, colon cancer, breast cancer, other cancers tend to dissolve in the mind of the freshly diagnosed patient wondering if the killer cells have progressed beyond the reach of medicine's extraordinary advances of the past twenty years. I remembered a statistic. About thirty-four thousand men die of prostate cancer every year, but at the same time, tens of thousands get through it.

Wendy and I shook hands in the driveway and I walked into the living room of my town home, flopped into a chair, and thought about putting on some music. I didn't. What did I want? Consolation? Some kind of reverie? No music today, I said. The wrong prescription. I prayed for a few minutes and stared at the sun. But when the shock dispersed and I accepted the truth, a pretty remarkable thing occurred. It was time to start doing things, confronting things. There'd been all those years of hovering fear of the cancer in my family, the seeming inevitability of it. Two of my grandparents died of cancer. A third had skin cancer at the time of her death. My father died of leukemia. Was that why I'd resisted the tests for early detection?

It probably was. But what had been depressing the last two hours was the unknown of it. One small way to deal with the unknown was to find people who could walk me through the decisions ahead, past the impressions of a lifetime, past the phantoms and into the clear air of what was probable. I dug out the phone numbers the nurse had given me and made some calls. Two of them were to doctors' offices. It was Sunday afternoon, but there were answering machines and I left messages. I felt better engaging in some kind of action. I felt better two hours later after talking it through with Mark Hanson, my minister, who told me about the scores of successful cancer patients he'd visited, whose doctors he'd visited. His own mother was given two months to live ten years ago. She accepted no treatment. She'd simply outrun the cancer with her faith and her unquenchable optimism.

How much do we really know about the power of belief and a healthy, positive mind in dealing with an illness once called incurable?

"But you can't by any stretch put all of cancer in that incurable category today," Dr. John Brown said. "Some of it is actually curable. A lot of it can be controlled." He glanced at my charts. "Early detection is the critical part, and that's easier now than it used to be. You might have been slow in getting yours detected. I'd say there's a 70 percent chance yours hasn't spread to the lymph nodes. If that's happened, you still have a good chance to live some productive years. I expect you to have success."

This was not the standard pep talk from a friend or relative. This came from an oncologist who'd spent his professional life as an expert on cancer. An oncologist. Walking into his office, observing the sign, I remembered the dozens of newspaper columns I'd written in which the word appeared. Some of those stories were obituaries. Some told of the strength of the cancer patient, and some told of survival. But oncology meant cancer, and when I opened his office door, some of the creeping terror evoked by the word—the impression—returned.

But how is the neighborhood grocer going to be an agent of creeping terror? That's how John Brown struck me. He had a round face and glasses and an affable manner that took me back to the days of the family market. But what we talked was cancer.

"You have what we call a stage A-2 cancer, which means it was detected earlier than some but still calls for radical surgery," he said. "Chemotherapy and radiation probably aren't for you."

And radical surgery means?

"Removing the prostate gland. It's cancerous. Get it out of there." He talked about divided opinion on these issues in the medical community. But the neighborhood grocer didn't seem to have much doubt. Nor did he have much trouble diagnosing the doubt he read in my face.

"All right, let's get into male anxieties about radical surgery."

I asked him if it was that obvious.

"All men think about that. First, removal of the prostate doesn't mean the man can't have a normal sex life. There's a fair chance that the nerve that produces arousal won't be affected at all." (My later anecdotal research in the prostate cancer fraternity suggested that the neighborhood grocer might have been slightly optimistic there). "But even if it is, there are systems and devices that aid nature there and allow normal sexual relations. Hundreds of thousands of men have learned that." (And several years later science had developed a drug that could produce the same result without tubes or syringes or implants.)

"But whether you use a method, or no method, I don't have to tell you," John Brown said, "that manhood means a lot more than acrobatics in the bedroom."

A man facing a prostate cancer operation is probably not going to argue with this premise, recognizing that debating points can be scored on either side of the argument. But there truly was a bottom line to this discussion, which made talk about methods and manhood academic and almost comical. The bottom line was saving my life.

My consultations broadened. One urologist who read the same charts said he would not immediately suggest radical surgery. But Rodger Lundblad, admitting he was aggressive about these things, agreed with John Brown. I drove to the Mayo Clinic, on a highway filled with traffic though on that day it was the loneliest road I'd ever traveled. The chief of urology there read my charts.

"Get it out of there," he said.

The scan for cancer in the bones came first. If it was there, the surgery would be futile. The horizontal x-ray machines hummed almost playfully as they moved back and forth across my body on the table where I'd been placed. The sound was innocent, but the verdict it would render would mean life or death. It came in three days. There was no evidence of cancer in the bones. Rodger gave me a briefing. Although I'd undergone bypass surgery four months ago, he said, my body was strong enough for another operation. He scheduled mine for the first week in May. He would perform it. He grinned. "It's BYOB."

BYOB.

"Yeah. Bring your own blood. I'll give you a phone number. They'll take some blood, which we'll have at hand if necessary. It's the new wave. Litigation and all that."

I did all the preparations before leaving for a weekend drive through western Minnesota to do some final reconnoitering for my annual group bike ride in June. Riding through the greening countryside, I made an accounting of the past six months. Some events, those. A quadruple bypass. A divorce under way. Next week, surgery for cancer. I'd learned something years ago about the human being's power of resilience. What you imagine in adversity is usually far worse than the reality of it. Keep remembering that, I told myself.

And a few hours later, five days before my operation for cancer, I was arrested for drunk driving.

The Maple Plain patrolman's rotating lights in my rearview window were vivid enough. Nothing much about the next few hours were. I'd been drinking sherry on my ride through western Minnesota, getting a lift, being dumb and reckless. It wasn't to blank out the coming surgery. It was getting a charge, feeling airy, the usual reasons. In the five-year period when I'd stopped drinking, I attended group meetings each week and felt confident about staying away from alcohol. I stopped going to the meetings. Two months later I drank again. I went years when my drinking took the form of one or two cocktails a month, other years when I drank from a bottle of brandy at home, or from a bottle of wine—or from a small bottle in the trunk of my car.

That bad. My drinking was irregular. I didn't do it every day or every week or every month. I did it, obviously, enough. Workdays I was sober. I wasn't drunk often, but when I was, I embarrassed everybody around me. Usually those times, ironically, were connected with pleasant events: my daughter's graduation from high school, her graduation from college, leaving on a trip to Europe.

Why? When there were so many positive parts of my life, when it had so much action in it, professional rewards, good people in it?

I drank because I was an alcoholic. The reason wasn't any more complicated than that. In the dozens of times I'd thought about it, in the hundreds of meetings I'd attended, in the three previous arrests when my blood alcohol content permitted a careless driving plea, I'd never made the admission.

I did in a column I wrote on the Monday after my arrest. I apologized to my readers and to those whose lives I'd endangered. The humiliation I felt on that day exceeded any pain I'd ever experienced. The embarrassment I felt didn't come from admitting the truth to my readers. I was embarrassed because I'd come face to face with the arrogant self-indulgence of it, drinking and driving, knowing the hazards I was inflicting on innocent people, on myself, and doing it anyway.

The newspaper put the column on the front page, accompanied by an editor's note by Tim McGuire explaining to the readers that the newspaper viewed this incident gravely and pledging that it would insist on my undergoing treatment for alcoholism as a condition of my continued employment. I don't know that the newspaper had to insist. The judge was going to do that, and at that hour of shame I was more interested in my own recognition of the gravity of it than in the newspaper's. I thought this might be my last piece in the newspaper, and I can honestly say the realization of that didn't affect me nearly as deeply as the need to bring some peace into my life. With a friend, I removed all the alcohol from my house in the midst of the predictable vow: never again. I'd made that vow before.

In surgery five days later, nothing was said about the drunk driving. The anesthesiologist, Jim Musich from my hometown, administered a spinal. In view of the events of the past week, I welcomed the descending mist. When it was over, Rodger said it went well. The cancerous prostate had been removed. He saw no evidence of the lymph nodes being involved. It would be a while before he could say for sure that the cancer cells hadn't penetrated the stomach wall, but right now it looked good.

I read my mail for hours every day. It came in bales, from people I'd never met. It said you made a mistake but we're on your side and you can recover. I'd never much aspired to simple humility before. I had no trouble embracing it now. The letter writers weren't saying it was all right. They were saying they forgave.

My court appearance was scheduled a few days after my discharge from the hospital. Before that I appeared in the office of a dependency evaluator. My daughter Amy and Mark Hanson accompanied me. The aftereffects of the spinal made it painful for me to sit up, so I made my deposition, and listened to Amy's, lying down. I told of the episodes and history of drinking in my life. My daughter, the lawyer, then gave her own testimony. It was not quite testimony. It was a prosecution. She told of the times when as a child she'd seen me tight at home. She told of the damage my divorce had inflicted on her, her sister, and her mother. She told of the lies she'd heard from me when she brought up the subject of drinking. She told of seeing me lift the trunk door of the car, pretending to examine something in the car, and taking a drink during the charade. She spoke with fury and sorrow and in tears. I was stunned by her arraignment, not by the power in it but by the litany of my deceptions. When she finished, she walked to the couch where I lay, took my hand, and said, "I love you. You can save yourself."

I couldn't alone. In court, Doug Kelley, my climbing friend and lawyer, stood beside me before the judge. I pleaded guilty. The judge looked at the evaluation report and then turned to me. He said making the plea was a start. He said he didn't normally give lectures at a time like this. He said I knew what was at stake, and that he thought my chances for success—for recovery—were good. It was a strong, positive statement that I will carry with me for the rest of my life. His sentence was the standard under the conditions: mandatory inpatient care at a treatment center, aftercare, temporary withdrawal of driving privileges, two days in the workhouse, and a seven-hundred-dollar fine.

The judge and I came together again two months later, as we now do each week of the year, at a meeting of recovering alcoholics.

I'd been in a treatment center near Cambridge, Minnesota. It was a small, sequestered clinic whose patients included men and women of the world, teenage drug users, middle-aged alcoholics, people in treatment for the first time, one in for the nineteenth time. We met in small groups five or six hours a day, attending nearby meetings of Alcoholics Anonymous, and wrote journals about our days at the center, examining how truthfully we were dealing with our dependency.

On the day I entered, I made a vow about drinking: I won't go down that road again. I won't hurt myself and others that way again.

It was a nice gesture, but within a week I think I understood the emptiness of it. Avoiding that road was no unilateral act. Avoiding that road meant needing help. Needing help began with an admission.

I'm an alcoholic. I don't have the power to handle alcohol. Faith in something higher was the answer. Was God the something higher? For most of us, probably. For others something higher was the combined strength of those in their circle, making the same daily struggle, recognizing the same vulnerabilities, chiseling away at the personality defects made so glaring by alcohol but not necessarily erased by sobriety. Sitting there appalled to the point of laughter at the pretensions that can delude a human being when he is drinking out of control.

Without that admission, without that cry for help, I know now I would not make it. I discovered that in my second week at the treatment center. It was my day in the dock. The counselor stood at the blackboard and drew columns and lines. The heading was Consequences of Drinking. He asked me to recite my history of drinking, how it began, how much it involved, and what it had caused.

The time for deceptions about drinking had passed. I gave him and the others my history, the progression of alcohol in it. At the end of each line on the board was a place for the result. I told first of embarrassments. Then I told of loutishness at home, no physical abuse but all of the mental injury I'd caused. I told of arrests, loss of money. I told of an automobile accident one drinking episode had caused. From there, I told of the first divorce, the disruption of my children's lives, their adolescence without a father. I began adding the cost of divorce, the friendships I'd lost, my delinquencies as a stepfather in my second marriage, the costs the two of us had absorbed in our separations. The cost included the damage to my self-respect from lying, the anger and lost years of companionship that I'd imposed on the two women I'd married. Finally I added the cost of my drunk driving conviction in personal humiliation, in money, and in the pain of those close to me.

The paralyzing weight of it came down on me with a shock. It was a ledger of horror, confronting a man now in his sixties, which is supposed to be an age of ripening wisdom.

When I finished, the counselor looked at the board, making a silent appraisal. He then looked at me, as though saying he understood how alcohol had devastated much of my life, and wondering if I understood too. He asked, "What do you think?"

I couldn't answer immediately because the hard and unforgiving accusation in front of me had sucked all of the pretense and rationalization out of my mind and left it naked. Staring at the board, I could scarcely comprehend the ugliness it recorded. I closed my eyes and remembered a line in "Amazing Grace": the hour I first believed.

I left the room in the first steps of the recovering alcoholic. That was more than four years ago. Alcohol is not part of my life today. I've set it aside as an act, drinking, that no longer is an option today. The recognition of that truth has not made me a candidate for enshrinement as a human being. What it's done is to dissolve illusions— that you can indulge yourself and manipulate your way out of the consequences, that you can keep doing this without busting up the game because everybody has to have some escape from the grind or from boredom or the intensity of life, a way to lighten up with a well-deserved trip to la-la land for a few hours.

But some people can't keep that game going because it will destroy them, or destroy another. That realization has not removed all of my warts, but it does tend to improve my vision. I can see them with reasonable clarity today. What else have I found? I found I've not surrendered some of the old capabilities, of quick judgment, sporadic rudeness, and grandiosity. One capability I've lost is insisting on identifying them as decisiveness and vision.

I've found an invisible companion to walk with me through the hard times. God. I've found something close to a calmer and I think a more responsive life, closer to a peace I'd only felt before in isolation in wild nature.

When this happens to a human being, he looks for sources. I remember those bags of mail I received from readers in the days after the drunk driving arrest, not excusing the act but telling me they cared and calling themselves friends. I remember the language the judge used in court, Amy's indictment, Rose's forgiveness, and Lois's inspired meddling. I also remember the patrolman in Maple Plain, and today I can say truthfully, "Thanks for the red lights."

10/ Yiga's Scarf Says Farewell

A white scarf made from cheesecloth has been draped over a small prayer stone in my memento cabinet for the better part of two years. It was given to me by a Tibetan refugee I scarcely knew, a young woman named Yiga, a few weeks before I left daily newspapering. The white scarf in the Tibetan culture carries intimations of farewell and good wishes. The young woman knew nothing about the shelf life of American journalists. But she did know something about the nexus of two lives from opposite ends of the earth.

The white scarf she placed around my neck one day is fragile. It can't absorb much sun or handling, so I keep it away from those hazards. The prayer stone is a miniature of the slabs that are endlessly stacked along every trail and passageway in the Solo Khumbu of Nepal, in Tibet, and in other Buddhist lands of Asia. The mantra chiseled into it in the Tibetan language reads "om mani padme hum": praise the jewel in the lotus. The meaning of the white scarf is less exact. A white scarf is often given to a traveler who has received the hospitality of village dwellers in the Himalayas and is going on. It tells the traveler, "God be with you, wherever you go and in whatever you do."

One of the perceptions of newspapering, and of police work, is that the business is populated with an excess of cynics and wiseasses and a sizable smattering of idealists, which doesn't leave a whole lot of room for normal people. First movies and later the television sitcoms fostered this idea. Let me offer a minority opinion. Most people who write and edit the news have the normal impulses to be touched or to be amused or aroused, and, of course, they are fallible. What most of them prize most dearly about the business is its gift of bringing them face to face with people like Yiga, those who season and expand our lives. They are the ones who make the reader's trip through the daily newspaper the revolving theater it ought to be.

There are two reasons why the white scarf will keep the Tibetan woman in my life long after she has forgotten the name of the newspaperman who recorded her ordeal in the late fall of 1995, when she collapsed near starvation in the freezing wind of a park in New York City. She had gone from her apartment in Minneapolis to join a half dozen other Tibetan refugees on a hunger strike near the United Nations headquarters. The strike was intended to dramatize the Tibetan struggle for freedom from Communist China, which had murdered thousands of Tibetans in the years of its occupation. Knowing of my sympathies with the Tibetan cause because of my travels in the Everest district of Nepal, which is the home of the Sherpas of Tibetan origins, the young woman's friends called me. They and she were part of the publicity apparatus to heighten American awareness of the Tibetans' struggle. I had no illusions about that. But knowing it didn't make Yiga's commitment—"I'm willing to die if it will help free other Tibetans"—any less convincing or any less a story.

But it couldn't have given the Tibetan refugees any realistic hope of success. I told the woman's friend in Minneapolis that they must know this was futile, that the world and the United States were in too deep commercially with the Chinese government to do any favors for the people of Tibet.

The woman's silence said she knew that. But acting and failing were better than doing nothing. I wrote of Yiga's appeal to the world's conscience. She wrapped a blanket around her to take the bite out of the wind and vowed to take no food. She held out for several days and then was taken to a hospital, nearing dehydration. The doctors persuaded her friends on the scene to advise Yiga to take nourishment, which she did. In the midst of this, some U.N. office said it appreciated the Tibetans' appeal and would do what it could (which was nothing) toward easing conditions in Tibet. Maybe this recognition of the Tibetan strikers was something for them to carry away. It wasn't going to put one ounce of generosity into the boots of the Chinese occupiers, but Yiga's story got onto television and she came home to the tiny Tibetan colony in Minnesota a kind of heroine, although she didn't seek that status.

Yiga's scarf will keep her and her struggle in my life because it is a palpable if sentimental link with the times I've traveled with the Buddhist Sherpas, walked with them on mountain trails to their shrines, and wondered what it is about them that lets them do the humblest kind of work without ever appearing servile, and without losing their buoyant goodwill. It will recall the chagrin I felt walking into the Himalayan clinic at Khunde and meeting two Tibetans whose toes had been amputated by a volunteer doctor from New Zealand a few hours earlier. They had walked over a twenty-thousand-foot pass in tennis shoes to escape the Chinese occupation and froze their feet. That had been three days before, at about the time my group had reached the base camp on the glacier of Mount Everest. We were Americans, well off, experiencing the thrill of the high Himalayas. A few miles away, at that very hour, they were two Tibetans slogging in desperation through the same mountains, their own. We saw their mountains as glorious. They saw them as death. Here were beauty and pain coexisting on the highest place in the world, which struck comfortable people with wonder and struck hounded people with fear. I tried to suppress a natural guilt when I met the Tibetans.

Guilt is available whenever the Westerner travels in Third World countries like Tibet and Tanzania. Maybe it ought to be. But if you are overpowered by it, you will never travel there. You can deal with it by trying to understand, and trying to be generous. You can also try to remember what you saw in the eyes of hungry kids when you get back home and hear folks wailing about impossible taxes and lousy playoff seats.

I shook hands with the Tibetans and fumbled in my pocket. I found a white scarf that had been given to me by an innkeeper in Pheriche and put it around the neck of the one nearest me. They shuffled away in their cloth foot covers, smiling and reciting mantras of thanks to be alive.

But Yiga's scarf on my mani stone is also a memento of the most lasting harvest of a career in newspapering: voices and faces like Yiga's, people who made a difference in my life and perhaps in the lives of thousands of others without realizing it.

Writing about Super Bowls gave me a wallop, and covering the ranting politicians made me tired or made me laugh. Walking thin mountain ridges high in the sky made me feel tiny, and watching Neil Armstrong step onto the moon made my heart feel proud and strong. But people like Yiga and Linda Phillips and Stan Mayslack put into the daily newspaper the blood and giggles of life, its glimpses into the nobility of the spirit and its casual goofiness. Something about them is different, and maybe extraordinary. It might be a crisis they faced or the character they became. One way or another they make life bigger or wiser or funnier. They were the people who filled my private gallery from a lifetime as a newspaper minstrel prowling the towns and country roads for their faces and their stories.

Workaday journalists meet people by the thousands. For this they should thank either God or their own bungled attempts to make it in a more dignified trade. The streams of humanity in which they mix is the rough benediction of their business. It's their daily nourishment and a tradeoff for their sleepless nights and the bad days when they get the name of the defendant mixed up with the name of the judge.

The new day, the first step into the newsroom each morning, was a liftoff for me for forty-three years, and I don't blush to say that. What calamities or screwballs do we have today? What drifter who wants to sober up or politician who wants to dismantle the government and let the marketplace take care of your heart attack?

The faces changed each day. So did the sounds of triumph, fear, hope, and apathy. Once in a while mild derangement got in there. A woman trying to publicize a new physical fitness shop she was opening walked into my office, introduced herself, and promptly stood on her head. She held this position despite my protests that the office neighbors were going to begin to talk and might call 911. She insisted that she was more comfortable conducting the interview upside down. What interview? I asked. I didn't invite her. She wanted to know what the chances were that I was going to turn down a conversation with an aggressive businesswoman standing on her head. She was right, of course. She talked for half an hour without her eyes getting above my ankles. I briefly considered starting the subsequent column at the bottom of the page.

I'm not sure this woman exerted any significant pull on the world's orbital path, but she *was* an original. Eventually she made it to television. Shrewder minds than mine, possibly belonging to the sponsors, convinced her she was going to make more viewers seasick than fitness-conscious by doing her monologue upside down.

But Linda Phillips not only was an original, she did make a difference. She was a scamp and a nag. She was brazen and tender and immortal. She lay on her back in a subsidized apartment, her speech and hearing gone and her body shrinking. We talked to each other with notepads. She was dying but her face was lovely and animated, her mind quick and still a little spacey. I'd remember her letters. Every few months she mailed me some of her original doggerel, which usually had a wry environmental message buried somewhere in it. She sent me cute animal dolls she stuffed herself, as if she were sharing a part of her secret menage. She plowed me into tears a dozen times while she lived. Sometimes she did it with her harangues against the bastards and impostors of the world. Paralyzed and living alone, she conducted her private little war, fiercely and without compromise, trying to protect the earth she was about to leave.

Yet when the time came to mourn her, it was hard to put on a decent face of solemnity. It was hard even when I acknowledged to myself that of all of those thousands, I don't think I met another human being like Linda Phillips. She was a fireball, and she was almost as beautiful in her fiftieth and last year as she'd been as a bride thirty years before, when the car she and her new husband were in skidded in the rain on their honeymoon in Baja California and plunged down a cliff. He escaped serious injury. Her back was broken, making her a paraplegic the rest of her life. They divorced after a couple of years. She never yelled any resentment about it. Their lives had taken different turns. So be it. If she'd stayed healthy she could have been anything she wanted—a politician, a saleswoman, a lawyer, a banker. She was that smart and that motivated. Wait a minute. Not a banker. She groaned at the thought of making money on other people's money: "God. There have to be limits." What she wanted to do most of all was to save the world, in the way the dreamers and the evangelists equally want to save the world. If she couldn't save it, she wanted to change it.

We met because she needed an advocate. The airlines were hassling her. She wanted to travel and they insisted that people traveling in wheelchairs needed a nanny or someone like that to care for them. She screamed about the condescension of that. Nobody heard. She called me up. "Make them hear," she said. So I gave Linda a forum for her wrath. In it, she spoofed the airlines and then hammered them. She confronted them with logic and wheedled them with poetry. Those were the Middle Ages of airline policies with respect to customers with wheelchairs. Eventually the policies changed. Linda may have sped the process. She never claimed credit. She did claim what was rightfully hers when she got on a plane after the airlines' reformation.

We came together again a few years later when, although she couldn't walk, Linda canoed in the Boundary Waters of northern Minnesota. The week was an epiphany for her: Linda lying in her sleeping bag at night, watching the lightning crackle through her tent flap, a thunderstorm transforming the north woods into a wild land of Oz. Like the northern sky itself, she was charged with energy and inner commotion.

We didn't know each other well by orthodox social standards. But on my next visit to her thirty-second floor apartment in the blighted Cedar-Riverside district of Minneapolis she grilled me about growing up in northeastern Minnesota. This was well before she lost her power to speak. She wanted to know if the world was always so magical in the middle of a storm in the northern woods. And was there any sound so filled with yearning as the yodeling of a loon at nightfall?

We became kin in a special way, putting our own private spin on nature's mysteries and sometimes on those of our own lives. On some days we talked as brother and sister. Other times, I played the sponge and simply absorbed her splutterings.

She assaulted the world's hypocrisies with her long black hair flying and four-letter words sizzling under her breath. She attacked the corporate powerhouses that were stifling her life in her wheelchair. She prodded the government to get the lead out and recognize that people in wheelchairs like shopping and strolling the sidewalks and going to an unbarricaded bathroom like everybody else. She damned the abusers of the earth and the profiteers who skinned the powerless. She denounced good, God-fearing suburbanites who shut their eyes to the struggles of the poor and the alienated. With Linda, there were no shades of innocence or guilt in these morality battles. Somebody was always guilty, and therefore there was always a victim. She had class and intelligence, but she was never slowed by one solitary admission that sometimes there might be room for doubt, nor was she swayed by voices—occasionally mine—advocating a sensible compromise.

Yet her anger never extended to her lifelong pain and her loss, her disability and her poverty. She decided very early to spend the rest of her life being Linda. This meant pushing her crusades and amusing her friends, who got the same stuffed animals and limericks I got. It meant never surrendering her rages and her hilarity and her protectiveness of the earth. If it had four legs or grew leaves, she loved it. If it had two legs, she would have argued, it always had a chance if it listened to some of Linda's advice. She had no money, but she found a way to give two dollars to Save the Rhinos and three dollars to Save the Anteaters, and to canoe the rivers of the north. I visited at her bedside two or three times a year after she was unable to use the wheelchair. I thought at the time I was doing it to renew a friendship with a brave woman, once so vibrant and self-reliant and now a charge of the state, dependent on caregivers, speaking in whispers or writing. I know now what was going on.

I didn't come just to sit with an invalid friend. I came on days when the phones at the office were full of bitchers and grinders, all with fresh evidence of how life in these United States had become unbearable. They blamed crooked politicians and money-grabbing CEOs. They blamed leeching landlords, road hogs, and the city alley inspectors.

Linda Phillips blamed nobody for her shrunken life. She blamed nobody for the loss of her marriage and her isolation. She found no scapegoats for the most terrible losses of her life: she could not be a mother; she could not be the physician or the lawyer she surely could have become if she'd been physically able. She blamed nobody for her approaching death. What she did was to plumb each day for what it brought into her life, or for whatever she could inflict on the spoilers. I always marveled at that. Here was a woman accepting the tragedy in her life and squeezing out of each day moments or hours that made her wiser or made her laugh. She did that with a certain bittersweet serenity, as though mocking her infirmity and the disappearance of her dreams, but still doing it with some tenderness.

What she did for me each time I saw her, apart from telling me her secrets and giving me her friendship, was to offer the newspaperman in me a fresh, clean page on which to explore the human spirit at its most compelling and sometimes at its best. I say sometimes. Linda could be a wall-banging shrew. She was waspish and intemperate for a while, but she wasn't hard to get out of those moods. She prized the earth's faraway places above almost all of her other passions, and she saw herself as a global rambler if a miracle ever happened to ease her paralysis. Because of that, she welcomed me as a kind of carpet-riding guru narrating the earth's exotic lands. We became co-conspirators and illusionists, picturing Linda Phillips riding a Land Rover on the Serengeti Plain. Some days we were serious, probing the meaning of the mantras recited by the Sherpas in the Himalayas. Sometimes we were mischievous. She said there were times when she felt she had the soul of a flower. We quarreled over whether flowers had souls. I was the curmudgeon. I said I could see her as a marigold but had to draw the line at nasturtiums. She stormed about that, if you can storm on a notepad. She thought I was trivializing her relationship with nature. I said I wasn't. I was just trying to understand what a nasturtium needs to do to get to heaven.

It went on that way until one of her friends called to say that Linda had died. One of her final wishes, the friend said, was to have her ashes scattered among the wild lady's slippers near one of the Boundary Waters lakes, where she'd fallen in love with the north woods and been lit by the night storm. The storm had been thrilling. But it was the wildflowers she found beside the trail that aroused the healer in her, and gave her peace.

When the spring came and her friends and relatives carried her ashes to the lake country, I remembered her bursts of glee and her silent withdrawals of reflection, and I wrote:

> The ladyslipper of the north's short summer is a kind of wild orchid, lovely and fragile and intricate but oddly tough. It is also Linda. Most of her life was pain and busted visions and scrabbling years of coping in a wheel chair. That and her undefeatability. It was the kind of life not bound by the markers of time or even death. She was the human spirit pounded by blows of grotesque unfairness. But like a wild flower growing out of scorched earth, she was redeemed by the sun of a new day.

And so her reunion with the wild orchids and thrashing pine boughs she'd met in her week of discovery in the canoe country was her requiem. No organs or harps were necessary. The music was the music she'd sworn she'd heard in the middle of the lightning and thunder.

I keep one of Linda's limericks around, where I won't forget it. I also keep a photo from Stan Mayslack showing a sellout luncheon crowd at his second buffalo burger feed in his Polish polka lounge in northeast Minneapolis. It carries an inscription: "It doesn't happen often, but I was wrong." Mayslack was in the foreground of the picture, of course, wearing his huge white chef's cap and wielding a butcher knife that he might have bought cheap in a Turkish bazaar. He was also wearing an apron that could easily have been converted into a hot air balloon. Mayslack weighed more than three hundred pounds and, in his black goatee and his fat baloney biceps, was fond of striking the glowering poses of the old wrestling villain. Almost all of this was an act, although Mayslack—born Stanley Myslajek— actually wrestled professionally until he hurt his back and went into the bar and restaurant business in the ethnic mishmash of northeast Minneapolis.

I need hardly tell you that Mayslack eventually became familiar to readers of the Minneapolis newspaper. He was northeast Minneapolis written about as large as the street ordinances allow. He was Polish first generation, pierogi, polka parties, big weddings, big wakes, and all. He bought an old tavern off University Avenue, the kind with a tile floor, large, distant booths that resembled dark alleys, and a bar that reached halfway to Golden Valley. The enterprise limped along until his wife, Butch, prodded him into putting on a daily roast beef feed as the trademark of the house. "Yeah," Mayslack agreed, "but we need some class to attract the white-collar trade. We can't make it with Polish truck drivers. We'll serve champagne with the roast beef."

It wasn't just a roast beef sandwich. What Mayslack served on his paper pulp plates had enough displacement to sink a tugboat. He had a recipe and a process. He marinated his beef for hours overnight. He would get up early in the morning and slather it with esoteric herbs and with garlic potent enough to scare off all of the vampires in Transylvania. He'd dress it out and stoke up the oven temperatures to serving heat, and then cut slice after ponderous slice for his serving trays. At 11:30 A.M. the line would begin to form. It didn't matter what season it was. The line stretched into the next block in the middle of January. Occasionally, on days when the windchill hit minus forty, customers on the outside would send an emissary into the lounge to ask Mayslack for permission to huddle on the dance floor instead of standing outside in the cold.

Mayslack listened to these pleas with the compassion of a brick wall.

"If anybody keels over," he'd say. "I'll take him in. The rest stand outside until the line gets shorter. Mayslack don't play favorites."

But nobody left the line, because dining on the roast beef sandwich at Mayslack's carried the same prestige as getting a ticket for the Stones. It conferred not only calories but also status. It was a badge of survival, too. Mayslack served tyrannically and without pity. The customer approached holding a paper platter. You had a choice of roast beef, ham, or turkey, but if you took ham or turkey at Mayslack's roast beef lunch it was like ordering pizza at Antoine's in New Orleans.

"Two hands under the plate," Mayslack barked if the customer happened to be a novice. Among his several virtues, Mayslack was frugal. He'd seen too many plates of good roast beef flop on the floor because the customer lacked the bench press strength to handle the weight of Mayslack's sandwich. If the customer insisted on showing off with one hand, Mayslack threw him out. So when Mayslack said "two hands," it was like a drill sergeant ordering left-face. Everybody complied. The reason was twofold. It gave the customers enough conversation material at the club for a month, and the roast beef stuck with them for days. Into a sesame bun five inches in diameter, Mayslack troweled slabs of beef without mercy. Wedged under the bun were four napkins: one for the table, and the other three the minimum deemed necessary to handle the drainage of garlic sauce that flowed from the stacked beef sandwich like the waters of a jungle cascade.

At the end of the buffet line sat an aging pixie, Mayslack's white-haired mother-in-law, banking the day's proceeds in a cigar box. This was the cash flow of the noon commerce at Mayslack's for years. Among Mayslack's hundreds of luncheon customers were two or three who were said to be IRS agents. To my knowledge, none of them ever raised any questions about the propriety of collecting the day's receipts in a cigar box instead of the conventional cash register. Clearly, they made the same assumption I did when I witnessed this remarkable marketing practice for the first time: When the waves of beefeaters subsided and the last drops of garlic sauce had been squeegeed off the old tile floor, Mayslack the dutiful citizen and tax-payer rang up every dime of grandma's cigar box receipts on the company register.

Mayslack insisted that he did. I believe that. The IRS agents were too entranced by the roast beef to ask. I also believe there may have been some undiscovered therapeutic benefits to the customers' gastric systems from Mayslack's roast beef sandwiches and garlic sauce. I've heard this thought expressed by one or two professional nutritionists who were among his regular customers. The theory was that Mayslack's thick seasonings may have acted as cleansing agents. It was literally true that I never saw one of Mayslack's customers with a sickly bearing. The scent of all of that massed beef rising up from the table might have been strong enough to clear sinuses by itself.

But as the proprietor of one of the town's marquee polka joints, Mayslack was not just another hustler, not just another beef slinger. As chef and impresario, the man bristled with art. I have never met a more instinctive promoter. Although his bar and lounge was unapologetically committed to orchestrating Polish happy times, Mayslack organized parties for the Chinese New Year, St. Patrick's Day, and the Hispanics' pride, the Fifth of May. He promoted football trips to Vikings games in Chicago, but to escape the clichés of the wild football party and to comply with his own codes of decorum, Mayslack insisted the bar on the bus would not open until the travelers reached St. Paul.

The bus usually left Mayslack's for St. Paul at 7:00 A.M.

In the 1970s one of Mayslack's customers called me with the news that the Harvard Glee Club, of which the customer's son was a member, was finishing a world tour and was scheduled to sing at the Guthrie Theater in Minneapolis as part of a two-day visit to Minnesota. He thought it would be a superb addition to the Twin Cities cultural scene to invite the Harvard Glee Club to sing at one of Mayslack's roast beef lunches. I certainly didn't want to be accused of obstructing new explorations in the performing arts, so I called Mayslack and suggested that he should invite the Harvard Glee Club to sing in his polka lounge. Mayslack was momentarily confused about the identity of the Harvard Glee Club.

"Are they the guys who row those skinny boats out east?" he asked.

No, I said, he was thinking of the Poughkeepsie Regatta.

When we finally pinned it down, Mayslack's yen for marketing the bizarre overcame his basic ignorance about the Ivy League. A few days before the event, I wrote of the looming collision of the cultures. The world-renowned choraleers from the citadel of higher learning would be singing their Elizabethan ballads amid the fumes of Mayslack's beef and garlic buffet. The day before the concert, Mayslack was deluged with phone calls from Twin Cities bankers, lawyers, and board chairmen, all of them sons of Harvard, asking for table reservations. "I don't give reservations at Mayslack's," he told them. "There's usually a line here. You have to stand in it."

It was one of those Minnesota February days. The north wind blew down northeast Fourth Street en route to the old Ritz Theater, but they stood. They stood in the snow until the line crept through the doors. The glee club was already there in swallowtails and cummerbunds, amply reinforced with Mayslack's roast beef and beer. Around 1:00 P.M. they mounted the risers and started singing. They were in splendid form. They sang from the Renaissance, from the Appalachians, and from Wagner. Rapt at the tables sat scores of the sons of Harvard, some of them with moistened eyes, their hearts reaching back to the Charles River. In an uncommon show of democracy, they shared the recital with scores of Mayslack's regulars, including the truck drivers, secretaries, and Marquette Avenue brokers. Scattered among the brokers were a few walk-on millionaires who were sons of Yale, looking noncommittal, undoubtedly preferring to hear "The Wiffenpoof Song."

The glee clubbers finished with an original written by one of the club's in-house composers, a rousing salute to Mayslack with a title borrowed from one of his kitchen slogans: "Nobody Beats Mayslack's Meat." The crowd rose in a standing ovation, clapping rhythmically. Mayslack took a modest bow, although in the excitement he forgot to put down his cleaver and nearly nicked the nearest tenor.

Remembering this gala, I called Mayslack a year later from Winner, South Dakota, where I was covering the first bison auction conducted in the American West in years. The American buffalo almost disappeared in the indiscriminate frontier slaughters of the 1800s, but it has made a comeback nurtured by federal protection in the Black Hills and other parklands and is now being raised by private ranchers. By the time of the Winner auction, the buffalo was no longer seriously threatened, and it was safe to do some limited marketing. Early in the evening of the auction, I telephoned Mayslack with the news that I had bid on half a bison in his name and won the bid.

"What are you paying for it?" Mayslack asked.

"I'm not. You're paying."

Mayslack made a glugging sound, as though he'd been stabbed in the parking lot.

"Why did you do that? I don't know nothing about buffalo. The last one I saw was on a nickel. Give it back. Don't bring a buffalo in my joint."

The freight handlers brought it into Mayslack's joint, one side of a dressed-out buffalo. He looked at it without enthusiasm, but in a few minutes his promoter's juices started flowing and he envisioned stacks of buffalo slices on his buffet serving table. A meat cutter divided the buffalo into workable sections and Mayslack got out his secret marinating recipes. He posted signs in the polka lounge, and on the designated 11:30 A.M. opening on a Saturday he got ready to serve his bison burgers.

The sidewalk queue was already a block and a half long by 10:30. Two hours after Mayslack started serving, the line still wound around the parking lot. By 4:00 P.M. he was out of marinated buffalo, demoralizing a couple of dozen customers who'd waited for hours. He scheduled a reprise for the next Saturday. When the roundup was over, Mayslack banked hundreds of dollars in profit. The following Monday he called me.

"When you planning your next trip to South Dakota?"

So why Stan Mayslack? the venerable newspaper columnist is probably going to be asked. People like Stan Mayslack make cameo appearances in the newspaper, and we might have survived one of those beef sandwiches, but in the larger scheme of people who affect our lives, was old Stan that important?

He was to me. Linda was, and Yiga was, and a few hundred others. When you look at the world around you, at its worth and its impermanence, you pretty much personalize it in terms of your own attitudes—your sense of what's tragic, what's funny, what's beautiful, and what's ugly. Is life fundamentally good or fundamentally miserable? You're not going to get the same answer from the trial lawyer in Bloomington and from the barefoot old man in Calcutta. We all have our own picture of life around us and our place in it. The world to me was and is round-the-clock theater, sometimes circus, sometimes morality play. The players can be duds or saints or crooks or heroes. But there is gallantry or something sinister in there someplace, a streak of genius or a swatch of the unique in all of these people. You, for example, are unique. You have something to tell us. Maybe you should be interviewed. That uniqueness defines who and what human beings are. Sorting through all of those mixed strivings and the comedy and the tragedy kept the wonder alive for me each day of my life in the news business. It also kept the bafflement alive.

The wonder came not only from strangers I'd encounter but also sometimes from a friend. Rod Wilson is a Minneapolis lawyer with whom I often climbed years ago. We were coming down from the summit of Nevado Huascarán, a twenty-two-thousand-foot snow mountain in Peru, and Rod wasn't doing it very well. He was a powerful, well-conditioned man who'd experienced dehydration and probable symptoms of pulmonary edema on the mountain. We reached the summit late in the day under a draining equatorial sun, the two of us with Fausto Cleva, a Peruvian native who was our guide and porter. Weakened, Rod lost his footing on steep ice in the descent and shot down the mountain. I heard his yell and drove my ice ax into the slope down to the head. Before the rope ran out I looped my end of it around the ax head and leaned hard against the ax. We were all going if it didn't hold. Fausto, a hundred yards farther down the mountain in the lead, couldn't help much. Rod slid over the lip of a ridge and out into space, over a crevasse and onto another slope. My ax held and the rope came taut. I yelled down the mountain to find out if he was still conscious. He waved slowly, and Fausto and I climbed down to him.

He was able to walk, although he was out of it mentally. He imagined seeing a Christmas sleigh in the distance. I told him he might be right, but it was hard to make out. We got down to our tent at nineteen thousand feet in the dark shortly before 10:00 P.M. I put my ear to his chest and heard a gurgling, at this altitude usually a mark of pulmonary edema, potentially fatal. It can be forestalled either with a quick descent to denser air, which was impossible for Rod at this point, or with oxygen. We had stashed a twenty-pound bottle of oxygen at our base camp at fourteen thousand feet. Fausto helped me remove Rod's crampons and boots and we made him as comfortable as we could in his sleeping bag. I told Fausto I'd try to keep Rod awake, and the guide disappeared into the Andean night with his flashlight and ice ax, heading toward five thousand vertical feet of ice seamed by crevasses.

A Swiss couple occupied a tent a few hundred yards away. I walked over and asked if they had anything for pulmonary edema. They gave me a syringe containing a diuretic, which might get some of the liquid out of Rod's system. In pulmonary edema, the lungs fill with fluid, a condition caused by too rapid exposure to a rarefied altitude. Rod was groggy and his eyes were unfocused. He couldn't have been aware of the crisis he was in. I unzipped his sleeping bag and loosened his climbing clothes. I told him I was an amateur at this, but I was going to give him a shot in the duff to try to give him some relief. I had no idea where I was going with the syringe, but I looked for a vein with my flashlight and emptied the syringe.

He didn't react, and he may have felt no pain. I'd be amazed if the little operation did him any good. He is a gentle and thoughtful man and he thanked me. He wanted to sleep. I didn't know if that was a good idea, although he was warm enough in the sleeping bag. I kept hearing the raspy sounds in his lungs. "Care to talk?" I asked. He didn't answer but dug around in his shirt pocket and emerged with a tiny black booklet about two inches square, a Bible.

"Could you read from this?" he said.

I elbowed over to him on the tent floor and sat wrapped in my sleeping bag. Off and on, I read through the night with my headlamp on the miniature pages. I read from Psalms and John and anybody that seemed right, although—listening to the avalanches—I did pass on Revelations. Rod was a believer, and an undoubting one. We conducted what might have been the highest Bible study ever, examining some of the passages, mostly in monosyllables. Rod remembered when he'd read them for the first time as a boy. Outside, the wind that had been wracking our tent fly had slowed. But every half hour or so we could hear the boom of an avalanche on Huascarán or the neighboring peaks. It didn't offer much comfort, although our camp was protected from the slides. When we dozed or drifted into self-absorption, the sound of the avalanches prodded us into renewed talk.

The night outside was deep and implacable. It seemed to last forever. But as it slipped toward morning my anxiety about Rod evolved into a feeling of brotherhood with him. Our talk was more personal than it had ever been. We talked about the right and wrong turns in our lives and about the days we'd shared that were nutty or hair-raising. We also tried to remember the last time we called on God when we weren't stuck in a mountain tent nineteen thousand feet high on a glacier. Rod laughed about that. So we talked about getting down when the sun came up, and as we did I understood pretty clearly why the ancients worshipped the sun, which shouldn't be hard to figure out. The sun is life. It brings deliverance and healing and hope. It might also bring Fausto and the oxygen bottle. We began a mental countdown to the sun, and I read more passages from the Bible. Rod said almost abruptly, as though it were written, "I think God will take care of us." Lying in his sleeping bag, eyes muddled, he nevertheless seemed almost serene, and that began to scare me.

The tent flap opened just after dawn, disclosing the tired brown face of Fausto Cleva peering in at us, half smiling, a large green canister on his back. Behind him was the rising sun. He'd walked through five thousand feet of glacial crevasses in the middle of the night and returned in six or seven hours with the life-preserving oxygen. Rod put the nosepiece to his face and I opened the valve. The needle on the gauge moved. The oxygen was flowing. Rod inhaled a half dozen times and gave us a thumbs-up. It was the best news in ten hours. He breathed pure oxygen until the bottle ran dry. With help, he was able to walk down with us to base camp. He got stronger with each step as the air thickened, and he was out of danger.

In the years that followed, I've often relived that night without being sure what saved him—the oxygen or his simple conviction that someone else was in the tent with us that night. I know now that one doesn't have to dig for answers. He believed it and prayed for it, and that turned faith into reality.

One life in the world's morality play. It changed my own life in ways that didn't materialize until years later, after a crisis of my own. But I think of that night in the Andes as one of those hours that lights and memorializes the times in our lives. This one was all about living or dying and the mysteries of why.

Ginger Rogers had nothing to do with mystery. Yet the newspaperman in me will remember an interlude with her because it's sealed in my mind as indelibly as the memories that are more solemn and significant. And when friends ask what celebrity I remember best, I usually skip through the Reagans and Carters and Namaths and tell them about Ginger Rogers. While I'm doing it, newspapering and my adolescent years and the world as theater all bump into each other, and I'm back at a table at the Sheraton Ritz Hotel in Minneapolis, ready to sing a song, which, thank God, I didn't.

For years, Barbara Flanagan and I were the hosts of the annual downtown style show, dividing the interviewing. Usually a Hollywood star was brought in to talk fashion and spruce up the show. This was early in the 1970s. Ginger Rogers was then in her late fifties, having concluded her sixth divorce. She was chatty and lovely, still dancing and playing dramatic roles in films and in the middle of a physical fitness surge. During our conversation backstage she mentioned staying over in Minneapolis for two or three days to do some clothing promotions. She asked if it would be safe to jog through downtown and what the best routes would be. I said it was safe and asked if she planned to jog alone. She did, but she preferred company. She smiled in a way that invited a gesture of chivalry. So here was a cue from Ginger Rogers, dancing partner of Fred Astaire, actress known to millions, but particularly by me from the old Ely Theater on the Range. It didn't seem the time to be fumbling lines. I said I'd be delighted to be her partner. I showed up at the registration desk of the Sheraton Ritz on Monday morning at the designated nine o'clock, wearing my running shorts and burgundy T-shirt. I asked the clerk to call Ms. Rogers, explaining that we had an appointment.

"Ms. Ginger Rogers?"

The same.

He telephoned her room and seemed surprised when she emerged from the elevator a few minutes later in her running togs and her buttermilk hair. We ran up Nicollet Mall, past the storefronts and through pedestrians who predictably gaped at the sight of a celebrated movie star running through the streets of Minneapolis. We diverted to Loring Park and came back through the city. The sun was out, and she was relaxed and talkative and slightly exuberant, and then she asked, "Care to do a couple of steps?" Meaning dance steps. I nearly froze. I dance like a rhino. Here was Ginger Rogers asking me to dance in the middle of the sidewalk in Minneapolis. She extended her hands. "Be kind," I said. She was. She led and glided and did a turn and then lifted her arms and bent her knee and it was over. May the saints be thanked. At the Sheraton Ritz before she went up to shower and change, we had a small breakfast. She was thoughtful. She asked about my work and Minnesota and a little about my life, and then I had to tell her about the Ely Theater. "The movie I remember best . . ." I started to say.

She finished. ". . .Was *I'll Be Seeing You*."

How did she know?

"Fellows your age remember it," she said.

I'm sure they do. It was threaded into my growing up and all of my moony notions of romantic love. And that somehow wrapped Ginger Rogers and a song into my life. She played a woman convicted of a crime that wouldn't get her two weeks of probation today, but it put her in the slammer then. She was out on furlough and met Joseph Cotten. The story was sweet and wistful and weepy, and the lyrics of the title song drew a picture that no teenage romantic of the 1940s is likely to discard.

Ginger Rogers teased me. "I suppose you remember some of the words."

"I do. 'In that small café, the park across the way . . .'"

She broke in, half singing, ". . . the children's carousel, the chestnut trees . . ."

The wishing well.

When she left she thanked me for the run and for the company and lightly gripped my arm, half teasing again. When she died twenty years later, I dipped back into that little scene and remembered her words as she left the table, giving her jogging partner a droll wink.

She said, "I'll be seeing you."

And when I sift through all that today, and the millions of words and seven thousand newspaper columns, my muses tell me that of all of the good and the indifferent and the electric days I spent as a workaday journalist, the best ones for me were the days when I told a love story. Love when it was joyous, when it was hilarious or heartbreaking or when it told of what human beings are capable of doing for each other.

Linda's was basically a love story: her love of the earth and her pursuit of life after her dreams ended at the bottom of a cliff. Andy's was too. He and Zel were in their eighties. They met decades before, coming off divorces. It's probably why they didn't do the vows again. They spent the next thirty-five years in a kind of permanent courtship, living apart but seeing each other every day, running around in their later years in Andy's beat-up Ford, and traveling together on vacations. He'd gotten sick after serving in World War I and never advanced occupationally beyond handiwork in a store. He was an energetic guy with an elfin humor but always a courtliness in how he behaved toward Zel. He pampered her and talked her out of her darker moods. She went into a nursing home when she was nearing eighty. He visited her on her first day there and day after day after she could no longer recognize him.

He came every day, wearing a white shirt and a tie, what men in his day wore on a date. He visited her every day for four years, on days when it stormed and on days when he was sick. They talked about whatever she wanted to talk about. When she got cranky with the world, he held her hand and said something sympathetic, and then talked her out of it. If she didn't feel like talking, he sat and waited for the aberration to pass. He befriended her and loved her, every day. An attendant said, "I don't think it mattered that one of them is eighty-four and one is eighty-one."

But maybe it mattered very much.

Thinking of them a while ago brought me back to Yiga's white scarf. It means good wishes and godspeed, which is another way of saying, in Tibetan or any language, You are loved.

It's something to keep.

Jim Klobuchar has spent forty-three years in journalism, thirty of them as a columnist with the *Star Tribune* in Minneapolis. He is the author of fourteen books, including *Over Minnesota*, *Tarkenton*, and *Heroes Among Us*. Retired from the newspaper business since 1995, he is currently president of Jim Klobuchar's Adventures, a travel club.